The User Manual Manual

How to Research, Write, Test, Edit and
Produce a Software Manual

The User Manual Manual

How to Research, Write, Test, Edit and
Produce a Software Manual

by Michael Bremer

UnTechnical Press, Concord, CA

The User Manual Manual

How to Research, Write, Test, Edit and Produce a Software Manual

by Michael Bremer

This book is dedicated to Linda.

It could not have existed without support and inspiration from
Barbara, Jeff, Wendy and the "other Michael."

Special thanks to Richard, Tom, Kevin, Debbie, Laura, Bob
and a few others who know who they are.

Published by:

UnTechnical Press

P.O. Box 272896 • Concord, CA 94527

Publisher's Cataloging-in-Publication
(Provided by Quality Books, Inc.)

Bremer, Michael, 1955-
    The user manual manual : how to research,
 write, test, edit and produce a software manual /
 by Michael Bremer. -- 1st ed.
    p. cm. -- (Untechnical Press books for writers)
    Includes bibliographical references and index.
    LCCN: 99-90430
    ISBN: 0-9669949-1-4

    1. Electronic data processing--Authorship.
    2. Computers--Handbooks, manuals, etc.
    3. Technical writing.   I. Title.

QA76.165.B74 1999   808'.066004
                    QBI99-1307

Contents

Foreword 9

Part 1—
The Software User Manual 11
Introduction 12
    About This Book 12
    About Manuals 14
    About Software Products 15
Writing 17
    Technical and UnTechnical Writing 17
    Manual Grammar and Style 18
    Other Topics 19
All About Manuals 27
    The State of the Manual 27
    Purposes of the Manual 28
    How People Read and Use Manuals 28
    The Software Manual Dilemma 30
    Manuals and Product Design 31
    Manuals and Interface Design 31
    Parts of a Manual 31
    Manuals for Kids' Products 47
    Manuals and After-market Books 48
    Beyond the Words 49
    Beyond the Manual 50
    Online and Onscreen Help and Documentation 53
Companies and Their Systems 59
    The Organization 59
    The Development Team 61
    Beyond the Development Team 68
    Design Documents 69
    Software Development Lifecycles 71
    The Tools 78
    The Cost of Changes 82
Special Topics 83
    Big Projects with Multiple Writers 83
    Rush Techniques 84
    Manuals for Multiple-Platform Products 85
    Writing for Console Machines 86
    Localization and Internationalization 87
    The Future of Manuals 89

Part 2—
The Sample Project 91
Project Overview 92
    The Project's Purpose 92
    The Sample Software 92
    Project Organization 93
    Projects and Different Companies 93

The Scenario 94
Before You Begin 94
Project Flowchart 95
Stage 1: Learning the System—Setup and Planning **96**
Establish the System 96
Establish Project Goals 101
Establish the Reader 104
Your Tools 106
Problems and Solutions 107
Complications and Opportunities 109
Stage 2: Learning the Product—Research **111**
Research 111
Problems and Solutions 115
Complications and Opportunities 117
Stage 3: Organizing the Information—
The Outline and the Structural Edit **118**
Thinking and Preparing 118
Writing the Outline 119
Pre-edit Feedback 119
The Structural Edit 119
The Finished Outline 120
Problems and Solutions 125
Complications and Opportunities 125
Stage 4: Writing the Manual—The First Draft **126**
Time to Write 126
Format and Presentation 127
The First Draft 128
Problems and Solutions 164
Complications and Opportunities 165
Stage 5: Validating the Information—
Content Editing and Testing **166**
Preparing the Draft for Content Editing 166
Testing the Tutorial 168
Tutorial Test Results 169
Mini Design Review 170
After the Edit 171
Problems and Solutions 171
Complications and Opportunities 172
Stage 6: Rewriting and Retesting **173**
Summary of Changes 173
Rewriting 175
Numbering the Graphics 175
Retesting 176
Final Draft 176
Problems and Solutions 210
Complications and Opportunities 210
Stage 7: Detailed Editing—The Line Edit **212**
Preparing for the Line Edit 212
Selected Sample Edits 213

Problems and Solutions 216
Complications and Opportunities 216
Stage 8: Preparing the Manual for Layout 218
What You'll Deliver 218
Preparing the Final Draft and Style Sheet 218
Preparing Graphics 221
Problems and Solutions 225
Complications and Opportunities 225
Stage 9: Making It Look Good—Layout and Final Edits 226
The Graphic Artist 226
Writers' Contributions to Layout: Editing, Index, Table of Contents 227
Final Edit(s) 229
Problems and Solutions 229
Complications and Opportunities 230
Stage 10: Printing and Final Production 231
Final Preparation 231
Blueline—The Last Line of Defense 231
The Payoff 232
Problems and Solutions 232
Complications and Opportunities 232
Stage 11: Producing the Addendum or Quick-Start Guide 234
A Project in Miniature 234
Problems and Solutions 235
Complications and Opportunities 235
Stage 12: Producing Onscreen Help 236
A Little Background 236
Timing 237
Extra Reading 237
Writing for the Screen 237
Onscreen Help for The Personal Newspaper 238
Problems and Solutions 238
Complications and Opportunities 239
Stage 13: Writing the Readme 240
The Last Word 240
Writing the Readme 241
Problems and Solutions 243
Complications and Opportunities 243
Stage 14: Cleaning Up—The Project Backup 244
Backup 244
Problems and Solutions 245
Complications and Opportunities 245
Stage 15: Looking Back—The Postmortem: Lessons Learned 246
The Postmortem 246
Problems and Solutions 247
Complications and Opportunities 247
The End 248

Part 3—
Exhibits 249
New Employee/Onsite Contractor Checklist 250

Parts of the Manual Checklists 251
Quick-Start Guide (or Addendum) Checklist 253
Key to Proofreaders' Marks 254
Preparing a Draft for Layout Information Sheet 255
About the Sample Project Documentation 256
Sample Project Proposal 259
Sample Project Initial Design Document 265
The Finished Sample Project Manual 280

Part 4—Appendices and Index 305

Recommended Reading 306
Contact Information 309
Author Bio 309
About UnTechnical Press 309
Index 310

Foreword

After 10 years of writing, editing, managing and producing software manuals, I have a few bits of wisdom I'd like to pass on to everyone in the software world. The first one is:

A lot of manuals stink.

Manuals have a bad reputation, often for good reason. The good ones don't get the credit they deserve because the bad ones get all the attention. The worst part of it is that writers get the blame, even when they are given inadequate time and support to do a good job.

This book will help writers produce better manuals. It explains how, what and when to write, plus how to organize and plan to get more done in less time. More than that, it helps writers understand the business and politics behind the project, so they can beg, borrow or steal the support they need.

The next bit of wisdom is:

The manual is an integral part of the interface.

Most writers understand this, but many others, including engineers, producers and various species of managers, including financial types, still don't have a clue about what a good manual is, or why it is worth the time and money to do it right.

Software is still in the process of evolving from something only a technical person could love into a mass-market commodity. But it still has a long way to go before it is as universally accepted and understood as a TV or a toaster. And good manuals are part of the solution.

This book will help writers improve products and the customer experience with the products by creating manuals that are worthy of—or better than—the products they are written about.

Next bit of wisdom:

Writers can and should be more than just "manual writers."

Writers, even technical writers, are creative people. Writers are skilled communicators. Writers are organizers and presenters of information. Writers are valuable members of a software development team, above and beyond writing the manual.

In addition, technical writers in the software industry spend years dissecting, analyzing and describing user interfaces. They spend weeks on each project trying and retrying each and every menu, button, function and control. They learn about user interfaces whether they want to or not, and if they put in some effort, they can become interface experts—again a valuable resource for a development team.

This book encourages writers to use their skills, gain more skills, ask the questions, help the project and expand their career options.

The last bit of wisdom is one that I recently had to swallow myself:

One book wasn't enough.

When I began writing the book *UnTechnical Writing,* I thought I could crystallize and preserve all my years of experience into a single book that would help all writers master all aspects of working in the technical world. But it wasn't enough.

That's why I wrote this book, one that focuses solely on the software manual, and that shows and explains every step of a sample project. Well, here it is. I hope it helps.

Part 1

The Software User Manual

The chapters in this part of the book are:

- Introduction
- Writing
- All About Manuals
- Systems
- Miscellaneous Topics

The first part of this book gives a complete rundown on software user manuals, including processes, tools and techniques used in their creation, as well as their purpose, their composition and their readers. It also introduces software development teams and development methods, and how they affect you, your work and your manual.

Introduction

This short chapter quickly presents some basic background information that puts the rest of the book into perspective.

The sections are:

- About This Book
- About Manuals
- About Software Products

About This Book

Purpose

This book was written to:

- Teach new manual writers about the process of writing a software manual, the systems they'll be working within, the pitfalls they'll face and how to overcome them, and the possibilities and opportunities they can find if they know where to look.

- Give experienced manual writers the benefit of another writer's experience, and to offer well-tested processes and solutions to common problems, and suggestions for challenges.

- Get everything I learned from 10 years of writing manuals, editing manuals, managing and coaching writers and running a writing department within a software development company down on paper, and share it with all the writers I didn't have a chance to work with personally.

Organization

This book is organized into three parts:

Part 1—The Software User Manual explains the state, the art, and the state-of-the-art of manual creation. It covers everything from reader analysis to writing style and grammar to software development systems to online documentation.

Part 2—The Sample Project is a complete, step-by-step example of creating a software manual from day one through postmortem[1].

Part 3—Exhibits contains useful sample documents, checklists and worksheets,

---

[1] *A postmortem is a review session, verbal or written, that is held after a project is finished. It is a look back at the project's processes and results to summarize what worked and what didn't. The goal is to learn from the mistakes and successes of the past to make future projects better and smoother.*

plus the sample project's proposal, design document and finished, laid-out manual.

Part 4—Appendices contains sources of useful information.

How to Use This Book

As an author who put a lot of work into this book, I'd love it if everyone who picks up this book reads every word, from the first to the last page. But realistically, I know that very few people read technical books that way. Everyone reads and absorbs information in their own way, so you're going to use this book any darn way you please.

But—just as a suggestion—if you're just starting to write manuals, I'd recommend that you read through Part 1 (The Software User Manual) and scan Part 2 (The Sample Project). When you're on a project of your own, read Part 2 carefully, a stage at a time, before you enter that stage.

If you're in a hurry to get started on a manual, focus on the subsection *Parts of the Manual* in Part I, then focus on the appropriate stages in Part 2 as you move through your project.

And feel free to use the exhibits as samples or templates whenever they can save you time and energy.

Assumptions and Methods

Some books on technical writing are actually courses in beginning writing. Some supply blank charts to fill in to help you write procedures. Some have whole chapters on active and passive writing.

If you need this kind of instruction, pick up a basic writing book—a few are listed at the end of this book in the Recommended Reading appendix.

This book isn't a beginning writing course. It assumes that you have basic writing skills. It touches briefly on style and grammar, but isn't filled with lessons on either subject.

This book teaches by supplying complete background information, extensive explanations and examples to analyze. More than that, it covers real-world subjects beyond the actual writing, including development systems, team dynamics and office politics, all of which have a major effect on your writing and your ability to get your job done.

The Sample Project

The project that this book follows all the way through is for a piece of software called *The Personal Newspaper.* It is a yet-to-be-developed product that was only halfway designed when this book was started.

It's perfect for this purpose because it is complex enough to demonstrate all the different aspects and stages of a manual's development, yet small enough that it's practical to include its multiple manual drafts in a book like this.

Design flaws and ambiguity have intentionally been introduced into the early stages of this project (that's right, I *meant* to do that), so the process of refining and finalizing a product can be shown in the sample project.

The early drafts of the sample project manual are based on the supplied initial design document. The journey from that to the final draft and final manual is documented step-by-step in the sample project.

A sample demonstration program that shows the screens and navigation of the program—but is not a functional model—is available for download from the publisher's website (www.untechnicalpress.com/downloads).

About Manuals

What's a User Manual?

User manuals are generally associated with software. Manuals for hardware products are more often called owner's manuals.

A manual of either type can consist of anything from a single diagram or paragraph on the product packaging to a one-page instruction sheet to a multi-hundred-page tome. It just has to explain what you can do with a product, and how to do it.

What Products Need User Manuals?

Unless a product is so completely clear and understandable that any proposed user can intuitively use it without more than a few seconds' pause to consider, it needs a manual of some sort.

There are very few software products today that are that clear.

And while many products don't really need a manual, some sort of documentation can still be useful. For instance, even something as simple as a toy ball could come with inflating and patching instructions, or contact information in case the ball is defective. And the legal department may want to include some disclaimers and protective warnings.

So just about every product could be accompanied by a manual of some sort, even if it's mostly legalese and incorporated into the packaging.

Manuals for Hardware Products

While the focus of this book is on manuals for software products, many of the processes and techniques presented here are useful for writing and producing manuals for hardware products. If you write about hardware, you'll get a lot out of this book.

But software, because of its fluid nature and constantly changing platforms, has a whole set of logistical problems, time constraints and complications for writers. Those problems and their solutions are integrated throughout this book, making this a far more valuable book for writers in the software world.

The Term "User"

I personally dislike using the term *user* to describe the person buying the product and reading the manual. After all, there's only one industry other than computers that refers to its customer base as users.

What options do we have? Operator? Too impersonal. Owner? While respectful enough, the term "owner" traditionally hasn't been used for software, probably because the people who buy software don't actually own it. They only buy the right to use it. It has to do with the nature of software and intellectual property. Read the license fine print on any package of software if you want to be further confused.

Whatever the future brings, the term *user* is universal enough today that I even used it in the title of this book.

About Software Products

What's a Product?

For the purposes of this book, products are what you write manuals about.

These products can be hardware or software (though this book concentrates on the special aspects of manuals about software products). Products can be for business or pleasure, utility or spectacle.

If there's no product, then there's no manual.

Product Complexity

Products can range from simple and straightforward to ridiculously complex.

A well-designed product will seem far simpler on the outside than on the inside. Though it may be the most complicated piece of coding ever created by a team of programmers, it should appear clear and simple to the user.

As the writer of a user manual, you explain the interface—what the user sees. If it's a well-designed product, no matter how complex, writing the manual needn't be difficult or complex.

On the other hand, if a simple product isn't designed well, it can be a nightmare of confusion, inconsistencies and idiocy for you to explain and justify to the weary reader.

Open-Ended and Close-Ended Products

Something to be aware of when you write about software is whether the program is open- or close-ended.

A close-ended program is entirely predictable. It does a limited number of things. You can cover every possibility and contingency in the manual, and cover every operation in a tutorial. (You *can,* though you may not want or need to.)

An open-ended program is so flexible that you can't possibly cover every operation that the user might do with it.

A loan amortization program is close-ended. It has a limited number of operations. You can input certain things and you get certain outputs. There can be an unlimited number of different outputs, but there are a limited number of operations and processes.

A spreadsheet is open-ended. It can be set up and organized (and programmed) to serve an unlimited number of different purposes with unlimited variations.

A writer trying to explain how to use a spreadsheet can't possibly give every possible use or process, but you can:

- explain the overall premise of the program
- explain the basic interface functions (windows, menus, toolbars)
- define and explain each of the built-in functions and calculations, and
- give a few varying examples of how to use the program.

Similarly, in a chess program, you wouldn't be able to explain every possible strategy that can be used on a chessboard, but you can:

- explain the overall premise of the game
- explain the interface
- define how each of the pieces can be moved and the results of various moves, and
- give a few sample strategies for different stages of a game.

Writing

This chapter gives a brief background in the basics of style and grammar you'll need to know when you write a manual. It also introduces the concept of *Un-Technical writing*.

The sections are:

- Technical and UnTechnical Writing
- Manual Grammar and Style
- Other Topics

Technical and UnTechnical Writing

All writing about technology isn't the same. The big difference is the audience: for whom it was written. Writing for the consumer audience—generally non-technical people living in our ever-more-technical world—is very different in process and practice from writing for highly-skilled technical people.

We at UnTechnical Press use the term *UnTechnical writing* to describe technical writing that is meant to be read by a nontechnical consumer audience. This kind of writing requires a little more diligence, a little more testing and a lot more patience, understanding and reader advocacy.

The sample project in this book is intended to be used by nontechnical customers, so many of the strategies and techniques of UnTechnical writing are incorporated throughout the book.

A few of the premises of UnTechnical writing are:

- Your job is to get the information into the reader's brain as quickly, easily and enjoyably as possible. The world won't end if someone actually enjoys reading your manual, as long as they gain all the necessary knowledge to use the product.

- Your main function is to communicate, not to write a manual. If you can get the message across quicker and more easily using another method of communication, then use it. This could range from comics to wall charts to improved interface design.

- Understand your audience. A lot of people are new to, uncomfortable with or afraid of technology. (You're writing about technology. It doesn't matter what the product or program is, if it's on a computer, it's technology.)

- Write for people, not for professors. Don't make people feel like they're back in school. A lot of people didn't—and don't—like school. People bought the product you're writing about to use the product, not to go back to school. If your manual makes them feel like they're back in the classroom, they won't read it.

- Be the reader's advocate.

- You are part of the user interface. You and your writing are a layer of the user interface. The more you know about user interface design, the better you'll do your job.

- Test your work, especially tutorials and instructions of any sort, with real, typical customers.

For much more on this subject and the necessary tools, skills, and processes needed to write about technology for normal people, see *UnTechnical Writing—How to Write About Technical Subjects and Products So Anyone Can Understand,*[2] available at better bookstores (physical and virtual) everywhere.

Manual Grammar and Style

For technical writing, and even more so for UnTechnical writing, grammar is important, but less important than communication. Writing can be correct without sounding academic or stuffy.

If you want people to read your manual (and you do), don't make them feel that they're in a classroom.

For instance:

- You can sound conversational.

- You can use *they* as a singular pronoun (sometimes) to avoid sexist language.

- You can use slang.

- You can end sentences with prepositions.

- You can even get away with starting sentences with *and* or *but*.

Of course, some things must be absolutely correct, including:

- Spelling,

- Proper word usage, and

- Punctuation.

There are few hard-and-fast rules any more. If you're working on an entertainment product, you have more leeway than if you're writing about project-management software, but even for strictly business products, it is better to have the manual read than collect dust on a shelf.

---

[2] *Yes, a shameless plug.*

What you can and can't get away with—or make use of—will depend on the company you're working for, your local editor and your boss.

Other Topics

Here are a few other helpful topics to know about when writing a manual.

Choosing Your Role

When you receive information for evaluation or absorption, you consider the source. When someone reads a manual, they also consider the source. Who is it that's talking (writing) to them? Is it someone who knows what they're talking about? Is it someone who's really trying to help them understand? Is it someone who "got stuck" with writing a manual, and only slightly prefers writing to getting a root canal? Is it a jerk who can't explain his way out of a paper bag?

When people read your writing and decide how seriously to take it and how much effort to put into understanding it, they take the source—you—into account. They don't know you, and most likely there's not a picture of the manual writer on the back of the book. But, whether you're aware of it or not, you are performing a role and are being defined—even if it's only in the reader's mind.

As long as you're being labeled, you might as well choose your own label. Choose your role.

It's a subtle thing. You usually shouldn't be obvious about it (unless it's a kid's game and you're writing from the point of view of a character in the program). But just knowing who you are (or want to be) to the reader can help flavor your writing. Choosing the role is something you do to help yourself; it's a tool for setting and controlling the document's tone, level of technology and rate of delivery.

As you think about how you'll tackle a project, try on these roles for size, and see what fits you and the project. If none of these roles works for you, find something that does. The idea here is to get into the right frame of mind to communicate with your audience at the right technical level.

- The Tech Writer—you are a technical professional explaining technology to other technical professionals. This writing is simple, to-the-point, unadorned and pretty much devoid of personality. This is the standard role that tech writers usually take. It is the best role to write from if you are writing for a highly technical audience. The rest of the roles in this list are better to take on if you are writing for a nontechnical, consumer audience.

- Writer as Translator—you're the link between a world that speaks Technese and people that don't know the lingo. Your job is to translate technical words, concepts and processes into normal language.

- Writer as Host—you welcome your guests to a new, scary, complicated place. Make them feel at home. Treat them with respect. Talk to them in words that they understand and feel comfortable with. Not only the words, but also the format, feel and media contribute to the comfort factor as well.

- Writer as Friend—you're trying to make your friends feel comfortable while helping them master this new experience.

- Writer as Neighborhood Nerd—you're the guy who knows and loves technology, and you're the one everyone on the block comes to when they have technical questions. You know the deeper inner workings of the technical universe, but know most of your neighbors don't care about that, so you reassure them, then tell them what button to push to get the result they want (tutorial) and give them more information if and when they ask (reference).[3]

- Writer as Teacher—not the cranky teachers you hated, but your favorite teacher that lit that spark in you and made you want to learn.

- Writer as Intrepid Explorer—you've been down this dangerous road before, and are documenting your discovery process for the readers, allowing them to follow and see the sights, yet avoid the pitfalls. This is especially useful for explanations of very complex systems.

- Writer as Tour Guide—you're guiding a group of tourists through a dangerous, foreign land. You've got to watch out for them, even protect them, while showing them a good time.

Non-sexist Language

Think about your audience. If it's mostly men, then you can use the pronoun "he" freely and exclusively. If it's mostly women, then you can use only "she." If, as usual, it's a mixed audience, then you have the potential to annoy them by choosing one gender or the other. While we proponents of UnTechnical writing may want to surprise or even shock a reader now and then, we don't want to annoy.

When you find yourself in the pronoun dilemma, you have a number of choices:

- **Use only "he."**

    Using "he" as a pronoun to refer to an individual who may be either male or female (but you don't know for sure) is the traditional English usage,

---

[3] *All those billion-dollar computer companies should set aside some sort of retirement fund for Neighborhood Nerds. Judging from the complexity of early computers and the incomprehensibility of many early computer manuals, if it hadn't been for those noble Neighborhood Nerds simply explaining what button to push to get the desired result, computers would never have caught on.*

dating from before political correctness. It isn't technically wrong, but it can make some readers think you're a jerk and pay less attention to you.

- **Use only "she."**

On the opposite end of the scale, you can take the attitude that women have had to put up with being called "he" for a long time, so why not turn the tables and let the men see what it's like. While fair, and technically legal, it can still alienate a good portion of your audience, both male and female.

- **Alternate between "he" and "she."**

This is the "fair" approach. Approximately every other time you use a pronoun to refer to a person whose sex you don't know, switch between "he" and "she." While it's fair, legal, and generally acceptable, it is also noticeable. The reader is very aware that the writer is switching back and forth. This can be distracting; the reader stops thinking about the subject and thinks about the switch.

- **Use "he or she."**

If a writer wants to cover all the bases without switching, he or she can use "he or she" each and every time he or she has to write "he" or "she." Again, legal. But there's something ... wishy-washy about it. And it's longer and a bit more awkward. You can usually get away with it once in a while without it seeming awkward, but continual use makes it stand out too much, and readers once again notice the writing instead of concentrating on the subject.

- **Pluralize and use "they."**

A very good way around the whole issue is to take advantage of the fact that in English, the plural pronoun "they" works for both sexes. Instead of writing something like:

If the reader likes the subject, then he or she should read the book.

You can write:

If readers like the subject, then they should read the book.

At least 80% of the time you can pluralize and use "they" to avoid sexist— and awkward—language without ruining your point. In those few cases where pluralizing just doesn't work, then you can fall back on one of the other options, or just use "they."

- **Just use "they."**

  Many editors and grammar mavens are now allowing the use of "they" as an any-gender singular pronoun for technical, if not for academic, writing. A reader may find that they are referred to as "they" even though they are one person. Most readers won't notice, and some editors are still sticklers. I use it over "he and she," but not very often.

- **Get cute.**

  A final possibility is to use some sort of combination of he and she, such as "he/she" or "s/he."[4] These work, but they seem like the writer is trying too hard. Maybe, if and when a combination like this comes into more common usage, it'll lose its cuteness.

Consistency

There are a lot of ways to be consistent—and inconsistent.

- **Names of Things**

Don't call it a doohickey in one chapter and a whatsit in another. Make sure the name you use in the manual matches the name on the actual product, and on the box.

- **Abbreviations**

When you use them, use them the same way throughout the whole document or series of documents. Consistently define them the first time they're presented.

- **Level of Detail**

If you're covering a number of similar subjects, they should all be covered in the same amount of detail—unless there is a reason that the reader needs to know more about a particular subject, in which case that should be made clear.

- **Look and Feel**

This includes the page-to-page and chapter-to-chapter look of a single document, including typography, tables and illustrations, and the book-to-book look of a series of related documents, including typography, overall design, and table of contents and index organization.

- **Presentation of Information**

Like information should be presented in a like manner. Always show the reader instructions within tutorials the same way. Always explain similar things in the same way—if you show a flowchart in one process, then show it for all processes.

---

[4] *I've heard it said that even the combination word "s/he," which means "she or he," is showing undue prejudice against non-sexual entities, and the proper combination word should be "s/he/it." Of course, it would never work in polite conversation.*

- **Lists**

Use parallel style and construction. Note that the headings on this list of ways to be consistent consist of all nouns or noun phrases. If this item's heading was "Be consistent with lists," it would be inconsistent with the rest of the list.

- **Overall Quality**

Don't make half your manual wonderful and slap the rest together. And if you're doing a quick cheapie, don't make part of it wonderful—it'll make the rest seem worse than it is.

The Rule of Threes

The standard rule of threes is:

Tell them what you're going to say, say it, then tell them what you said.

For each chapter, topic, section or segment, you first explain what will be contained in that chapter, topic, section or segment. Next, you present the body of information. Then, you summarize or review it at the end of the chapter, topic, section or segment.

While many manual writers and editors adhere strictly to this rule, you may prefer to (and be allowed to) play fast and loose with it. You should almost always stand by this rule in a tutorial, but for introductions, reference sections and other parts of the manual, you may choose to use it or not depending on the technical difficulty of the subject. The more difficult the subject is for the reader to understand and master, the more you should stand by the rule—and the more often you should use it within a document, breaking the subject matter into smaller and smaller chunks of information presented in threes.

If the subject is light, and easily mastered by the reader, you may want to avoid the repetition and imposed format to either simplify and shorten that part of the document, or use the saved space to add flavor and entertain a little.

All in all, you really can't go *too* far wrong by adhering to the rule of threes. At worst, you might miss an opportunity to simplify and entertain.

Keeping the Reader Reading

If nobody reads the manual, we still get paid. But most writers—even technical writers—want to be read. And it's not just a matter of ego. It's wanting the work we do to be useful, to be worth the doing.

Most people don't read technical books and manuals for pleasure. They only do it because they have to. And they're looking for any excuse to stop, to take a break, to get a cup of coffee or to throw the book across the room in frustration. Anything we can do to keep readers reading is good. Anything we can do to help them get through it quickly and painlessly, we should.

Here are some helpful tools to keep readers reading:

• Write in Bite-Sized Chunks

Keep sentences, sections and paragraphs small—write in bite-sized chunks. This forces you to be clear, to keep your explanations simple, and stops you from rambling on too much. And it keeps the reader reading longer.

A small, simple-looking paragraph smiles at the reader and says, "I'm quick and easy. Come on and read me, you'll be done before you know it." A large, densely written paragraph says, "I dare you to read me, and to try to wrest meaning from the dark, twisty caverns of my many long sentences."

It is especially important to keep the paragraphs at the beginnings of each chapter or section small and inviting. If they're inviting enough, the reader will put off stopping until the end of the next chapter or section.

You should also present the writing in bite-sized chunks, even in early drafts. Make it as easy as possible for the people who have to read those drafts, and you'll get better feedback.

• Use Lots of Headings and Subheadings

Using a lot of headings and subheadings serves four purposes:

1. It keeps the book divided into small, easy-to-absorb chunks.
2. It allows the reader to zero in on the exact section they want to read without fishing around.
3. It familiarizes readers with all the sections—as they look for the topic they want, they read all the other headings. When they need to look up something else, they'll often remember that there was a heading about that subject.
4. It makes it easier for you to organize the book and explain each subject independently.

• Advocate a High-Quality Layout

The quality of the layout can also help keep the reader reading. Lots of white space on the page and a good space between paragraphs makes the page look inviting. A page crammed full of solid text looks scary. Do what you can to ensure that the layout is done by a good graphic artist.

• A Little Humor Goes a Long Way

By this I mean both that some humor is good and that too much is bad.

A little humor, spread thinly throughout a manual, is a good way to get readers to at least page through the whole book once. Too much—or inappropriate—humor and you lose the point of the whole book.

Humor diffuses a tense situation. If you can laugh at it, you're no longer afraid of it. Many readers are afraid of the technology you're writing about and afraid of breaking it and afraid of how it will change their lives and afraid of having to read your manual. They need a good laugh. If you can get them to laugh at something, they'll no longer fear it.

That said, here are the inevitable caveats...

Humor Caveat #1: Know when not to use it.

Don't force jokes about something that you personally can't comfortably joke about. Even more important is how the reader, and your client or employer feel about the jokes. Some people, including bosses, have no humor. Know when to keep your humor to yourself.

Humor Caveat #2: Test your jokes.

Try out your jokes on some trusted—and honest—friends and family members before putting them into a manual. If the general response is bad, kill the joke— even though you love it.

Humor Caveat #3: Ask for help.

If you don't have—I won't say good, but how about—a widely accepted sense of humor, get someone else to supply a few jokes or comics. There's bound to be someone around the house or office that can help.

> "Men will confess to treason, murder, arson, false teeth, or a wig. How many of them will own up to a lack of humour?"
>
> **— Frank Moore Colby**

Humor Caveat #4: Watch your mouth.

Unless the product you're working on is intended for adults with an adolescent sense of humor, stay away from insults and bathroom humor. Again, it's important to know your audience to know your limits, but when in doubt, go the tasteful route.

Humor Caveat #5: Humor is often a cultural thing.

Much of humor is culturally based, so what's funny to you may not be funny to someone in Japan or Germany or France. Some subjects that we casually joke about here may be seriously taboo elsewhere. If you know that what you're writing will be translated to other languages, be prepared for your humor to be chopped out. Make sure this chopping won't affect the usefulness of the document.

Your Duties—Above and Beyond Writing

Of course, your obvious duty is to write the manual. That's what you're being paid to do. But there's more to it. All of these, and more, can come into play, conflict, and compete for attention as you work on a project:

- Duty to self—your desire to do the best work you can, to write a master-piece, to create art and to promote your career.

- Duty to employer—your need to satisfy the boss for continued or future employment, *and* have a positive impact on the bottom line. A positive impact on the bottom line includes minimizing costs to the company by controlling the time and cost of writing, as well as the size and cost of documents and their related shipping costs. It also involves the cost of after-sales support (eliminating as many tech support calls as possible), and improving the opportunity for future sales of updated versions and other company products. (If a customer buys a product and doesn't understand it or can't use it, they won't buy another from the same company.)

- Duty to team—whether you've been on the project since the beginning or just joined weeks before shipping, the design/development team has been working on the project for months or years. They deserve docs that "do right" by the product: show it in a good light, make it more useful and pro-mote it. (And mention all their names—properly spelled—in the credits!)

- Duty to product—often the product itself, whether spreadsheet, computer game, VCR or whatever, is such a good piece of work that it deserves to be given a good chance to succeed. And that means it should be well-docu-mented, so it can be used and enjoyed as quickly and easily as possible.

- Duty to customer—marketing will identify with and represent the custom-ers up to the point where the product is sold, but it's up to you to be there for them once they get home with it. Beyond their absolute *needs,* what does the customer *deserve?* What would you demand, expect, or want if you just brought the product home or to the office and opened the box? What would satisfy you as a customer? What would satisfy your mother (assuming your mother isn't a technological wizard)?

All About Manuals

This chapter delves into the art, science, politics, composition, analysis, variations, extensions and future of the software manual.

The sections are:

- The State of the Manual
- Purposes of the Manual
- How People Read and Use Manuals
- The Software Manual Dilemma
- Manuals and Product Design
- Manuals and Interface Design
- Parts of a Manual
- Manuals for Kids' Products
- Manuals and After-market Books
- Beyond the Words
- Beyond the Manual
- Online and Onscreen Help and Documentation

The State of the Manual

Technical manuals—especially software manuals—have a generally dismal reputation. Most people ignore or avoid them.

At one time, not long ago, this reputation was universally deserved. Now, as companies realize that the people buying and using technology are not technogeeks, but are "normal" people, things are starting to change. There are enough products on the market and enough competition so that companies that provide inadequate documentation lose market share. Consumers will no longer buy software because of novelty or because there are no options. They demand a product that works: that does what they need it to do, and that they can understand and understand how to use.

Today, consumer magazines that rate technical products (camcorders, VCRs, computers, software) are beginning to rate the documentation along with the rest of the product. This is a good trend for consumers and for conscientious manual writers.

Purposes of the Manual

Product manuals can serve all of these purposes:

- Introduce the customer to the product and its capabilities.
- Help the customer install and use the product.
- Give the customer enough background in the product's environment (for instance, giving background or basics in the operating system, which is above and beyond the program) to properly use the product.
- Add value to the product by supplying background, scientific, historical or entertainment information.
- Add weight to the box (heavier boxes feel like they're worth more).
- Give the customer a reason to like the company.
- Help the customer feel secure about buying another product from the company.
- Eliminate as many calls to customer service and technical support as possible.

The more of these purposes the manual serves, the better. The only limitations are time, budget and company attitude.

How People Read and Use Manuals

How people read and use manuals depends on who they are: how new they are to the product, their level of technical expertise, their previous knowledge of the subject, their available time and their personality. Whoever they are and however they read the manual, it has to serve their purposes. You have to write it to meet the needs of a lot of different people.

Here's a small sampling of reader types, and hints on how to make sure their needs are covered:

• Thorough Readers

These are people who read everything cover to cover, and work through all the tutorials.

This type of reader may be new to the product or technology and want to read everything to avoid mistakes. Thorough readers may also be very experienced people who want to know everything there is to know about the new product or tool.

For these readers, you need to present the document as a whole, linear unit. The organization must be logical, and must build from beginning to end. The tutorial must be well designed, and well written, thoroughly tested, and well laid out.

• Thorough Dry-labbers

These are people who read everything and dry-lab the tutorial.

This type of reader is similar to the thorough reader, but is familiar enough with the product or type of product that they just read through the tutorial, without actually performing the steps.

For these readers, you need to be sure that your tutorial not only lists the tutorial steps that the reader is intended to perform, but also tells—and shows—the results of each step.

• Foundation Seekers

These are people who only read the introduction section, work through (or dry-lab) the tutorial, and figure out the rest on their own.

For these readers, make sure the introduction section completely describes the product and its capabilities, and that the tutorial covers all the basic knowledge the readers will need to use the product on their own.

• Self-starters

These are people who dig into the product on their own to figure out the basics, and only look at the reference section for specific topics and questions.

For these readers, the table of contents and index need to be very complete. Lots of well-named subheadings help, too.

• Scanners

These are readers who quickly glance through the whole book and only read the headings and picture captions, and anything else that catches their eye.

Give these readers lots of things to catch their eyes: pictures, headings, drawings, quotes, etc.

• Avoiders

These are people who avoid the manual at all costs.

For these readers, you have to be sure that the one time they resort to opening the manual, they have a good experience. That means it looks good, it reads well, they can find exactly what they're looking for quickly and easily, and, if all goes really well, you catch their attention so they spend a little extra time paging through the manual, and consciously or not, get a sense of the book and what's in it. If these readers have a good experience they might come back.

The Software Manual Dilemma

The big dilemma of the software manual is that the manual has to be done before the software is done.

Manual writers are faced with the following questions:

- How do you write about something that isn't there?

- How do you check and test and perfect your manual if you can't check and test it against a finished product?

- How do you get the engineers, who really only want their product to be as wonderful as possible, to stop making changes and stop improving the product once the manual has been sent off to layout? (Especially on a large project with multiple engineers or multiple teams of engineers, there are so many possible ways and means and reasons for an engineer to make one single little change that will make your manual obsolete.)

Gold Master—

the final, totally tested, QA-approved, ready-to-duplicate-and-ship master copy of a program.

Feature Freeze—

the point of a project at which the powers-that-be declare that no new features will be added to a program. Henceforth, only refining and bug-fixing will take place.

Before discussing solutions, let's first look at why the manual has to be written before the product is done. It starts with manufacturing time and cost. A large run, 50,000 or more of manuals, can take weeks to print (without paying extra for rush charges), while that many disks (floppies or CDs) can be duplicated in a couple of days.

You've got to have the manual and its graphics edited and ready for layout at least one month (if not two) before the disks are ready, in order to have finished manuals ready on time for manufacturing. And if you have to have the manual ready a month or two before the *gold master,* then there must be a *feature freeze* at least a week, if not two, before that.

Of course, the logical thing to do is to schedule time *after* the program is done for final manual writing, testing, editing, layout and printing. That way you can be sure to be accurate and complete. But both for financial reasons—the company has hundreds of thousands, or even millions of dollars invested in this project, and getting it to market as quickly as possible is a reasonable goal—and for attitude-related reasons—it's only the manual; it has no right to delay shipping—this just isn't the way things are done.

One option you have to give yourself more time is to pay a premium to the printer. For enough money, they can speed up their delivery, giving you another two to three weeks. But for the sake of the company and your future employment, you don't want to be the one held responsible (whether it's your fault of not) for the considerable extra cash outlay.

It looks and feels hopeless, but time after time, those manuals are ready on time—and they're often very accurate. The saving grace? Complexity.

Software that is complex enough to require a large manual is complex enough to take quite a while to debug. Even after all the features are in—and frozen—it usually takes weeks or months to get everything working and looking good enough to ship.

Of course, there are times when, complex or not, the program will be ready quickly and you've got almost no time to do a wonderful job on a huge manual. When this happens, there are no easy solutions, unless you have a time machine. If there's no way you can get more time, then all you can do is try to pare down the manual's contents to the most important parts, be as accurate as you possibly can and forget about sleep for a week or two.

Manuals and Product Design

For a customer to understand a product, it takes good product design—especially the interface—and a good manual. Universally improving these two things will change the customer's experience with technology for the better.

While generally treated as separate processes, performed at different times by different people, interface and documentation are, and should be, intertwined. As writers of manuals, we need to study interface design. And interface designers should be equally concerned with the manual.

Manuals and Interface Design

The manual is part of, or a layer of, the interface. It can even be looked at as the interface to the interface. Writers who write manuals for technical products should learn all they can about interface design.

Parts of a Manual

Manuals come in all shapes and sizes, but they're all made out of some or all of the same parts.

Go to your shelf and pull out all your software manuals. If you don't have a good assortment of manuals of different lengths for various types of products, then borrow some from friends or enemies. As you go through this section, look through all the manuals to compare them.

The different parts of a manual are:

The Front Matter

Definition

Front matter is the first few pages of a manual. It contains some very important information, both for legal reasons and for the reader's convenience. Try to keep it fairly short, so the reader gets right to the meat of the manual quickly.

Front Matter Parts

- **Title page**

  The title page states the title of the book, the author[5] and the publisher. For a software product, it may also have the name of the program's designer(s) or producer, whoever is the product's driving creative force.

- **License page**

  The license page hold the copyright and license information for both the manual and the software. Check this carefully with your legal department. The license page also has the name, address and other contact information for the publisher, trademark declarations for all trademarks that appear in the book or product, and the ISBN number. There may also be a dedication here.

- **Credits and special thanks**

  These can be quite lengthy for a large software product. If you can afford the space, put all the names here that you can. People love—and deserve—to get credit. *Make sure you spell everyone's name correctly.* Depending on company policy, those mentioned in the special thanks section may be people in or out of the company that contributed something directly or indirectly to the project, or they may be a listing of the company's management staff. Sometimes credits appear in the program and are left out of the manual. As a minimum, put the manual credits in the manual: author(s), editor(s), designer(s), graphic artist(s), etc. Sometimes credits are put in the back of the manual, in an appendix.

- **Table of Contents**

  This is essential in a manual or any technical document. If you are allowed the pages, consider taking the contents down two heading levels below the chapter level. Anything to help readers zero in on the information they want. Don't make it long for the sake of making it long, but make it as long as it needs to be to guide the reader. In general, the more

---

[5] *Most manuals don't have the author's name on the title page. As an author, I think it belongs there.*

complex or technical the product, the longer the table of contents needs to be.

- **Acknowledgments, etc.**

  There may be other things in the front matter, like acknowledgments, but most of this is usually covered in the dedication or credits.

Writing Front Matter

There's really not much writing involved in front matter. It's more an act of carefully gathering information than writing. You'll need to check with previous company products and manuals to see how it is usually handled. It wouldn't hurt to check with the legal department, if there is one, to make sure the license is up-to-date. Be careful to spell all names correctly. Let your word processor or the page-layout program build the table of contents.

The Introduction

Definition

The introduction is the orientation meeting for the product and the manual. After reading the introduction—which shouldn't take more than five or ten minutes at the most, preferably one or two—the reader should know where they are, what the product is, how the product fits into their life, what they have to do to get the product going, what they can do with it, how the manual is going to help them, and that they are safe, welcome and in good hands.

The main information to convey in an introduction is about the product, the company and the manual. Beyond that information, you also want to use the introduction to establish the tone of the manual: serious, humorous, relaxed, silly or whatever is best for the product. Whatever you do, you'll set some sort of tone, so be aware of it and set the tone you want.

Introduction Parts

- **Welcome**

  This can be a single word *(welcome* or even *hi),* a single sentence, or as much as a paragraph that thanks the customers for buying the product and welcomes them to the product, the product line, the family, the world that the product provides, etc. While not absolutely necessary, it doesn't hurt to be nice. The amount of space it takes up doesn't cost much. Just don't lay it on too thick.

- **Description of the Product**

  All you need is a sentence or two explaining what the product is or does. If you can't say it in less than a paragraph, then either the product is confusing or you don't really have a grasp of its essence. This description can be combined in a single sentence with the welcome.

Some may think this unnecessary, but it's worth the 10 minutes and three square inches of space on a page. Sure there's a description of the product on the box (we hope), but boxes get thrown away. People come into jobs and inherit the software at their workstation. Software is sometimes bundled in a suite or with a computer—and without its box.[6]

If there are a number of books, disks or other objects in the package, then give a listing of what's in the box. Its just a courtesy so people don't spend hours trying to make something work only to find that they're missing a part.

If there is any prerequisite knowledge, or additional software or hardware required to use the product, say it now, define what's needed and where to get it. This isn't the same as system requirements, which are covered under installation instructions. This should just mention hardware and software that isn't a standard part of the computer or operating system.

Here you might also want to briefly point out how the product fits into the product lineup or works with a suite of products that the user may have or wish to buy. You may also want to mention how the product has changed or improved since the last version, if it has.

Finally, there's the description of the manual and its organization. Tell them how the manual will help them, and briefly explain what each section or chapter contains.

This product description is actually marketing—marketing the product, the company, the next version of the product and the manual. If the introduction drags, bores or confuses, or comes on too strong as a hard sell for other products, the reader won't read on.

• Installation and Startup Directions

If it's software, it has to be installed and started, and you have to tell the customer how to do it. Even if it's as simple as "Shove the CD into the CD drive and pray that AutoPlay works," you have to say it. And tell them what to do if their prayers aren't answered.

Installation and starting instructions are often put into a separate document, smaller than the manual. It can be called a Quick-Start guide, an

---

[6] *When I upgraded my copy of Director® from version 3 to version 4 (or 4 to 5?), I opted to buy their whole suite of programs. It was a good deal. One of the programs that comes with it is called XRES. I didn't know what it was, and couldn't tell for sure by its name. I grabbed the manual and flipped to chapter 1. It didn't say. It talked about terminology and creating swap disks. I flipped back to the table of contents. It wasn't until the 6th page of the table of contents (chapter 5) that I found out what the product actually did.*

Installation card, a Getting Started booklet or any number of similar things. This is done for a couple of reasons:

1. It's easier and less intimidating for the customer to use a little booklet or one-page instruction sheet than to have to page through a big manual just to get the product started.

2. The installer is often the last thing done on the program (slapped on at the end), and may not be ready for testing by the time the manual has to be sent off for printing. A small booklet or instruction sheet can be printed quickly at the last second.

If it is in a separate guide, you should say in the manual's introduction that the program must be installed before use, and to look for the Quick-Start guide or Getting Started booklet or whatever it is, for instructions.

• **A Plea to Fill Out the Registration Card**

A last option for the introduction is a plea to fill out the registration card. Names in the database are money in the bank. Besides selling the names, companies can find out where their products are and aren't selling, and, if you leave room for comments on the registration card, you can get some excellent feedback, positive and negative, about the product and the manual.

Writing the Introduction

Writing the introduction is more like marketing writing than technical writing. Check with marketing to see if they already have well-worded product descriptions and information on the product line.

Look to previous company manuals to see if there's any boilerplate text that you'll be expected to include.

While the introduction is at the beginning of the manual, it needn't be the first thing written. Often it's easiest to write it last. It's easier to describe the manual's structure after most of the manual has been written and you're sure the structure won't be changing.

If you're including the installation and starting instructions, test them with typical users. Have people who are new to the product actually install and start it using your instructions. Watch without offering any help. See where they pause, stumble, get confused or mess up. Then fix it. Then test it again.

Tutorial

Definition

Tutorials are the follow-the-bouncing-ball sing-along of manuals.

Whether they're called tutorials, lessons, learning guides, exercises, explorations or torture, they are often the new user's first real experience with the product. It's up to you to make sure that the first experience is a good one.

Face it, tutorials are usually pretty darn boring. Boring to read, boring to work through and boring to write. Do yourself and your readers a favor and lighten up the tutorial.

Keep the tone light and fun. Use humorous or entertaining examples whenever you can. You might even be able to couch tutorials in a story or case study as long as you don't leave the point for more than a sentence or two at a time. (Be careful with this; it's easy to overdo it and lose your audience.)

Sometimes, when a manual is organized into a number of separate topics, small tutorials may be spread throughout the book, instead of having one tutorial chapter or section of the manual. In these cases, make sure each individual tutorial is completely self-contained, and doesn't depend on any other tutorial for starting instructions or sample data.

Tutorial Parts

- **Tutorial Introduction**

   This short introduction welcomes the reader to the tutorial and to the program (again), explains what they will learn in the tutorials, and describes the structure of the tutorial chapter.

   You should also point out here that within the tutorial there are two basic types of text:

   Text that looks like this describes and explains things.

   Text that looks like this is an instruction for you to follow.

   It's up to you to make this clear to the graphic artist who lays out the book as well as to the reader.

   A reason to keep manual introductions short is to get the reader to the tutorial as quickly as possible. Once they get to the tutorial, get them working on the program as quickly as possible; that means you should keep tutorial introductions short as well.

The tutorial introduction sets the tone for the tutorial, which should be consistent with, though not necessarily identical to the rest of the manual.

• **Lesson Introduction**

If there is more than one lesson or section within a tutorial, then each one should have a little introduction telling what the reader will learn in the lesson. A sentence or two should be enough; a small numbered or bulleted list works well.

Each lesson introduction should include something to the effect of:

Before you continue, your computer should be on and the program should be running. For help with this see ...

• **The Lesson**

If this isn't the first lesson, you have to allow that the reader may have turned off their computer since the last lesson, and instruct them to start it up and load any work in progress needed to continue the tutorial.

Once you actually start a lesson, the general form for each step or series of steps follows the rule of threes:

1. Tell them what they are going to do.
2. Tell them how to do it.
3. Tell them what they did.

For example:

The first thing to do is to load the sample file called *Tutorial 1*.

1. Open the File menu.

2. Select Open ....

3. When the Open File dialog appears, click on the file called *Tutorial 1*.

4. Click OK.

The file *Tutorial 1* is now open and ready to use. Your screen should now look like this: (screenshot)

Numbering instructions isn't necessary, but it doesn't hurt, especially if there are more than three or four in a row.

Graphics are very important to tutorials. In the example above, it wouldn't hurt to have an additional graphic showing the Open File dialog box with the cursor pointing to the highlighted file *Tutorial 1*.

Graphics in series are very helpful, too. There are many times when showing pictures of step one, step two and step three of a process with short captions explains things better than paragraphs of text.

Always add an instruction to save the file in use at the end of *each* lesson in case they stop the tutorial and need to return to this exact point later. (It's also a generally good deed to instill in computer users the habit of saving often.)

• The Lesson Summary

At the end of each lesson, summarize what the reader accomplished or learned in the lesson. Invite them to continue on to the next lesson or to come back later and take up where they left off.

• Tutorial Summary

At the end of the tutorial, summarize what the reader accomplished and learned through all the lessons. Perhaps congratulations are in order. Invite them to jump in and start using the program, and that whenever they need help, to use the help system and look in the reference section of the manual. And if they wish they can repeat the tutorial at any time.

Tutorial Rules of Thumb

- Tutorials are a must in manuals for the consumer audience. In more-technical technical manuals, such as those that accompany computer languages, the tutorial may be replaced by a section with sample code.

- Keep each tutorial, section of a tutorial, or lesson to 20 minutes or less. If it's longer, divide it up. You can separate tutorials into smaller parts by dividing them into beginning and advanced tutorials, by separately covering different modes or functions of the program, or by dividing them into progressive lessons.

- Always allow for the reader to go directly from one tutorial or lesson to the next *or* to approach each lesson as a separate session.

- Make sure that any instructions or actions that the reader is actually to perform are clearly marked, preferably in large, simple, bold type, separated by a little space from the surrounding explanatory text.

- Make sure your graphic artist knows what to do about the instruction text.

- Explain through text or graphics what should happen after each step or series of steps the reader performs. This helps those who actually do the steps understand if they're doing it right or wrong, and enables dry-labbing for those in a hurry or away from their computers.

- Tutorials for kids should be more extensive than those for adults, and should be written as a series of goals or challenges.

- Try to make it fun. Fight the boredom.

Writing Tutorials

Tutorials are often the last major writing done on a software manual because the program has to be nearly finished before you can write exact step-by-step instructions and take the accompanying screenshots.

Once the program is far enough along, writing tutorials is a multi-step process.

1. **Determine who the tutorial is for.**

    The audience influences both the tone and the content. Experienced computer users who know the operating system can just be told to load or save a file, while newcomers to computers will need step-by-step instructions. Kids will need longer, more goal-oriented tutorials.

2. **Determine what the tutorial must cover.**

    What will the user need to know, and know how to do, in order to use the program? What are the absolute basics of the program? What are some of the more difficult tasks to master?

3. **Outline the tutorial.**

    This needn't be very detailed. It can be a simple list of the things that the person working through the tutorial will do. For example, a first outline for a tutorial for a very simple word processor might look like this:

1. Turn on computer	9. Paste text
2. Start program	10. Highlight another way
3. Load sample file	11. Cut text
4. Type in text	12. Paste text
5. Highlight text	13. Save file
6. Change text	14. Print
7. Highlight another way	15. Quit program
8. Copy text	

4. **Get feedback on the outline.**

   Run this outline by whoever is doing your structural edit and as many people on the project as you can, including producers, product managers, testers and engineers. This needn't be a formal distribution of the document. You can either corner the people you want, one or two at a time for 10 minutes and ask them what else they think should be there, or call a 20-minute meeting and talk to everyone at once.

5. **Write the first draft.**

   Write the tutorial using the rule of threes for each major step. Mark where there should be graphics, and take the screenshots, even if they're *FPO* (for position only), and will have to be replaced later.

6. **Test the first draft.**

   Locate at least a couple of test subjects. Ideally, they should be typical prospective users of the program, but you can usually get away with finding people around the office for this first round. Choose people who aren't on the project, and are seeing the program for the first time. Also make sure they are at about the same technical level as the typical customer. If you can't find people at work, try family, try friends, try friends of people at work. If you can't find anyone, have the marketing department find them for you.

   Print out copies of the tutorial. The graphics can be embedded in the text, or on separate sheets of paper. Gather the test subjects in a room and supply them with computers, disks of the program in progress and your printed tutorial.

   Give them instructions like these:

   This is the very first draft of the tutorial, and we've brought you in to help us find out what needs to be fixed.

   If you have any problems, it's not your fault—it's because the tutorial still needs work. If you have problems or questions, that's good, because we'll know what we have to fix.

   Think out loud if you can. Ask questions that occur to you, but don't expect any answers or help. We have to find out just how much work we have ahead of us.

   Watch and listen and take notes. Don't help. Don't answer questions unless they get totally stuck, but write down every question that's asked, as well as anything you notice they have problems with.

7. **Rewrite the tutorial.**

   Take your notes and incorporate all the necessary changes to the structure and information. Update any screenshots that changed or were FPOs
   the last round. Clean up the writing to the best of your ability and run it
   through a spelling checker before sending it off for an edit.

8. **Reality check.**

   Be sure to continually update your tutorial with the latest version of the
   program. It could change, making some of your tutorial steps or
   screenshots wrong. Besides checking it yourself, run your ready-for-edit-
   ing copy, complete with graphics by a few people on the project, including the producer and a tester. They may know about changes that you
   missed or that are about to happen.

9. **Editing.**

   This a very thorough line edit, hopefully performed by a good editor. The
   point here is to clean up the writing, perfect the punctuation, check your
   consistency and make sure you're meeting the company style and quality
   standards.

10. **Final testing.**

    Pretty much the same as the test of the first draft, but, if possible, with
    real customers as test subjects. Often, you won't have the time or budget
    to run this second test, but if you can, you'll be sure that your tutorial is
    going to serve its purpose.

11. **Final rewrite and editing.**

    This round of writing and editing could be a matter of minutes if you and
    the editor were careful on the previous rounds, and there were no sur-
    prises in the final testing. The main thing that'll cause problems here are
    if the program functions or graphics changed yet again, requiring you to
    rewrite or retake screenshots.

    Once this is done, you're ready for layout.

Reference Section

Definition

The reference section is the product's bible. It defines and explains every window, every mode, every function and every control. It is usually the largest part of the manual.

Reference sections, depending on the product and the writer, may also include an explanation of how the program works, as well as strategies or practical applications to get the most out of the program.

Reference Parts

Reference sections may include any or all of the chunks of information listed below: (These parts aren't necessarily separate sections within the reference. They can be combined, mixed and matched to present the information to the reader in the best possible way. But most, if not all, of the parts should be covered.)

- **Introduction to Reference**

  Once again, this introduction should be short. It need only explain the organization and contents of the reference section, and direct the reader to other potential sources of information: Help system, tutorial, etc.

- **Functional Overview**

  Describe the program's major functions and division into modes (if it has modes).

  This isn't a detailed explanation of how the program works behind the scenes, but what the user does with the program and what the program does for the user. Don't get too flowery here. This is wetting the sponge for the detailed information to come, not pure marketing writing.

- **Detailed Mode Description**

  If the program has different modes of operation, explain them, what they do, and what the user would do in each one.

- **Detailed Menu Description**

  List each menu, menu item, submenu and submenu item, and explain what each choice does. You want to explain what choosing the menu item does, not necessarily what you do after you have chosen the item.

  For instance, say you are writing about a database program with a View menu that contains choices such as Design view and Table view. In the detailed menu description, you would explain that choosing those menu items presents the user with the Design or Table view, and maybe even include a screenshot of what is displayed when the item is selected, but you wouldn't describe the entire workings of the two views within this menu section. Putting all that information here breaks up the usefulness of the menu description. There should be a separate section of the manual that describes Designing Databases and Using Tables.

On the other hand, if you are writing about a word processor, and are describing the Find ... item in the Edit menu, you may want to put a complete explanation of this function here. Since it is short and simple, it won't break up the menu description too much, and there just might not be another good place to put this information.

- **Detailed Toolbar Description**

    If there are toolbars in the program, first define and list them, then give the information that is common to all toolbars in the program, such as moving, hiding, reshaping, tool tips, etc. Next, display a picture of each toolbar and describe what each button on each toolbar does, to the same level of detail as a menu item in the detailed menu description.

    It is especially helpful to show a graphic of the toolbar with callouts explaining what each button is. (Many button icons do more to confuse than communicate.) It is also helpful to put a small graphic of each individual button next to its description so the reader doesn't have to refer back, sometimes a few pages back, to see what button matches what description.

- **Detailed Window and Dialog Description**

    Identify each window and each dialog box and describe what the user will be doing in this window or dialog, and how to do it. Explain what each and every button and control does.

- **Detailed Control Description**

    Every button, every slider, every fill-in text box should be named and explained. If there are any that aren't covered somewhere in the menu, toolbar or window and dialog sections, make sure they're covered somewhere.

- **Keyboard Commands and Shortcuts**

    A chart listing all the keyboard commands and shortcuts may be included in the reference, or may be in an appendix or even a Quick-Start guide.

Writing the Reference Section

References are usually the first part of the manual you can start writing, because at least some of the look and function of the program should be finished and nailed down by the time you start writing. They are often the last thing finished, since you have to update them to cover every functional and graphical change until the product is done.

The actual writing is far less painstaking and requires less testing than a tutorial, but getting the information from busy team members can sometimes be a lot of work. Features and functions and their accompanying graphics can change wildly if you so much as blink. The biggest challenge of writing a reference section is accuracy.

The second biggest challenge of a reference section is organization. There are as many ways to organize this section as there are products. A couple of ways to organize are:

- **General to Specific**

  Start with an overview, the big picture. Next give the menu window and function overview. Next, the detailed descriptions of buttons and functions, then how to put it all together and actually use the product.

- **Work Patterns**

  Start with the overview and functional basics, then cover the rest in an order that follows typical working patterns—ways someone would normally use the product. In some ways this would resemble a long, very detailed tutorial. But it won't replace a tutorial.

Beyond the organization, the next most important thing about writing and presenting a reference section is consistency. All the lists should look the same, all the buttons should be presented in the same way, all the window explanations, all the mode descriptions and all the segments of like information should be organized and presented consistently.

Additional Information

Definition

Depending on the product you're writing about—and your budget and schedule—it may be appropriate or necessary to include in the manual information that is above and beyond the product.

- With a historical battle simulation, you could include an historical account of the actual battle and biographies of the better-known participants.

- With a simulation of any sort, you might want to include an *inside the simulation* section, explaining the limitations of and assumptions used in the simulation.

- With a strategy game (or any game) you might want to include hints, tips and strategies.

- With educational products of all sorts you could include background material.
- With many products, it may be appropriate to list other references, in print and on the Web, that could be useful to users of the product.

Writing the Additional Information

Sometimes it may be up to you to suggest this additional information, other times it may be called for in the product design. In any event, writing this additional material is generally a matter of research, writing and editing. Most of the information, unlike the product, is static, and won't change if you turn your back. Because of this, you can work on this material in bits and pieces, while waiting for feedback or edits on other parts of the manual, or while waiting for the product to near completion.

Generally, you won't be writing the equivalent of a book on the subject, but more of an introduction to the general concepts or a list of "interesting facts" on the subject. If you can, find some experts in the field to look over your work, and verify the content. Use illustrations or photographs to highlight the important points and make the section of the manual more interesting.

And, as always, it should be edited carefully.

Back Matter

Definition

Back matter is all the rest of the stuff at the back of the manual. Depending on the project, there may be a lot or almost none at all.

Back Matter Parts

- **Appendices**

    Appendices are supplementary pieces of information that are added to the end of a book or manual. They're all the extra stuff that you know should be included but that doesn't fit anywhere in the main body.

    Lists and resources—like the recommended reading list in this book—are best as appendices, so the reader can find them easily and all in one place.

    Other chunks of information that work well as software manual appendices are:

    - Troubleshooting tips
    - Help with the operating system and operating system extensions that the program depends upon
    - Company and support contact information
    - Detailed technical specifications beyond the average reader's interest

- Technical theory of operation
- Data file formats
- Frequently asked questions
- Command summaries, keyboard shortcuts
- Warranty information
- Explanation of the program's error messages

• **Credits**

If the credits aren't part of the front matter, they can be part of the back matter. Sometimes, even though the human credits are given in the front matter, credits are given to the tools used in the back matter. If a particular graphics program was instrumental in the creation of the product, it may be mentioned here. I've even seen the layout program for the manual—and even the fonts—listed now and then.

• **Glossary**

If the manual has a lot of technical terms, it's a good idea to add a glossary at the end of the manual. Even if you define each term on the page where it first appears (and you should), having a glossary at the end makes it easier for the reader to find the definition the second or third time the term is read.

• **Index**

A good index is as important as a table of contents for enabling readers to find the part of the manual they want.

Indexing is simple—if the manual is small and the subject is simple. A long manual about a complex subject requires a detailed, multi-level index.

Most word processors and page-layout programs have built-in facilities for creating an index, even a multi-level one. If you're writing the manual with the same program that will be used for the layout, you can mark items for inclusion in the index in your word processor. If your work is imported into another program for layout, don't bother marking the index—your marks will most likely get lost in the import process.

In this case, wait until the graphic artist gives you the first draft of the layout, and mark the items to be included in the index with a pen or highlighter. When you see the second draft of the layout, there should be a first draft of the index, ready for you to edit.

An option for indexing is to hire a professional indexer. A professional can do a very quick, very good job, for $1 to $3 per page (of the book, not of the index). The difficulty is scheduling a couple of days for the indexer to work at the end of a rushed project.

Writing the Back Matter

As with the front matter, back matter is largely a process of gathering information, and being nitpicky about details (especially the spelling of names).

If the appendices contain complex technical information, make sure a couple of local experts check their accuracy and completeness. If they contain troubleshooting, installation or operating system information, run them by tech support and customer service and test them with typical readers.

If you're creating the index yourself, allow enough time to do a careful job. Expect at least two revisions in the layout process, and recheck each and every page number during the final edit.

Manuals for Kids' Products

When you're writing a manual for a kids' product, be sure you write for the right person. Is the child—the user of the product—the one who reads the manual, or is it the parent or teacher?

When you write for kids, these are the points to keep in mind:

- The younger the reader, the simpler the vocabulary. (Books that list common reading vocabularies by grade level are available at libraries and bookstores.)
- Define any big, new or technical words, preferably on the same page that the word is used. Definitions can be in the text or in a sidebar or callout. An additional glossary in the back of the manual helps as well.
- Use your grammar checker to analyze the grade level of your document, and simplify if necessary.
- Keep both sentence and word length short. Don't talk down to the reader, but keep it as short and simple as it needs to be.
- Avoid using words and phrases that parents may not want their children to use.
- You may want to be a little more diligent about grammar when writing for kids than for adults.
- Be careful with slang. If you use it, be sure you use it correctly, that you use the right slang for the reader's age, and that it hasn't passed out of common use. Slang is a good way to spice up and personalize a manual, but if you mess up, you lose your audience.
- Structurally, kids' manuals need a higher tutorial to reference ratio than

adults' manuals. An adult generally uses a tutorial to get started, then uses the reference when necessary to move on from there. Some kids need a little more hand-holding, and therefore more tutorial. But it's more than that. Children will use the product more if they have a mission, a goal—or many goals—to accomplish. Writing the tutorials as missions, goals or tasks rather than just steps to complete makes it more fun for the kids.

- When it comes to technology, most children, unlike their parents, have no fear. Adults who are unfamiliar with technology need to be led by the hand to give them the confidence to deal with this newfangled gadget, and get over their fear of breaking it. Kids will jump in and start pushing buttons to see what happens.

Manuals and After-market Books

More than 10 years ago, when asked for advice on buying software, it was a good idea to tell people never to buy software that their business depends on or costs more than $100 unless there's at least one after-market book available for it. At that time, you couldn't count on getting enough information with the product to use it. And the fact that someone took the time to write the book and the publisher invested the money in the book meant that they thought the program was good enough and would be around long enough to make their investment pay off.

More than 10 years later, the same advice still applies.

After-market or third-party books have been part of the software industry since the dawn of software. Look at any bookstore. There are hundreds of books about how to use different programs, and sometimes dozens of books for a single program or operating system.

This market was probably started because of software piracy. People who had copies of programs without the manual found they needed help. Publishers and authors met that need by supplying after-market books—basically replacement manuals—at a lower cost than actually buying the product. But the market for these books boomed because the authors added a lot of useful, in-depth information that the manuals—even the good ones—didn't have.

A few years ago most after-market books were actually released *after* the product. The author(s) had time to work with the finished product to find out what problems users would have, to read the original manual to see what information is missing, to experiment to find useful ways to use the program, then to write the book.

Now, many after-market books are made under agreements with the software publishers, which is usually fine, unless the publishers demand the right to censor any criticism of the product. What's worse for the usefulness of the books is the fact that many of them are released along with the product—or even before it. This tells us two things:

1. The publisher, knowing about the after-market books—and getting royalties on them—knows it doesn't have to provide, and actually loses money if it provides, a manual that has everything a customer would want to know about their product.

2. The authors of these books haven't had much, if any, time with the finished product and finished manual to see what really needs to be in their book.

On the other hand, these authors often work closely with the development teams and the manual writers and often cover subjects and techniques that the manual writer would like to cover but can't, due to either time or budget constraints.

Does a good manual remove the need for after-market books? Absolutely not. While some simple programs might not need any additional explanation beyond a decent manual, many, if not most, will—especially open-ended programs. After-market publishers and authors needn't worry that good manuals will cut into their business.

Is an after-market book that is released the same time as the product always bad? Not necessarily. While some—even some actually published by or approved by the software publishers—are intended to be merely replacement manuals for pirates (if you can't charge them for the software, charge them for a manual), many actually do give a lot of useful information and practical examples.

The fact that programs are getting bigger and more complex and take longer to debug after all the features are in gives authors of books *and* manuals more time to do a good job.

Beyond the Words

By the time you're starting your rewrite, if not when you're working on your outline, you should think of how the words will appear on the page.

Unless you're responsible for layout, you won't be expected to do the graphic artist's job. You don't have to worry about the actual font or font size, but you should be concerned with the more basic aspects of the manual's look:

• What size will the printed pages be?

• How many pages are you allowed as a maximum?

• Can you cover a subject on a single page or a two-page spread?

• What chunks of information will be useful to present as a chart or table?

You are also responsible for the graphics—at least for identifying and specifying them, if not for creating and editing them. A software manual will generally contain a number of screenshots. Both Mac and Windows have a built-in rudimentary ability to take screenshots, but there are a number of utilities that make taking, cropping and managing screenshots much easier. While writing, think about the screenshots you'll need, including series of shots that show the steps of a process.

Beyond the Manual

In addition to the manual itself, there are other documents you may be responsible for:

Quick-Start Guide

If required, the Quick-Start guide should be a short (24 pages or less) document, that may be formatted like the manual, or may be formatted to fit into the CD jewelcase. If it's longer than 24 pages, then chances are it contains information that really belongs in the manual. It could be a single piece of paper or card stock folded to make four pages, or even a single card. Only what's needed.

The Quick-Start guide should contain:

- **Short welcome**

    A single sentence will do. You can stretch it to three or four sentences if you want to remind the reader how the product will make their lives better.

- **System requirements**

    List the hardware and software needed to run the program. If users don't have what they need, they should find out before they spend hours trying to make the program work on a computer that won't run it.

- **Program installation instructions**

    This is the most important part of the Quick-Start guide. Make sure it is short, simple, clear and well-tested.

    If the program is available for more than one platform, you must include machine-specific instructions for each platform. Generally, cost as well as inventory and manufacturing hassles will lead toward having all platforms covered in one Quick-Start guide, even though it forces readers to do some extra searching to find the information they need.[7]

---

[7] *In the not-so-good old days, when programs were distributed on multiple floppy disks, software was manufactured in separate packages for each platform. The cost of the disks prevented having multiple platforms in a single package. As long as there was a separate build with a separate parts list, it made financial sense to keep each document as short as possible and not mention other platforms. But today, with programs being distributed on*

- **Program starting instructions**

    This is the second-most important part of the Quick-Start guide. Even if it's only a single sentence, make sure it's there, easy to find, easy to read and well-tested.

- **Where to get more information**

    Mention the manual and the help system, if there is one. Also mention the Readme file if it exists.

- **Where to get help (customer service and tech support)**

    It never hurts to include technical support and/or customer-service contact information (phone, fax, email and website).

In addition, you may also want to include:

- **Machine-specific file loading and saving**

    If the program doesn't strictly follow the standard Windows or Mac file-loading and -saving procedure, point out the differences.

- **Handy reference charts**

    A listing of all the keyboard shortcuts is helpful, but less necessary when keyboard shortcuts are listed in the onscreen menus.

    A graphic of each toolbar with callouts can be helpful, but can be left out if the programmers have activated tooltips (so leaving the cursor pointing to a button or icon for a few seconds pops up the name of or other information about the button or icon).

    Include program or process flowcharts to help guide users through typical—or particularly difficult—tasks. Include any other charts or tables that will help the user master the program.

- **Corrections or additions to the manual**

This is where the Quick-Start guide serves the function of an addendum.

Wall Chart, Poster or Other Display

Reference charts and other data, including flowcharts, may be reformatted to a wall chart or poster. Wall space is usually at a premium, so other kinds of displays, often cards that can be folded so they can stand up on a desk or atop a monitor, are common.

CD-ROM, it doesn't cost any more to manufacture a CD with both Mac and Windows versions of the program on it. To keep costs down and inventories smaller, combining platforms is the standard—at least for Mac and PC-based software. Software for consoles (Nintendo or Sony PlayStation, for instance), even if it's on a CD, must be separate in every way. Console manufacturers have very strict standards for packaging, including manual dimensions and allotted pages, and don't allow the competitor's name or product to be mentioned in their materials.

Generally this will be designed and put together by a graphic artist from information you supply.

Addenda

Addenda are extra pages or an additional booklet of information that either was missing from the manual or is wrong in the manual.

Addenda are, of course, to be avoided if possible. They're an admission that the manual was approved for printing before it was tested or that the programming staff changed the program after the manual was approved.

If there are only a few small points to cover, then they can usually be slipped into the back of the Quick-Start guide. If there is a lot of material, then it might be best as a separate insert in the package. If there's a massive amount of material, then something went wrong with the writing or the development process.

In any event, an addendum should be temporary. After the first printing and shipping, update the manual to contain all the correct information and remove the addendum from the manufacturing instructions. If there is a small addendum section in the Quick-Start guide, update that, too.

Online and Onscreen Help

Help systems are a standard part of almost every piece of software today. They may be the standard Windows Help system, HTML, or a proprietary system. They may exist on the distributed CD or on the company's website.

In any event, it will be up to you to provide the content. Much of it may be a condensation of the manual, but you may have to do some major rewriting, if not new research and writing.

As much as most computer users dislike and distrust (and even fear) onscreen help systems, they deserve a useful help system.

Other Onscreen Text

In addition to the help system, there may be a little or a lot of text on the screen. Instructions in dialog boxes, error messages, window and button names, etc., should all be checked for spelling, grammar and consistency, if not totally rewritten to be clear and to seem to be coming from a single, consistent voice.

Readme File

The Readme file is a software tradition. It is found on the program disk, floppy or CD, and can contain just about anything, from addenda material to tech support information to the entire documentation.

Its best uses are for last-second information like:

- Late-breaking hints and tips, and
- Incompatibilities with certain hardware

It is a handy, quick, inexpensive way to get information that is too late or too new to be printed to the audience. But it is not a replacement for a manual or a Quick-Start guide or even an addendum. It's not even a half-decent replacement for a help system or electronic manual. Don't do a sloppy job on the manual because you can "fix it in the Readme."

If you're writing for a computer-savvy audience, it can be a good place to stick last-second info and corrections. But the average new computer user has no idea where or what it is, and will generally ignore it.

Box Copy

Box copy is often written by copywriters in or contracted by the marketing department. But sometimes you may have the chance to take a crack at it.

Writing box copy is in some ways far more fun that writing a manual, and in other ways far more tedious. You'll have to rewrite for size as much as for content, since a box has a finite size and you don't want the text too small.

Even if you don't write the copy, you can forward notes, suggestions and important features and benefits that you, as someone who had delved the depths of the product, will know far better than someone who is working from a marketing product description.

Online and Onscreen Help and Documentation

This is a subject that deserves its own book, but I'll cover it briefly here.

Some Facts About Online Docs and Books

While highly technical people, especially those that work with computers every day are used to and accept reading from a computer screen, most people hate it.[8]

- It can be hard on the eyes, and difficult to see clearly.
- With most screens, you can't see a full page at a time, so you're constantly messing with the mouse and scrolling.
- You're tied to your computer—and many people like to read in their favorite chair in the living room, on the hammock in the backyard or even while using the sanitary facilities.

---

[8] *This information came from numerous informal conversations and from a phone survey done in conjunction with the Maxis Customer Service department. (Thanks, Roger.)*

- Books are familiar, computers aren't.
- Nontechnical people consider a help system or electronic document to be "yet one more software program they have to learn," and don't want to spend the time.
- Most people find help systems difficult to use.
- Most people can't find the information they want in a help system. And if they do find it, it isn't understandable or useful.
- Books are wonderful things. They've been with us for hundreds of years. They feel good in your hands. Turning pages is something we've grown up with. Onscreen text doesn't give the familiar feedback that a book or manual does. Just holding a book in your hand and taking a glance at it gives you a lot of information that an onscreen document doesn't.
- With a book, you know how much information there is by the size, weight, number of pages and type size. With an electronic document, you usually can't tell if it's the equivalent of 10 pages or 10,000—and page size isn't necessarily a constant, so numbering them doesn't help.
- With a book, you know where you are within the range of pages, how much you've read and how much you have to go. With an electronic document, you don't know where you are or where you're going. On the Web you could even be in another document and not know it.
- Lately, companies have been working on the feedback problems, and soon (hopefully) far more useful and useable systems will appear. Already, some websites are dealing with this, but many, if not most, leave you feeling like you're on a page somewhere in limbo.

Some Definitions

Help or a *help file* is a supplement to a manual. It is (or should be) written to be shorter than a manual, and focus on definitions and step-by-step procedures, leaving out a lot of background material and explanations.

Online or onscreen *electronic documentation* is a complete manual in electronic form.

Onscreen help or documentation generally resides on a disk—floppy, hard or CD—at the user's location. It is read onscreen.

Online help resides in a single location—on a server or website owned by the software company. It is reached by the user going online and reading it on their screen.

The advantage of onscreen is that you don't need to tie up a phone line to use it. The advantage of online is that the document is (in theory) always kept up to date.

Of course there are variations on the above themes, involving combinations of onscreen, online and automatic updating.

The Writer's Role in Electronic Documentation

First and foremost, the writer is responsible for the content of the online or onscreen document. For a help file, this is usually a matter of paring down the existing manual,[9] and making it shorter and more focused on the step-by-step process. If you write a manual strictly for onscreen reading, then it can be a little more expansive than a help file, but try to keep it extra short and extra simple. For a complete onscreen duplicate version of a printed manual, you shouldn't need to do too much rewriting.[10]

Beyond that, writers should think about the presentation and organization, the browse sequence and how the user will access the information in the document.

If the program has context-sensitive help, you supply the programmers with the information they need to write the code to send the user to the correct section of the document under the correct conditions.

In some companies, help files are compiled by programmers or other staff experts. In some companies the writer may be responsible for delivering a ready-to-ship help file.

Whether you do it all yourself or work with others, the more you know, the better.

The Help Systems

There are a few standard help and electronic documentation systems, and they're constantly changing and evolving.

---

[9] *Manuals are usually written before help files because they need to be written weeks before the program to allow time for layout, editing and printing. Help files need less layout/compiling time and no printing time. They still need editing and testing.*

[10] *A practice among entertainment software companies is to prolong the life of an older product by lowering the price and making it part of a "budget" or "classic" line. In order to lower the price and still make a profit, the cost of manufacturing and packaging must be lowered. One way to do this is to eliminate the printed manual and put the manual on the CD in electronic form. If you know that the product will someday "go budget," you might want to prepare an electronic version of the manual along with the original release (in addition to the standard help file) even if it doesn't ship with the product. That way you won't be hit a year or two later with a rush job on an old project that you don't remember well, and have to dig up archived files that may have escaped or been corrupted.*

Windows Help

For a long time, Windows has included a help system. While not perfect, it works. There are many commercial and shareware products that make it easy to arrange and compile a Windows help file.

Over the years and versions, many features have been added to the system, including sound and video.

Tooltips, while part of the interface programming and not technically part of the help system, is a great thing. When the cursor sits motionless over a toolbar button or other control for a couple of seconds, a text explanation—or at least a name—for that button pops up. It has eliminated the need to have a separate chart of the toolbar next to the computer so you can tell what all those buttons do. Of course, in theory, you should be able to tell what the buttons do by their pictures (icons). In practice, most of them are incomprehensible, but are used anyway to make localization and internationalization easier.

A nonstandard but very nice variation on Tooltips, first used (as far as I know) by Bullfrog Productions Ltd. in the game *Dungeon Keeper,* turns it into a two-part information system. When the cursor is motionless over a button for a couple of seconds the usual Tooltips name-the-button information pops up. But if the cursor stays motionless for another few seconds, more information—how and why to use the button—appears.

The **What's This?** feature is activated by clicking a toolbar button marked by either the words "What's This?" or a question mark (?). Once active, you click on a menu, button or control to receive a pop-up explanation of the button or control. This generally has more information than just the name of the button or control—at least a sentence or two on what it is and/or how to use it.

Cue cards are a set of small windows that can be used to guide the user through a series of steps or a whole tutorial. The problem with them is that you either have to trust the user to follow the instructions and click something like "Next" or "Done" once they've done it, or arrange for a lot of dedicated programmer time so the program can communicate directly with the cue cards and automatically signal that it's time to move to the next step. If your program has a lot of short processes, cue cards are worth checking out.

HTML Help is the newest (so far) variation on Windows Help, and uses HTML as the raw data file instead of .RTF. The data is still compiled into a single compressed file before shipping.

Macintosh Help Systems

Macintosh hasn't had a widely used standard help system like Windows Help.

For the last few System versions, they have included Balloon help, which is what Windows' What's This? was most likely inspired by.

Very few Mac users I know use Balloon help. It's modal nature flies in the face of Macintosh interface standards.

A number of years ago, Macintosh introduced *Apple Guide,* a complete system for creating interactive help, including many-stepped tutorials. I personally haven't had much experience with Apple Guide. I was excited when it was first released, but never got a chance to use it—at least not yet. In order for the user to use Apple Guide, they had to load the viewing program into memory. At the company where I worked, our average Macintosh-based customer didn't have enough memory to run both Apple Guide and our programs. So it was useless for us at the time.

The latest version of help for the Macintosh is called Mac OS Help, and is HTML-based.

If you are creating help systems for a product that is made for both Windows and Mac, you may be able to save yourself some time and effort by first creating a Windows Help file, then using that file's raw HTML data with Mac OS Help. Apple provides developers with the tools and information to do it.

Alternative systems for converting Windows help to Macintosh help include QuickHelp and E-Help. They're third-party programs that take Windows Help file data and turns it into small, efficient Macintosh applications.

Adobe Acrobat

Adobe Acrobat has become a standard format for online books, manuals and general electronic information distribution.

Acrobat is wonderful for reading, even onscreen. It allows printing on any computer system.

Acrobat is not good for a help system or software manual that must be seen on the screen along with another program. It's a full-screen product. Unlike HTML or Windows Help, it doesn't reflow the text to match the width of the window it's in (but you can somewhat make up for that by viewing the Acrobat file at a percentage of its actual size).

HTML

Now, with the widespread use—and free distribution—of web browsers, HTML is becoming a common format for online and onscreen help and documentation.

Its main advantages are:

- (Almost) total cross-platform compatibility

- The fact that it reflows text to fit the space allotted, so it can be used alongside another program
- It can be prepared using tools that are similar to those that writers and graphic artists are familiar with
- It allows printing for those who wish to read away from the computer (though the printing isn't as nice as with Acrobat), and
- It doesn't require compiling

Its disadvantages are:

- It doesn't have any easy-to-use ways of interacting with a program to create interactive tutorials (yet)
- Different browsers display things differently, so if your product doesn't include a browser, you've got to test your documents with all the major browsers on the market

Both the newest version of Windows Help and Mac OS Help are HTML-based.

Companies and Their Systems

A big part of knowing how, what and when you'll be writing is understanding the company you're working at and the system you'll be working within. This chapter explains how different systems work (or don't work), and how to live with them.

The sections are:

- The Organization
- The Development Team
- Beyond the Development Team
- Design Documents
- Software Development Lifecycles
- The Tools
- The Cost of Changes

The Organization

This section of this chapter covers both the organization you are writing and working for, and the way that organization is organized.

There are as many different organizations as there are projects. Each group within a company can work differently. Each team will have its own way of doing things.

What is important for you as a manual writer to know are the answers to the following questions:

How does writing and the writing group, if there is one, fit into the company structure?

Chances are, you (or the writing group) will most likely be part of product development, part of marketing, or part of a separate corporate services group. If you're an employee, you should know where you fit into the company structure. Even if you're contracting for a single project, you should know where the staff writers (if any) belong, and know what "box" people put you in (whether they're right or not).

Depending on the company, writers may be an integral part of the development team, responsible for communicating information between team members during development, communicating with the rest of the company on behalf of the team, and communicating information about the product to the customer, through the manual and through the product itself.

And there are companies where writers are kept in a different department, possibly in a different building (or city) than the development team. Their job is to write the little booklet with installation instructions that goes in the CD jewelcase, and they barely talk to anyone who actually worked on the product.

What is the company attitude toward writing and manuals?

There are companies where writing is considered important. Manuals have to be good for the sake of the product and the customer. And there are companies where manuals are considered a necessary evil: something you have to include with the product because the customer expects it or because the competition does.

Who's your boss?

This is one of the most important questions to know the answer to.

You will no doubt know who hired you, and who is giving you direction, but dig deeper. Find out who makes the decisions that affect your work. Who has the ultimate control over what you do?

You may report directly to a producer, a writing manager or a product manager. But there is usually at least one other person that can and will affect how you do your job and how well you can do it. It may be a marketing manager or VP who wants to control all tone and veto the use of humor. It may be the manufacturing manager or CFO who wants to keep the documents to a certain size and cost. It may be the VP of product development or an executive producer for a line of products that wants a deadline to be met, no matter the sacrifices. And it may be any one, or none, of these people mentioned that believes that the quality of the product and its documentation are important factors in the product's success.

Is your ultimate boss—the one who pulls the strings—actually *on* the project? Or off in corporate headquarters counting beans? Is this person primarily concerned with quality? Or with the schedule? The cost? Might there be cross-purposes between this person and your immediate boss? Do the "powers that be" trust your immediate boss enough that they won't interfere?

Knowing the answers to all these questions will help you plan your work to meet the *real* requirements. Whoever is running the project will always say that you have to write the best manual ever. But the reality is that you have to write the best manual possible in the allotted time within the allotted budget, and it has to fit perfectly into the allotted page count.

The Development Team

Here's a brief description of the members of a software development team. This is by no means a complete description of each of these jobs—just enough of an introduction so that you, the writer, will know what everyone is responsible for and what information you can get from each of them.

On a small project, two or more of the jobs mentioned may be covered by a single person, but all will be covered. If it's a very large project, then each of the positions may be covered by a group of people, with one as the designated lead for that group.

Producer

In the software world, the title *producer* can mean almost anything, depending on the company and depending on who else is on the project.

Some projects have a very strong designer/engineer who runs development, and the producer basically acts as an assistant, taking care of paperwork, progress and status tracking, and representing the project at meetings, so the rest of the team can continue to work on the product undisturbed. There are also projects where the producer has ultimate control of the project, from design to completion, and makes all the important decisions.

In entertainment software, it was traditional that the producer was also the designer, although that is changing. It is becoming less and less of a creative position and more and more of a business and management position.

In general, as software gets more and more complex—and more and more expensive—and is produced by larger and larger teams, the organization is becoming more and more like the movie industry. Software producers are moving toward the model of movie producers, and are basically responsible for getting the project done, on schedule and within the budget. They are responsible for the quality and sales potential of the product as well. More and more, the producer is becoming deluged in contracts, meetings, negotiations, spreadsheets, project tracking and general business, and less and less has actual "hands-on" contact with the product they are in charge of.

To make up for this isolation of producer from product, there may be levels, or hierarchies, of producers on a single project (as there are in the film business) ranging from executive producer to managing producer to producer to associate producer to assistant producer—a chain of management through the project, always reporting upward.

Producers may also go by the name *project manager,* but they generally prefer *producer,* because it sounds more important.

As a contract writer, you will most likely report to one of the producers. As a staff writer you will most likely be reporting to a writing manager, but assigned to a project, and working closely enough with a producer that it will feel like that producer is your boss.

The main information you will get from a "pure" producer is about scheduling, budget, and the amount of pages you are allowed. A producer who is also the creative lead can supply you with information about the actual product.

Product Manager

Producers and pro*ject* managers are generally part of the product development department. Pro*duct* Managers, on the other hand, are from marketing. Remember that: when you hear "product manager," it means marketing.

This isn't necessarily good or bad—but it will let you know what type of background and experience this person brings to the project, and what type of information they will base their decisions and opinions on. Depending on the individual, a product manager can be a very valuable asset to the team and product, or a pain in the rear. (Of course, that goes for everyone on the team to a certain degree.)

While there traditionally is friction between product development and marketing, someone from marketing who is on the development team can and should be a valuable asset.

Depending on the company and the type of product, a product manager may have a little or a lot to do with the product's development. Many product managers simply drop in from time to time, so they know when to start their marketing functions: focus groups, presentations to the sales department, competitive analysis, marketing and advertising campaigns, package design, etc. Other product managers may actually run the whole project, taking on the role of producer.

Product managers are more likely to be in charge of application products that can be evaluated by marketing techniques. For instance, a word processor is a very market-driven product. It's pretty well understood what a word processor is and does. The main differences between different word processors are the feature lists and the interfaces. A good marketer can put together a comparison of all the major word processors, list each of their features, and run some focus groups to find out:

- which of the features customers consider most important,
- what new features they would like, and
- which features—of your current product and of the competition's—need to be improved.

From this information, a design and development plan can be formulated, and the product can be cranked out—keeping an ear out for any additional features that you may have to add at the last moment because the competition added them.

With newer, less-defined types of software, and entertainment software in general, it is less likely (one hopes) that the product manager is making all the decisions based on marketing techniques. They should have a lot of input and offer a lot of useful guidance, but you can't use a focus group to find out what people think of things they haven't seen or used.

And you can't rely entirely on focus groups or marketing techniques to design entertainment products. If you could, then there would never be a high-budget movie or computer game that flopped. But there are. You really can't tell if something's fun until you try it. Very experienced, very successful game designers understand this. A year into a project, you'll hear them say something like, "I think this is going well. I just can't wait until it's far enough along to actually play it so I'll know if it's fun."

Product managers, in addition to the packaging and other traditional marketing responsibilities, may be responsible for organizing and running focus groups that test the product's interface and the manual, including the tutorial. Since this is something that needs to be done, it's nice to have someone who will take care of it. (And there is the possibility of this work being billed to the marketing budget instead of the product development budget, if you're concerned with that sort of thing.)

As a writer, you will be in contact with, and possibly report to, the product manager. If writers in the organization are part of the marketing department, then the odds of you reporting to the product manager go up. At the least, you can make sure that the product manager understands the product, and pass on any descriptive and introductory material you've written about it, and in return, you will get as much information about the customer as you can.

At times, the product manager may feed you introductory or descriptive material to use in your manual. The product manager may also have control over the size, look and feel of your writing, so it fits into a product line.

To a certain degree, the writer straddles the bridge between product development and marketing. It can be a precarious position, requiring some political skills, but it puts you in a good position to really see and understand the big picture of the product and the project, which is good for your career and for the customer's ability to use and enjoy the product.

Designer

There may or may not be someone with the title *designer* on the team. But someone—hopefully—is designing the product and creating the design document that will be used as the basis for planning the whole product. Find out who it is. They are your source of the real workings of the product—something you'll need for your manual and help files.

If there are designers on a project, they may have varying titles and duties.

In entertainment software, there may be a "game designer." This is the person who, obviously, designs the game: defines what the player will do and experience, what will happen under what circumstances, and blueprints the world that the player will exist in during the game. Good game designers are few and far between. To design a good computer or video game, it takes an understanding of games, programming, operating systems, interfaces, and various forms and methods of communication, including writing.

Non-entertainment products may not have the exact equivalent of a designer, but there will be someone—you hope—who will be writing down and defining in detail what the product will be. This may be a producer, an engineer, or possibly a writer.

Beyond designing the overall product, there may also be one or more interface designers on a project. Or an interface designer may be brought in for a short period of time on contract to work on particularly tricky interface challenges.

Interface designers are specialists in human-computer and human-machine interface factors, which are a combination of mechanics, physiology, psychology and design.

You will learn a lot when you work with any good designer—about the product you'll be writing about, and about design.

There is a lot of overlap in knowledge and skills between writers and designers, especially interface designers. Expand your skills into the area of design to open up new career possibilities, or just to give yourself a more varied set of tasks, and a little more control over the product you work on.

A number of books on design and interface design are listed in the Recommended Reading appendix.

Engineers

Who was once a programmer is now an *engineer*. The difference is both a matter of a more impressive title and a reflection of the fact that today, those who program, even on games, are often degreed engineers.

There is usually more than one engineer on a project, with one being the lead engineer, responsible for the program's architecture and the technical design. The lead engineer will also manage and assign tasks to the other engineer(s).

Notice that the product design (or script)—the responsibility of the designer or producer—and the technical design—the responsibility of the lead engineer—are two separate items, usually documented in separate design documents.

As the writer, you may need to spend some time with the technical design document and at least one of the engineers to get the information you'll need. If you write any technical descriptions or theory-of-operations sections in your manual, be sure to have an engineer check it for accuracy.

Artists

There are two very distinct types of artists involved with almost any product: computer artists and graphic artists.

Both types of artist work with computers, but those known as computer artists are usually part of the product development department, and create art that is meant to be displayed on the computer, as part of the program. Graphic artists, on the other hand, are usually part of the marketing department, and design mostly for print, including the packaging and the manual design and layout.

With their expertise in dealing with type, graphic artists are often consulted on or tasked with the design and layout of onscreen and online manuals and Web pages, bringing them closer to the development process.

Computer artists, once mainly involved with entertainment and educational software are now working on all types of software, even serious business products.

As a writer, you will be dealing with both types of artists.

You will need a good rapport with the computer artists in order to get accurate information on what art is final and what isn't. When you take screenshots for the manual and online help, you need final art—your shots must match the final product. But in the world of software, you have to have final screenshots for the manual weeks before the screens have to be final for the product. One option you have is to buy a little time by taking a temporary, placeholder shot (known as FPO, or *for position only*), so the graphic artist can start the layout, then replace it when it's final. Another option—if you're on really good terms with the artists, especially the lead artist—is to let the artists know what remaining shots you need—and when—in order to meet your deadlines, and they may shift around their work schedules to accommodate you.

You'll be working closely with graphic artists on the design and layout of all the printed documentation. This process is described in detail in The Sample Project section of this book.

Testers and QA

A tester's job is to break the product in every way possible. It sounds like fun—and it is, for a while. But after weeks of banging away at the same product, going over and over the same things to see if a bug was fixed and if fixing that bug broke something else, it can get boring and tedious. Even with games.

And then there's the hardware compatibility aspect of testing. A product has to be able to work with an almost infinite and always changing number of possible combinations of graphics cards, pointing devices, storage devices and networking options—not to mention the other software that may be running concurrently. That means testing the software on hundreds of different machines, or on a few machines, swapping cards and parts every couple of hours.

Organized field beta testing is another way to test the software on a lot of different computer configurations. Of course, this type of testing program takes a lot of time and effort to organize and administer, plus, the average field beta tester isn't a trained tester who is able to track down and document the exact /sequence of events that causes the problem, and write up a report that an engineer can use as a tool to help fix the problem.

Testers are usually brought onto a project en masse in the later stages, although a lead tester may be assigned to a project at its inception, to track progress and know when to kick in with the testing and write the test plan.

A good lead tester may also have good input into the design and development process—they have years of experience in finding mistakes and software problems, and can help you avoid many pitfalls.

On a very technical product, testers may need to be skilled programmers to understand what to test for and how to explain what went wrong.

In some companies Testing and QA are the same thing. In others, they are separate: testing is part of the product development, and QA is a final pass/fail test performed by another group.

For writers, testers are a good source of information about the product and about aspects of the product that may need extra explanation. Testers are good people to have read over your writing for an accuracy check. They're usually more willing to help than producers or engineers, and they're up on all the latest product changes and additions.

Writers may want—or have—to spend some time as a tester, officially or unofficially. As you learn the product and use all its functions so you can document them, you should report any bugs or problems clearly to whoever is collecting that information, often the lead tester. And if you're full-time on the project, there will come a time when you are pretty much done with all your writing, editing and layout, and the program is still in final testing. You are a prime candidate to pitch in with the testing. You know the product's every mode, function, button and control, and you can clearly document bugs and the steps that caused them.

Writer

As with all the other jobs, there is no standard job description for writers in the software industry.

Writers may be staff, temporary or on contract. Each of these options has its advantages and disadvantages.

The responsibilities, status, power and reporting structure of writers is different in every company.

Under ideal circumstances, a writer is part of the development team from the project's inception, responsible not only for printed documentation, but all onscreen text, including interface text and help systems. And more than that, the writer's duty is to aid communication—within the team, between the team and the rest of the company, and between the company and the customer. By increasing communication, the writer helps the project run smoother and finish sooner. The writer contributes to design. The writer helps with the testing.

In some companies, writers aren't considered part of the development team. Many of the responsibilities mentioned in the paragraph above are delegated instead to designers or producers (who would both do a better job if they were better writers).

If a project requires a lot of writing—large, long manuals, extensive help system, lots of screen text, etc., then there may be multiple writers on a project, and one will be the lead writer. The lead writer is responsible for the writing plan: a definition of all the writing that will need to be done for the project, how it can be divided between writers, how long it will take, how many people will be needed, what the schedule will be, etc. The lead writer will then divide the work between writers and gather and combine it when it is done.

Beyond the Development Team

Two usually overlooked resources for the product development team are the technical support and customer service departments.

These groups may report to marketing, product development or corporate services. They may be two discrete departments or combined into one. They may be located near the development team, especially in a small company, or they may be in another building or another city. In some cases, all customer service and tech support is contracted out to other companies in states where it's cheap to rent a big building with a lot of phone lines.

The closer these groups are to you, the easier it is to use them as a resource. It's worth the effort. Even if all the actual customer contact is farmed out to another company, there will be somebody locally at your company who is gathering and organizing the information for the outside company to dispense. Find this person and establish a working relationship.

Technical Support

These are the people who are on the "front lines." They take calls all day from customers that are having trouble with your company's products.

Their job is made harder by each and every mistake or omission in the manual or onscreen help. They know about all the confusing onscreen text, badly designed dialog boxes and clumsy interfaces, because that's what they have to help the customers overcome.

Most people in technical support will be glad to look over your manual—especially the installation instructions and the tutorial—and help you find potential trouble spots. Not only will it make their jobs easier by eliminating problems before they happen, and not only will it give them a head start on understanding a program that they'll eventually be explaining to customers, but reading and testing documentation gets them off the phone lines for a precious few hours.

Be sure to work through the technical support manager—don't assign outside work to someone else's department without going through channels. You could make enemies where you need friends.

Spend some time working in technical support if you can—and if you dare. It'll open your eyes, and really put you in touch with the people you're writing for.

Customer Service

Customer service is also a bank of people on phones. Their main duty is to distribute information, take some orders, and check on the status of orders—not answer technical questions. But many customers will try to get their technical questions answered by customer service first, because it's usually a toll-free number, as opposed to technical support's number that often has long distance charges.

While it's most important for technical support to check over installation instructions, it may also be useful to have representatives from customer service test your tutorials.

Design Documents

Design documents have been mentioned briefly in previous sections, but not described in enough detail—until now.

As always, different companies have different standards and methods when it comes to design documents. Some use them like religious texts, others don't bother with them at all. The times, contents and approval processes in this chapter are generic, and will no doubt be different from those where you work.

If you can get your hands on any design documents for products you're writing about, do it. But always double-check all the information with the actual program. Most companies stop updating the design docs in the later stages of development, and they can be extremely out-of-date.

Typical design documents to locate and use as resources are:

Product Proposal

This is usually a short (one to five pages), nontechnical document that is used to sell the idea of the product to the management team. If it sells, then the producer gets the funding to put together enough of a development team to produce the Initial Design Document.

The proposal will generally include a one-sentence, a one-paragraph and a one-page definition of the product. You'll want to read it if you can, to get a basic understanding of exactly what the product is—or what it was going to be and what the management team may still think it is.

New versions of existing products will rarely require a proposal. But you can look at the earlier version of the product, especially the package and the introduction section of the manual to get the basic "what is it" information you need.

Initial Design Document (or Script)

This document, often accompanied by artwork and programmed prototypes, is the product's proof of concept. A small group of people will generate this document in one to three months, plus or minus, depending on the company and the product.

Mental Models

People understand how things work by creating mental models. The models we make are based on what we see at the time *and* on preexisting knowledge—whether or not the knowledge is accurate.

There are actually three mental models involved with any software product:

1. The interface model—the mental model that the interface designer is presenting to the customer to explain how to understand and operate the product.

2. The engineer's model—the true, technical inner workings of the product as understood by the person who engineered or programmed it.

3. The customer's model—the mental model that the customer forms, based on what they learn (and don't learn) about the interface model and what they already know (or think they know) about the subject.

All three models can be very different. Your job as the writer is to try to align the customer's model as closely to the interface model as you can. Explaining things in terms of the technical inner workings is counter-productive, unless the reader has a very strong technical background, and knowledge of the technical inner workings will be useful.

This document is sometime called a *script* in entertainment software companies, because it describes what the user or player will see, do and experience, serving the same purpose as a movie script in the film industry.

The project is once again evaluated on the basis of this document, and if it passes, then the project is funded for the next stage. If it doesn't pass, then either the project is canned or the design team goes back to the drawing board.

In an update of an existing product, this stage may be skipped.

What you can learn from this document is what the underlying structure of the program will be. It won't have details down to every dialog box or every menu item, but it will explain all the modes, all the major windows and the most important functions.

Reading this document, it is interesting to note how the product has changed since the proposal.

Detailed/Final Design Document (or Script)

Once the initial design has been approved, or if this is an update of an existing product, the team is enlarged and the Detailed Design Document is prepared.

This stage can take anywhere from three months to a year or more, then once again, the project is put up for review. If the final design as specified in this document and the technical design as specified in the technical design document (see below) are approved, then the project is staffed up for production.

This document, in theory, will describe the entire program—at least the part that the user will see and experience—down to the last button. In practice, 70–80% coverage is very good.

For some programs, you may want to have every design detail nailed down ahead of time, but for most, especially entertainment programs, you need the flexibility to make additions, changes and improvements during the final stages of the project.

Of course, flexibility causes problems with schedules and budgets, but it generally leads to a better product.

This flexibility can improve the product, but it can also complicate the writer's job. Don't count on a detailed design document—even one that seems very complete and is well-maintained—to be totally accurate. Recheck everything with the program itself.

Technical Design Document

This document is prepared by the lead engineer based on the Detailed Design Document.

The technical design is the theory, method and division of labor that will implement the design. What the customer sees and what the computer does to create what the customer sees are very different from each other. As a writer, this document may be useful for your own understanding of the product, as well as for writing manual sections on theory of operation or explaining the parameters of a simulation.

But be careful not to explain the outer workings of the program (what the user sees and interacts with) in terms of the inner workings of the program (what's actually going on inside the computer), if there's any chance of confusion.

Software Development Lifecycles

The previous section on design documents hinted at a simple development process. It implied that software is partially designed, then approved, then completely designed, then approved, then produced.

While not totally wrong, that impression isn't completely accurate. In reality, developing software is more complicated, and even if it were possible, this simple method wouldn't necessarily be the best for every product.

Product development lifecycles—the way the project is planned and carried out—is another subject that can, and does, fill many books. What will be covered here is a quick overview from the writer's point of view. The more you know about the lifecycle processes, and what your team is doing and how they do it, and what *you're* expected to do and when, the easier your job will be.

A Little History

Software development is a new industry, but it has borrowed development methods from other, established industries.

Way Back When

In the earliest days of software, development followed the model of the book industry. Because of the memory limitations (both RAM and permanent storage), programs were smaller than they are today, and there was very little graphic content.

Software was usually "written" by a single programmer/author, sitting alone in a room, much the way books were, and still are, written. Perhaps a couple of people worked together—two programmers co-authoring a program. Or a programmer worked with an expert in the field that the program was about, each person lending their expertise, whether knowledge of subject or knowledge of implementation.

As computers advanced and became capable of displaying graphics (or people realized the computer's existing graphical potential), the team may have called in the equivalent of an illustrator to improve the visual aspect of the program.

Development times ranged from mere days to a few months. Development budgets were either nonexistent—the lone programmer worked on spec—or there was an hourly or weekly wage paid. In any event, the total cost of development ranged from hundreds to thousands to tens of thousands of dollars.

Documentation, if there was any, was a Readme file on the disk, or at most a printed page of keyboard shortcuts.

The Middle Ages of Software

As memory and disk capacities increased, and computers gained sound and more graphical abilities, computer programs became bigger and more complex. The skills needed to take advantage of all the computer's capabilities were rarely mastered by any one person.

The software development model evolved into the rock-band model. A small group of three to five (or so) specialists huddled together, often in a garage or spare bedroom in one of their homes, and created software. They called in friends and family to help test the finished product.

Development time expanded along with the complexity of the programs and the size of the team. A project could take many months, or even a year to finish, and total expenses could exceed $100,000—occasionally reaching as high as $250,000.

Documentation was generally handled by the publisher, added to the product after it had been handed over for packaging and sales.

Today

Today, with the low-cost computer sporting many megabytes of RAM, gigabytes of disk space, CD ROMs, millions of colors, onscreen video, and surround-sound audio, the software industry is emulating the movie industry, in team size, development methods—and in budgets.

Now, a project will have teams of specialists to perform the tasks of each of the previous stage's rock-band members. One or two programmers have become a team of programmers consisting of any or all of these specialties: interface programming, database programming, network programming, 2D graphics programming, 3D graphics programming, sound system programming, video programming, simulation programming and an ever-growing number of other areas of specialization.

Add to that teams of people to handle design, project management, testing, art (with 2D and 3D specialties), music composition, sound effects creation, audio engineering, and writing, plus the voice talent, actors and the video crew—and sometimes even a rock band to record the music—and you've got a credits list as long as those seen at the end of many movies.

Development times are typically a year or more. Often much more, though it's usually not planned that way. Budgets are in the millions of dollars.

The growing complexity of programs requires more and better communication between the program makers and the program users. That's where we come in. Documentation today is more and more becoming integral to the product, appearing on the screen, online and in print.

Throwbacks

There are still a few "lone wolves" creating software with the book model. But they are few and far between. There are more instances of rock-band development. But more and more, competitive commercial software is being developed by large teams of teams with big budgets and lots of time.

Is this necessarily a good thing? Yes and no. There are some programs that really require big budgets and armies of people to be made well. And there are other programs that are best served by a small, tight-knit group working quickly. Paralleling the movie industry, this is the difference between the big studios making huge blockbusters and small independent companies making smaller, lower-budget films. Each has a purpose and fills a need.

Code and Fix

An all-too-common method—or non-method—of developing software is called code and fix.

It is basically a three-step process:

1. Decide roughly what you want the program to do.

2. Dive in and start coding.

3. Look at it. If it's what you want and need, ship it, otherwise send it back for more coding.

Code and fix works for small test projects and proofs of concepts. If you're on a large project that is managed this way, then you're in trouble.

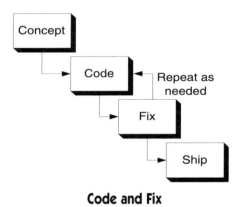

Code and Fix

Waterfall

The original development system that was called a development system is the waterfall.

The waterfall is a method where everything is done in order, putting one foot in front of the other and moving forward. Notice that the diagram indicates that it's possible to back up the waterfall, returning to earlier stages. It's possible—but very expensive and time-consuming. There is usually some sort of review process between each of the steps to avoid having to go backward, but they aren't always foolproof.

This development method works for very simple programs, for upgrades of existing programs, and when the product is very well understood, with no technological

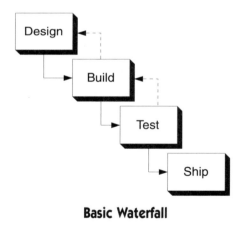

Basic Waterfall

challenges. It doesn't work well for games or entertainment software.

The waterfall method is totally document-driven. All the design has to be done up-front. A writer on such a project may be intimately involved with creating and maintaining the design documents, in addition to the "normal" writer's duties.

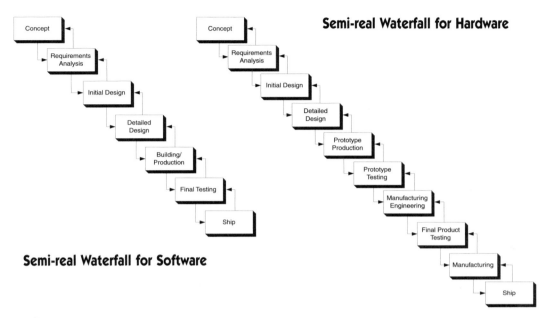

Semi-real Waterfall for Hardware

Semi-real Waterfall for Software

Spiral

The spiral development method is far more complex than the waterfall. More complex to manage, more complex to plan, and more complex to execute.

It is also a far better method for creating complex software.

The spiral method is iterative: you develop the project in repeating loops, or iterations, of activities. It is also known as a risk-reduction model, because each iteration is based on understanding, evaluating and solving risks.

For each iteration, the team performs (roughly) these five steps:

1. Determine the current objectives and constraints

2. Identify and (hopefully) resolve risks

3. Evaluate alternatives

4. Produce and test the deliverables for this iteration

5. Plan the next iteration

As a writer on a project run this way, if you're involved throughout the whole process, you may be able to participate in the documentation for each iteration. It's for in-house use, and shouldn't be too extensive, but this documentation must be absolutely clearly written and clearly communicated or the iteration can go astray. Here's a chance for a writer to act as communicator, beyond writing a product manual.

If you're just coming in on the end of the project to write the manual and help, make sure you know if the team's on the final iteration. If you base your writing on an earlier round, you'll have a lot of updating to do. If you can follow an iteration or two before the final one, you'll get a head start on understanding the product.

Waterfall Variations

There are a number of updated variations on the waterfall method. A couple of common ones are the waterfall with subprojects and the waterfall with risk reduction.

The waterfall with subprojects starts as the basic waterfall, but breaks up into separate teams tackling different areas of the project.

The idea behind this is to speed things up by spreading out the work and finishing all the easy, though possibly time-consuming, parts of the project as quickly as possible.

Waterfall with Subprojects

The biggest problem here is if the teams don't continually communicate with each other, they can design each other into corners when it comes to reintegrating all the subprojects.

As a writer throughout the project, you can maintain and disperse the different groups' design documents, making sure that everyone knows what's going on with the other groups, and avoiding problems at integration time.

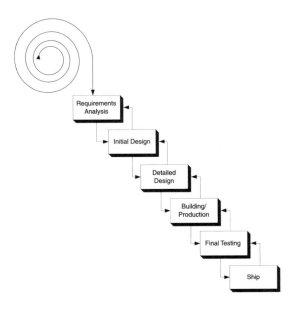

Waterfall with Risk Reduction

If you join the project near the end, try to get involved at the subsystem testing stages to give yourself enough time to learn the program.

The waterfall with risk reduction starts as a spiral project, iterating through a few stages of requirements analysis, architectural design and prototyping; then, when the project is very well understood, it breaks out of the spiral into a waterfall for final design, implementation and testing.

As a writer, you may be involved with internal documentation during the spirals, then leave the project for a few months (or more) until the rest of the team reaches the system testing stage, when you return to work on the manual and help.

Other Methods

There are a number of other common software development methods, including:

- Evolutionary prototyping—start with an initial concept, prototype it, then keep updating the prototype until it is "good enough" to ship.

- Staged delivery—design and build a very simple version of the program, then design and build a slightly more complex version of the program, and repeat until you run out of time or budget.

- Design to schedule—design the program to be built in stages, putting all the most important features in first, and cleaning it up to make it deliverable. Next, start adding some of the medium-priority features and clean the program up to make it deliverable. Keep repeating the process, adding less and less vital features and fixing all the bugs until you run out of time or budget.

What these development methods mean to the team is that they may suddenly find themselves done, usually before they are really satisfied that the product is the best they can make it. What this means to the writer is that you might not have much warning about when to start on the project. With everyone else on the project frantic to finish the next iteration on time or suddenly being told that the previous iteration is the shipping product, nobody is thinking about the documentation. If you're on staff, then it's up to you to keep track of the project and be ready to jump in and get your work done. If you're a contractor, and brought in at the last minute and expected to do a good job in almost no time, good luck. (Raise your rates and brew a big pot of coffee.)

One more method, evolutionary delivery, is worth knowing a little about. This method, a variation of evolutionary prototyping, adds an extra step to each iteration—actual delivery to sample customers for evaluation and feedback.

A writer on this project may be expected to provide some sort of simple documentation, and possibly a presentation, to the test subjects for each version. This is a good kind of product to work on. You become intimately familiar with the product, and you have a head start on the final documentation.

The Tools

Manual writers, as do all writers in the technical world, have and need a number of important tools to help them do their jobs.

Word Processor

Your word processor is your best friend and most indispensable tool. Know its quirks and strengths. Take some time to explore its features.

These days, there are only a few major word processors that are standard throughout the software industry and technology in general. It is important that you know how to use the word processor that is the standard at the company you're working for, or have a simple, accurate (and tested) way to convert documents.

Here are a few word processor features every writer should know about:

- **Spelling Checkers**

  Spelling checkers are wonderful, but they're not a replacement for looking over your own work, much less a reason to bypass an editor. Spelling checkers don't correct instances when you've used the wrong word as long as the wrong word is spelled correctly. Be careful about adding your own words to the custom dictionary—once you add in a typo or misspelled word by mistake, your spell checker will never catch that mistake again.

- **Grammar Checkers**

  Grammar checkers are as close to controversial as you can get with a word processor. Some people love them, others hate them. If you use them for nothing else, they are very handy for evaluating your writing for readability and grade-level statistics.

- **Outlining Mode**

  If your word processor has an outlining mode, try it out. Outlining is very useful for organizing and navigating long documents.

- **Tables**

  Just about every word processor made in the last 5 to 10 years can make tables. If you're writing in the technical world and your word processor doesn't do tables, it's time to upgrade. But be careful: tables can be lost when exporting and importing files from program to program. Some word processors drop the tables when exporting to .RTF (rich text format, a standard interchange format that almost all word processors and page layout programs can read and write), and some layout programs may ignore or butcher them.

- **Revision Tracking**

  Revision tracking is a way of life for some writers and a lot of lawyers. Others never use it.

  It can be used with email to solicit comments and corrections to a document from multiple people without printing copies and routing.

- **Macros**

  Macros, both those that run processes and those that add boilerplate text can be amazing time-savers. No point in doing extra, repetitive, boring work. That's what computers are for.

- **Templates**

  Templates are also time-savers, and can help a group of writers keep a consistent look and feel.

Other Tools

Besides word processors, there are a number of other tools that are useful for writers.

- **Page Layout Programs**

  Most companies will have graphic artists who put your writing into its final form, but sometimes you may have to do it yourself. If you are responsible for layout, then you'll need to know how to do it. If you're not doing the layout, then it's still worth knowing at least a little about the popular page layout programs—if you work with graphic artists, the more you know about their tools, the better you'll be able to communicate.

- **Flowcharting Programs**

  A nice, simple flowchart can help explain complex processes. Some word processors have built-in or add-on flowcharting, and there are a number of fairly low-cost, useful stand-alone flowchart programs.

- **Email**

  Whether you're communicating within a company or between locations, email is asynchronous communication at its best. Know how to use it and how to attach and retrieve documents.

- **Presentation Software**

  Sometimes teams, groups or companies need to put on a dog-and-pony show. As a writer, you may be asked to put together a presentation. Presentation software, whatever its shortcomings, speaks the language of board meetings.

- **Spreadsheets**

  For huge tables, tables with calculations, and for charting and tracking projects and progress, spreadsheets can't be beat. They're also handy for budgeting projects.

- **Scheduling Software**

  If you have a lot of meetings and deadlines, a scheduling program that reminds you when it's time to go somewhere or do something can save your life. Well, at least your job.

- **Project Management Software**

  If the project is big enough and you're managing enough people, you may need project management software. Of course, once you reach this level of management complexity, you're likely a full-time manager and not writing anymore. Project management software can be a black hole for time, requiring constant care and continual updates. Before you invest your time and money on a high-end package, first try using a spreadsheet, a wall calendar, and a simple Gantt-chart drawing program.

- **Graphics Programs**

  Most writers aren't expected to be visual artists, but you are usually responsible for screenshots, and will have to crop, edit and touch them up now and then.

- **Help System Creators/Compilers**

  If you're creating help systems for Windows-based software, you'll need to know your way around one of the systems for creating and compiling the help file. There are many shareware and commercial products that make this job fairly easy—unless you want to add all the bells and whistles.

- **Web Publishing Programs**

    If you write for the Web, or you want to supply a help system that can be read with a Web browser, you'll need to know how to create Web pages and links.

    You can use anything from text-based HTML editors to visually based programs similar to page layout tools to huge, fancy-schmancy Web design programs that include many project management and database features.

    HTML is becoming very popular for help systems these days (because of its cross-platform compatibility) as well as for publishing all manner of information on the Web.

- **Prototyping and Multimedia Programs**

    HyperCard, Director and other software tools are very useful for prototyping interfaces of both software and hardware products.

- **Reference Books**

    Old technology, but they still work.

- **Wall Calendars and Whiteboards**

    Wall calendars for scheduling and whiteboards for thinking.

- **The World Wide Web**

    These days the Web is actually a useful research tool. Besides general information on almost any subject, there are a number of sites that have specialized dictionaries and other useful information for writers.

- **Pencil and Paper**

    Agonizingly slow, and often nearly illegible, but there are times when nothing beats it. At meetings it's quieter and more dependable than a laptop for taking notes. Some writers still like to write their first draft by hand. Others mostly use paper for quick notes or rough drawings to help them think.

- **Tape Recorder**

    Sometimes you need to capture information faster than you can write or type. That's when a tape recorder is essential. It's also useful when you are dealing with people who are busy, or lose their train of thought while waiting for you to catch up in your note-taking.

    If you are taping, you can concentrate on the meaning of the words, and not on the writing or typing. It's better to catch errors and missing facts if you are listening closely, and ask for clarification during the interview, instead of days later after you've gone over your notes three times and the person you need to talk to is out of town.

Of course, the problem with tape recorders is that you have to transcribe the tape, which can be laborious and lengthy. A transcription machine helps by letting you keep your hands on the keyboard and move the tape forward and backward with your foot. It also lets you speed up or slow down the tape as needed. Having someone else transcribe the tape for you is also an option. You may be able to draft an administrative assistant or secretary.

• **Yourself**

Sometimes you need to communicate with your team, with other teams or with senior management. You'll have to talk, and possibly make presentations. This takes preparation and practice. Consider yourself a tool to be mastered.

The Cost of Changes

Here's a business lesson:

Making changes early is cheap. Making changes later is expensive.

This lesson covers your manual project and the whole development project. Changing text, correcting a fact or adding a chapter to your manuscript during the early writing stages of your manual costs you a few hours and the company your salary for a few hours. Making the same changes later, during the layout stage, costs you, the graphic artist and the editor each a few (or many) hours, and costs the company all of your salaries, plus any materials (film, etc.) that have been used and will have to be trashed. And if you make these changes even later, after the manuals have been sent to print, there's the added cost of trashed manuals that have to be paid for. Not to mention the cost to your reputation and career.

At the project level, making huge, sweeping architectural changes during the early design is relatively inexpensive. But making a far smaller change—for instance, changing the interface of a single window—in the final testing stage rings up huge costs. Not only the designer's time, but the programmers' time, possibly artists' time, definitely testers' time. Of course, the manual will have to be updated, causing more work and expense for writer, graphic artist and editor, and if it's late enough, there may be printed material to trash.

The lesson here is to check and recheck at every stage of development. Be sure you've got it right and the whole group is in consensus before moving on.

Special Topics

This chapter touches briefly on a few topics that you may confront some time in your technical writing career.

The sections are:

- Big Projects with Multiple Writers
- Rush Techniques
- Manuals for Multiple-Platform Products
- Writing for Console Machines
- Localization and Internationalization
- The Future of Manuals

Big Projects with Multiple Writers

If a project is very complex, a manual is very long, or the time to do the writing is very short, there may be a team of writers working together on a single project.

This is handled in different ways at different companies, but basically there will be a lead writer or project editor who breaks up the work and assigns writing tasks to multiple writers, then gathers everyone's work and molds it into a finished product.

If you are the lead writer or editor in charge:

- Your goal is to have the finished product seem as if it were written by one person, in one voice. Be prepared to heavily edit or rewrite everything.

- Limit your rewrites by giving writing style and tone examples to each writer. Make sure they understand what you want.

- Consistent structure throughout the document is as important as consistent style. Be absolutely clear about the structure you want, even if you have to actually outline each and every section.

- Be strategic about what you assign to whom. Giving each writer an assignment that they will like is great if you can do it. Happy writers work faster and better. Giving each writer an assignment that they can handle is absolutely necessary. If the assignment is late, missing or inadequate, then you've got to find someone else to start over or do it yourself.

If you're a writer on the project:

- Take some time to absorb the lead's desired style. It may not be your own, or even one you particularly like, but it's the job. If nothing else, it's a good challenge for your writing skills.

- Follow the lead's structure carefully. You may have a better way to organize the information in your part of the document, but if it's not consistent with the rest of the book, you'll have to rewrite it to match.

- Meet your deadlines.

Rush Techniques

Sometime in your career (if not every time) you will hit a deadline so hard it throws the whole company out of alignment. Suddenly, reasonable people are running in circles in panic, and demanding the impossible.

There are three basic techniques for speeding up a late project:

1. Pay rush charges to the printer.

   With a 25% premium, a printer may be able to deliver mass quantities of manuals in a week or two instead of four to six. Of course, you want to avoid this option.

2. Leave less-important sections out of the manual.

   You can reduce what you cover to the absolute basics, and try to include the missing information in the addendum, the Readme, the onscreen help, online help (over the net and always updateable), or ignore it completely and forever. This is usually the option that management prefers, but the customer pays the price.

3. Push the manual in unfinished form into layout before it's really ready.

   This option is often used in conjunction with one or both of the others. It's a false economy because it actually means more work for you and a lot more work for the graphic artist. The cost is higher than waiting to begin layout until everything is ready, and the time savings is smaller than you'd think. Starting layout a week or two early may deliver a finished product a day or two sooner.

Of course, sometimes a day or two is very important in meeting deadlines, especially in a public company that needs to ship within a particular fiscal quarter. But perhaps the most important thing about it is that it makes management think that things are moving faster, and gets them off your back so you can get your work done.

For this to succeed, you'll have to work very closely with your graphic artist and editor.

The first thing you can do is provide FPOs (for position only) for graphics that aren't final. The graphic artist can use these to get the layout as finished and polished as possible, then drop in the real graphics when they're ready. Be careful to supply FPOs in the proper size and shape or the document will require a lot of pages of rework. And be sure all the FPOs are marked, listed, and eventually removed.

If the document isn't finished, divide it into parts and forward those parts *that are finished and edited,* so the graphic artist can work on them separately. You may be tempted or asked to send the parts that aren't finished and edited to layout as well, but that's always a mistake that requires a lot more time and energy in the long run. Making edits and major changes during the layout process takes much longer and involves more people and ridiculous logistics.

Be ready to sit with the graphic artist (sometimes all night) and set up a bucket brigade of pages. The artist will input the changes from the editor, and print out each page—and the following page—as it is done, then will go on to the next page to edit. You check the newly printed page against the editor's edits to make sure they're right, and that they haven't caused other problems, like messing up the flow of the following page or losing part of a paragraph in layout limbo. You allow the graphic artist to work solely on correcting the document by taking over the duty of collecting all the final, finished pages and collating them into a completed draft that the editor can sign off.

The ability to handle rush jobs and finish on schedule without panicking is the measure of the writer, editor and graphic artist. The ability to avoid rush jobs is the measure of the producer, upper management and the company culture.

Manuals for Multiple-Platform Products

These days there are two basic flavors of personal computer: Windows and Macintosh. There are a few small, possibly growing alternatives, but at this time, not much commercial software is being developed for them. Keep your eyes open—things change fast in this industry.

The fact (though many people won't admit it) that Windows and Macintosh are so similar makes the writer's job of covering both platforms much easier. In the olden days of software, a whole six or seven years ago, there were many more platforms to cover: DOS, Windows, black and white Macintosh, color Macintosh, Amiga, Atari ST, Acorn, and others. And each looked, felt and operated differently. Even if they all had a menu bar along the top of the screen, all the menus acted differently. Life is much easier now. But it'll change.

As recently as five or six years ago, software was distributed on floppy disk. Sometimes on multiple floppy disks. It cost too much to put disks with versions of the software for multiple types of computers into one box. There would be separate products in separate boxes for each computer platform. Each box could have a customized platform-specific manual.

To save time and energy, the manual was often made generic, covering only the program functions, and staying away from any platform- or interface-specific information. An addendum or Quick-Start guide would be written for each computer, and cover the installation, starting, interface functions (opening and closing windows, using menus), and other idiosyncrasies of the machine.

Nowadays, with the advent of CDs for software distribution, and the ability to put not only a lot of data, but also multiple computer formats (at least Macintosh and Windows) on a single disk, it is much cheaper to put multiple versions of software into a single box. Retailers like this as well as publishers, since they can carry fewer different boxes. And as the Macintosh market dwindled (though it is now experiencing a reemergence), the only way to get stores to carry Macintosh software was if it was in the same box as the Windows software.

When dealing with manuals for products that work on both Windows and Macintosh, the standard is to cover both platforms in one manual. Hopefully the engineers for both platforms communicate and make their versions as identical as possible, so the only differences you have to cover are installation, starting, keyboard shortcuts and a few minor window-control buttons.

Complications set in when one version is done first, and the company wants to ship it alone, then add the second version a few months later. In this case, you've got a few ways to handle it. You can write the manual about the first version and mention in a few places that if customers have the second version they should look in the addendum or Quick-Start guide for details about using the program on their computer. Or you can try to cover both platforms in the manual, even though one isn't done yet, and you can't test every detail. Or you can just write the manual for the first platform, then add in the information on the second platform for the second printing.

Writing for Console Machines

Console machines are dedicated game computers, like Nintendo 64 and Sony PlayStation.

The manufacturers of these machines have tightly controlled, strict rules and regulations on the packaging, including the manual. There are specific page sizes and page-count limits. They have required graphics and text that you must include, further limiting your useable space.

To produce games for these machines, you have to pass the manufacturer's internal quality assurance. If you don't meet their specs in any way, you don't ship a product. Since the companies do all the actual manufacturing of the software for their machines, you don't have the option to ignore them. There's nowhere else to go.

Since these companies expect the games on their machines to be generally mindless shoot-em-ups, they don't allow for much of a manual within their specifications.

Don't even think about making a generic manual for multiple platforms of console machines. Not only does each platform require a different size and format, but your product will be rejected if you mention another platform in "their" manual.

There is no standard help system built into these systems, so you'll be supplying the team programmers with text to be included into the program. Because these machines display on a television—a very low-resolution display—if onscreen text is to be readable, it must be large. That means all your onscreen text, help and otherwise, has to be very short and precise.

Fun with Console Game Manuals

I worked on a complex simulation game that was first on a PC, then ported to two different console machines. The original manual for Macintosh and Windows was 200+ pages, laid out on 7 x 8.5-inch pages. For one console machine, the manual had to be cut to fit on 60 8 x 4-inch pages. It was horrible, heart-wrenching work to try to preserve enough information so the customer would understand the game. For the other console machine, the manual had to be further reduced to fit onto 40 5 x 5-inch pages. This was pure butchery. It was inadequate in every way. And to add insult to injury, this was the manual that won an award. Go figure.

Localization and Internationalization

The world is a shrinking place. Many US companies, even small ones, earn 50% or more of their money from sales in other countries. This means that everything you write, every manual, every bit of text on the screen, has to be translated into French, German, Spanish, Italian, Japanese, and many other languages.

Once just called translation, *localization* became the term for translating and possibly repackaging products for various local (to them) foreign (to us) markets. In recent years, this process has been expanded to include, when necessary, major redesign of the product to fit the culture of various countries, and is now called *Internationalization,* known in the industry as *I18N.* Since internationalization is an international word, professionals in the industry can't agree whether it should be spelled with an "s" or a "z." What they can agree on is that it starts with an "i" and ends with an "n" and there're 18 letters in between. That's where the abbreviation I18N comes from.

Good internationalization sometimes requires a major cultural conversion. Things we normally wouldn't think about can cause big problems. For instance, in some countries, the sight of a severed hand is incredibly repulsive. Makes sense. But this means those cute little hand cursors we all have on our computers have to be changed.

I18N is a book unto itself (a number of them, actually—check out the recommended reading appendix), but basically, it involves timing, organization, and working with a number of other people: translators, project managers, engineers, designers, programmers, international quality assurance, foreign publishers and accountants, and on and on.

As a writer potentially involved with I18N, you need to be ready to work with a translator, who may be local or in a foreign land, to explain and reword any cultural references that might not make sense in other countries. And there are more than you think.

Be conscious of the length of text that you write to be displayed on the screen. Some languages take up more space than others. On the average, German takes approximately 30% more space than English. Individual words may be far longer than their English equivalents. And the German publishers I've worked with tend not to like abbreviations. If you don't write it short enough, the translator will shorten it, and possibly miss the point.

When taking screenshots for a software manual, try to use shots that contain as little text as possible (if it still gets your point across), so they won't have to be recreated, re-shot and replaced for each language. This might be tough in a word processor, but in a paint program or even a spreadsheet, with a little forethought, you can keep words to a minimum. Here's a hint: include the icon or button bar, but leave out the menu bar (words) whenever you can.

In your graphics list, keep track of which graphics may need to be replaced (almost all with words). You may be asked to supply all the screenshot versions for the different languages. There are two basic ways to do this:

1. Take new screenshots with each of the newly translated versions of the program, hopefully with someone who speaks the language sitting next to you. At the very least you'll need a page or three with a translation of all the menus, windows, etc.

2. Touch up the original screenshot, using a paint program to change the text to the various languages. Before you do, make sure you have a good, final translation that will match the actual program and the foreign language docs.

If you are sending files back and forth to someone in Europe, you may have trouble printing documents they send you, because your printer will be waiting for you to insert size A4 paper. A4, the standard size in Europe, is slightly thinner but longer than our standard letter size. To avoid this problem, open the Page Setup dialog and change the paper size. (I've seen a whole office grind to a halt when the network printer stopped and waited for someone to change the paper. A dozen people had to scour the office, looking for the person who sent an A4-sized document to the printer and then left for a few hours.)

Be careful with humor. I encourage the use of humor in this book, but when it comes to translations, humor has its own set of problems. The best way to preserve humor is to have a translator with a sense of humor that can censor, change, rewrite or replace lines as needed. Translators like this are hard to find.

One last point. American English and British English are not the same language. You may be able to ship an unchanged British product in the US, but *not* the other way around. This translation is much easier and cheaper than, for instance, an English-to-French translation, but should be done. The main things you need to do are run a spelling check with an alternate dictionary and have a native British-English speaker give it a careful once-over for slang.

The Future of Manuals

For both financial and technical reasons, technical documentation is heading away from being printed on paper and toward integration with the product itself.

The financial reasons are that paper is getting more and more expensive, while memory, both RAM and disk, is getting cheaper. The technical reasons are that products—both hardware and software—are getting smart enough to contain their own help systems. And we also hope that the products will be designed well enough that they'll be able to be used intuitively, and not need as much documentation.

Video is another direction for instructional materials that will be around for a while. While it is fairly cheap to manufacture a VHS tape (and DVD will be cheaper), video, too, will head toward integration with the product whenever the product has a display screen.

As the rate of data transfer speeds up, documentation and instructions will more and more go online, as opposed to just onscreen. A master copy of the docs, tutorials, instruction video or whatever will reside on the net, and the product will pull it down and display it as needed. This master copy will always be up-to-date.

Of course, any product that uses online help will have to be hooked to the phone lines or cable or some other connection to the net, and will need some sort of display. This may seem far-fetched now, but it'll happen. Houses will be networks. Appliances will talk to each other for timing, coordination and energy efficiency, and to the factory to get updates, help screens and warm fuzzy messages and helpful hints for the owner. Appliances will also be networked to the TV for displaying messages, instructions and manuals.

It will be a while before printed technical and instructional books and manuals are totally gone. They just work better much of the time, and customers are still much more comfortable with them. Then again, technical information is growing and changing at breakneck speed. Printed material is stagnant, and can quickly become outdated. Over the next generation or two, printed technical information will become rare.

In the meantime, as both hardware and software become more self-contained, printed manuals—or the parts of the manuals that give basic operating instructions—generally become smaller. This doesn't mean that there's less for the writer to do. There's still:

- Online and onscreen help systems,
- Background and added-value material, and
- Interface and product design—integrating the needed knowledge into the product itself, instead of into a manual.

Remember, your job is to communicate, to get the needed information into the customer's hands and mind as quickly and easily as possible. Don't get left behind by thinking that your method of communication must be in a printed manual.

Part 2
The Sample Project

The chapters in this part of the book are:

- Project Overview
- Stage 1: Learning the System—Setup and Planning
- Stage 2: Learning the Product—Research
- Stage 3: Organizing the Information— The Outline and the Structural Edit
- Stage 4: Writing the Manual—The First Draft
- Stage 5: Validating the Information— Content Editing and Testing
- Stage 6: Rewriting and Retesting
- Stage 7: Detailed Editing—The Line Edit
- Stage 8: Preparing the Manual for Layout
- Stage 9: Making It Look Good—Layout and Final Edits
- Stage 10: Printing and Final Production
- Stage 11: Producing the Addendum or Quick-Start Guide
- Stage 12: Producing Onscreen Help
- Stage 13: Writing the Readme
- Stage 14: Cleaning Up—The Project Backup
- Stage 15: Looking Back—The Postmortem: Lessons Learned
- The End

This part of the book presents a sample software manual project, from the point where a writer enters the scene, all the way through production and even to the postmortem.

Project Overview

This chapter briefly describes the sample project, the way the project is organized, and the typical working situation it demonstrates.

The sections are:

- The Project's Purpose
- The Sample Software
- Project Organization
- Projects and Different Companies
- The Scenario
- Before You Begin
- Project Flowchart

The Project's Purpose

The purpose of this sample project is to give you an idea of what it's like to write and produce a software manual as part of a software development team.

It was written to try to bring you into the action—referring to the things *you* have to do and deal with—but it isn't a workbook. You personally won't be asked to do any writing, just reading and understanding.

The Sample Software

As mentioned at the beginning of this book, the sample project is based on *The Personal Newspaper,* a nonexistent program that was partially designed a while ago, then expanded for the purposes of this book. It is a simple program, close-ended, with only a few screens and controls to describe. But, as you'll see, there is still a lot of work needed to document even a simple program.

The early drafts of the sample project manual are based on the initial design document, found in the Exhibits section. The journey from that to the final draft and final manual is documented step-by-step in the sample project. A demonstration program that shows the screens and navigation of the program—but that is not a functional model—is available for download from the publisher's website (www.untechnicalpress.com/downloads).

Some design flaws and ambiguity have *intentionally* been left in the early stages of this project, so the process of refining and finalizing a product—and the effects on the writer and the manual—can be demonstrated in the sample project.

Project Organization

The project is divided into 15 stages, each covered in a chapter. At the end of each stage are these subsections:

Problems and Solutions—all the things that can go wrong with your part of the project during the stage and what to do about them, and

Complications and Opportunities—things that can go wrong with a project that are usually considered outside of the writer's responsibilities (and how to handle them), how to contribute to the product (and your career) by keeping the project moving forward, and how to watch for opportunities to learn, to do something new or to have fun.

Projects and Different Companies

Every project is different. Every company is different.

This sample project is presented in a fairly generic way, so it should stand as a reasonable example that you can follow on any of your own projects. Of course, you'll always want and need to play around with the steps and the schedule to match your particular needs. You'll add more time for some things, allow less for others, add extra editing stages, and change the order of or combine some of the steps.

If you work for a large, well-organized company, you *might* come onto a project as a new writer, and everything will go smoothly from your first day until your work is done. Everyone will know their jobs and there will be no bickering between departments. All your tools and information will be supplied, and your work will be clearly defined. And then again, things can get confusing and disorganized during the later stages of a project, even at the biggest and best of companies.

If you join a smaller software company—or start your own—things are almost always a little more hectic. The company is growing (or shrinking) and changing on a daily basis. Many people wear multiple hats. There may be no clear line of command, and policies aren't established. You face more confusion, but also more opportunity to contribute to the product and take on more responsibility.

The Scenario

The sample project refers to you as if you were a new staff writer, who doesn't know the people or the ropes yet, and who has joined a project already near its completion. For a contractor, the actual work would be the same, but there would be some additional negotiation and contract stages. The business, negotiations and contracts for contracting deserves its own book, and will not be dealt with here.

The company situation in the sample could be a small, growing one, a less-organized larger company, or a slightly less-organized project within any company. This approach was chosen partly because there are so many of these companies and projects, partly so this sample can cover as many problems, complications and opportunities as possible, and partly because the energy and chaos of a small, fast-moving, slightly out-of-control project is a lot of fun, in spite of the inevitable problems.

The best way to survive chaos is to know what you're getting into, and know how to deal with the issues as they come up.

Before You Begin

Before you begin reading through the stages of the project, you may find it helpful to first read the following documents in the Exhibits section of this book:

1. The Sample Project Proposal
2. The Sample Project Initial Design Document
3. The Finished Sample Project Manual

In addition, you may want to download the demonstration program that shows the screens and navigation of the finished program, and put it through its paces. (Available at www.untechnicalpress.com/downloads.)

Being familiar with these documents and the demonstration program ahead of time will help you get the most out of the sample project.

Project Flowchart

Here is a flowchart showing the steps of this project:

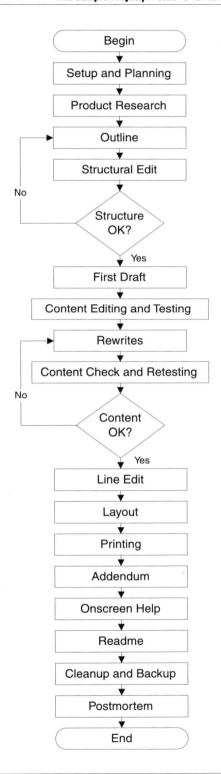

Stage 1: Learning the System—Setup and Planning

This chapter covers starting a new project, learning the ropes and planning the project.

The sections are:

- Establish the System
- Establish Project Goals
- Establish the Reader
- Your Tools
- Problems and Solutions
- Complications and Opportunities

Establish the System

Before you begin any writing, or even start familiarizing yourself with the product that you'll be writing about, there is some basic information about the working environment and the system that you should know.

You may know some of the answers from previous experience and from the interviews you went through to get the job. Finding out the answers to the rest can take a little time and effort. You'll have to talk to a number of people, including your boss(es), other writers in the company, the graphic arts department, and possibly someone from Human Resources.

Here are the questions, and the answers for the sample project.

The Very Basic Questions

What's the company structure, and how do you fit in?

The company has four main departments: finance and administration, product development, marketing and creative/corporate services. You are in the writing group, which is a part of creative/corporate services, acting as vendor for both product development and marketing.

Who's in charge? Of you, of the project, of anything else you should know?

You ultimately report to the writing manager, who is responsible for your reviews and your assignments, and who will also be your editor. But while you are on this project (for an estimated four months), you will be reporting to the project's producer.

The producer is leading and managing the project, and will be the judge of whether your work is appropriate for the product.

Also involved on an intermittent basis will be the head (VP) of development who the producer reports to, and the head of marketing. You find out that the VP of development has a lot of faith in the producer and won't interfere too much unless things start to go wrong or fall behind schedule. You also find that the head of marketing has a lot of faith in the graphic arts department to maintain company standards and quality, but is trying out a new product manager on this project.

What is the corporate culture, and what are the working conditions and atmosphere like?

This is a small but growing software company. It is in the process of growing from a group of friends on a mission to a large, serious company. The newer people, like you, are impressed by the friendly atmosphere and some of the perks, but the long-timers are bemoaning the "good old days" of last year.

The feeling on the project is casual but intense. Hours of operation are flexible (you don't have to show up until 9:00 or 10:00 am, but you stay until the work is done, no matter how late it is). Dress is casual. The project is nearing the end, and everyone is working long and hard to finish on schedule.

What is the product development lifecycle that is being used—and what do you know from it?

You don't get a clear answer to this, but gather that it probably started out as a waterfall that jumped into production too soon and turned into a code and fix project. Because the project is fairly simple, and the producer has a good grasp on what the final outcome should be, the project is actually nearing completion, and almost on schedule.

From this, you know that there won't be a very up-to-date final design document that you can work from, and that the team is loosely managed—beware of last-second changes.

What is the company's tone—what about humor?

The company has a bit of a maverick, startup reputation, and the long-term employees like to think of themselves as rebels, but the company is changing, becoming a little less radical. And this product in particular is meant for kids and parents, so the tone will have to be a little subdued. Humor is all right as long as it's rated PG, it fits into the feel of the product, and doesn't detract from the quality or usefulness of the manual.

Team and Personnel Questions

Who else is on the project, and what do they do?

The team for this product is fairly small. You put together a team info/contact sheet that includes everyone—even those not technically on the team—that you'll need to contact or deal with to get your part of the project done.

You print this out and keep it near your computer and phone. Leave some blanks so you can add people by hand as needed.

Name	Title	Ext.	Email	Comments
Chris Orny	Producer	5512	COrny	Team leader, product designer
Brian Rainier	Lead Eng.	5527	BRain	Architecture, database, tech. scheduling
Joe Okenso	Engineer	5529	JOken	Interface, installation, help system
Sue Topper	Artist	5533	STopp	All screens, icons, some interface design
Dan Amity	Lead Tester	5609	DAmit	Test plan
Horace Ecksley	Prod Mgr.	5540	HEcks	Marketing link, focus groups
William Ordyss	Writing Mgr.	5521	WOrdy	The boss, all editing
Linda Earnest	GA Mgr.	5555	LEarn	Keeper of graphic standards
Richard Bagel	Graphic Artist	5556	RBage	Lunatic assigned to this project
Fred Osilin	Manufacturing	5581	FOsil	Schedules printing
Barry Eeren	VP Prod. Dev.	5503	BEere	Wants notification of completed stages
Della Fenster	VP Marketing	5502	DFens	Wants to see only after layout

Once you know who will be involved, try to meet everyone, especially those who will need to approve your work. Find out if they have any special points, pet peeves or issues that they want to have covered. It's better to know now than to have to start over two months from now.

Who and what are the editing resources, who will do the structural edit, who does the line edit, who has the real control over the content?

As mentioned before, the writing manager will be your editor, both for structural and line edits. While your manager has a lot of control, you and he are both acting as service providers to the development group. The producer and his bosses will have the final say, but the writing manager has worked with them all for a while and won't steer you too far wrong.

What is the writer's role/responsibility here? Is it strictly the manual and the other specified text, or if you have the time and knowledge and opportunity, will you be expected or allowed to do more for the product, including contribute to interface design and smoothing out the overall development process?

This isn't a question you generally ask your boss directly. You may ask peers what their take is, but generally, it's a question that you answer by feel. In this instance, your gut feeling is that you'll be stepping on toes and causing problems if you forcefully suggest changes to the product or the system. But if you handle it subtly, and phrase issues more as questions than as suggestions, you'll be able to help out.

Process Questions

An organized writing manager should actually handle all the process questions and bring you up to speed along the way, supplying information as it's needed. Process, or lack thereof, can be confusing for experienced writers entering a new company, and doubly so for entry-level writers.

If there isn't someone on the job to handle this for you, or you just want to know everything you can about the project ahead of time, then it's worth your while to try to find the answers to as many of these questions as you can.

Is there a company style guide, and if so, where can you get one?

You find that there is one, but it hasn't been updated for years. You can get a copy from the company network.

Where can you get copies of the documentation for other company products, especially those that might be similar to this product?

You are told that this product is a new type for this company, and that the docs won't be similar to anything that they've already done. But you go to the mail room, where extra copies of earlier products and their docs are kept, and pick out a few different copies of manuals and Quick-Start guides anyway. You also get a couple of CDs of earlier products so you can look at the screen text and the Readme file.

How many edits should be scheduled?

One structural edit, one content edit, and one pre-layout line edit, plus more as needed, including at least two rounds for the layout.

How long will each edit take?

The writing manager promises two to three days turnaround for the structural and line edits. He suggests counting on a week for the content edit, and a couple days each for the post-layout edits.

Where is project information stored and how is it distributed?

Each project has a folder on the company network. The folder contains subfolders for code, graphics, documentation, transfer, etc. Most of the existing documentation on this project is on the company net.

How long is the standard printing time?

This will help you set your schedule. According to manufacturing, a non-rush print job for this product (assuming it is a small manual) will be four weeks. Print time for a very short Quick-Start guide is two weeks.

Who does layout?

There is a graphic arts department (part of marketing) down the hall. An artist will be assigned to this project. Deal directly with this artist for project-related issues, and with the graphic arts manager for standards and templates.

How long will graphic arts need?

According to the manual size estimates (made before you came on the job), graphic arts believes they can do the layout, complete with edits in two weeks. The Quick-Start guide will take an additional week.

How and where do you deliver what?

Edited text and screenshots should be delivered in electronic form, by placing a copy in the transfer folder in the project folder on the net. Email or call the artist when it's ready.

What format for text and screenshots?

You will use the company's standard word processor, and deliver in that program's format. You can go ahead and assign styles to the headings and a few other parts of the text. The page-layout program will read them in, and the graphic artist will redefine the styles through global changes. Graphics are best in .TIF format, but .BMP or PICT will do.

What are the standards for the manuals? Formats, sizes, templates?

Those will be provided by the graphic arts manager, as needed.

Long-term Issue Questions

Again, these questions and issues are generally handled by a writing manager, not an entry-level writer.

Is there a budget line?[11] Is this product likely to "go budget"?

Currently, there is no budget line, but you never know. So don't spend time creating a complete onscreen manual, but keep a complete copy of all the content locally in case there's a rush request for it.

Might this product be sold over the net in an entirely electronic version?

There are no plans for this at the current time. But you never know. Be ready for a future rush request for an onscreen manual.

Will this product be translated, localized and sold in other countries?

Because the product is so text-heavy, and relates to US grade levels, localizing this product would be very expensive and time-consuming. It has been decided to "wait and see." If the product sells well enough in the US, then the powers that be will make some foreign sales forecasts and make a decision then. For now, you don't have to worry about providing the localization group with anything.

Establish Project Goals

Now that you have an idea of what's going on around the project, it's time to define exactly what you'll be doing.

What Is the Project?

The project is *The Personal Newspaper, First Grade Edition,* a database-driven product that generates and prints a daily personalized newspaper for kids. It is very customizable, using names, pets, dates and ages supplied by the user. It is the first in a series, and will cover the first grade.

What Are You Writing?

Your main mission is to write the manual. Early estimates are that the manual will be about 40 pages, and no more than 60. It will be the standard company manual size, 8.5 by 5.5 inches.

There will also be a Quick-Start guide, same dimensions, but ideally only four pages, and no more than eight if absolutely necessary.

---

[11] *A standard practice among software companies—especially entertainment software companies—is to extend the life of older products by lowering their prices and repackaging them as part of a "budget line." Because companies charge less for budget product, they need to spend less to manufacture them. One way to lower costs is to supply an electronic version of the manual instead of a printed one.*

In addition, you will be responsible for editing all the interface-related screen text, writing the Readme file, and for supplying the content for the help file.

One of the programmers on the team will handle the actual help-file compilation, but you have to help design it and supply the content.

What's the Schedule?

Today is June first. The software is planned to go golden master (be ready for duplication) on October first and manufacturing is to start by October fifth. That means that the manuals and Quick-Start guides have to be printed by October first and delivered to manufacturing by the fifth. If the project slips much, it'll have a hard time being in the stores for the big holiday buying season—so the pressure is on the team to deliver. That leaves you four months to get your part of the job done.

The List of Deliverables

From this information, you establish a list of deliverables, milestones and delivery dates. The writing manager may give you a template to use, or even fill it out for you. It looks something like this:

Deliverable	Outline (Structural Edit)	1ˢᵗ Draft (Content Edit)	Final Draft (Line Edit)	To Loc.	To GA	To Printer	To Prog.	To Test	To Mfg.
Manual	6/7	7/24	8/10	n/a	8/15	9/1	n/a	n/a	10/1
Quick-Start Guide	8/15	8/24	9/1	n/a	9/7	9/15	n/a	n/a	10/1
Help Content	8/24	9/1	9/10	n/a			9/15	9/21	10/1
Screen Text	n/a	7/23	8/9	n/a	n/a	n/a	n/a	n/a	n/a
Readme file	9/14	9/16	9/20	n/a	n/a	n/a	9/24	9/26	10/1

It always helps to start at the end, with your absolute deadline, then work backward, adding in the times that you know others are going to need. What you have left after subtracting all the others' time is yours for the writing. And it's usually a lot shorter than you'd like.

You (or your manager) may later add extra columns to track the scheduled times vs. the actual times for future reference, but for simplicity, we'll leave that out for now.

Note that the interface screen text is scheduled to be done just ahead of each of the major manual edits. At these points, the manual and screen text should be consistent. Any changes to the screen text after the Final Draft point need to be reflected in the manual.

This is a good chart to let you know your deadlines, but some people like Gantt charts, because they show what you're doing when, and help point out overlaps in tasks.

Here's a very simple Gantt chart for this project. Note that a number of things are on your plate at the same time.

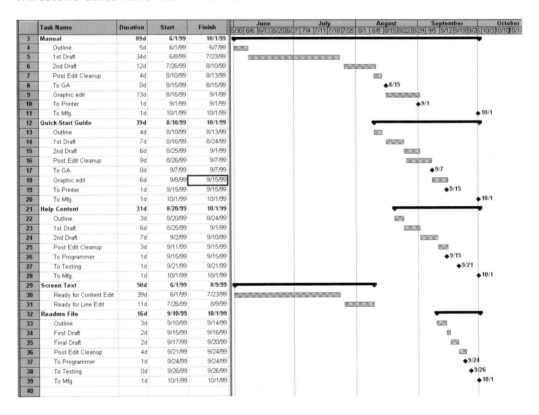

Here's a more complex Gantt chart, including a table of durations, start dates and stop dates. Each task has been broken down into its component parts, and milestone dates have been marked.

This chart makes it look like you have 10 times as much work to do, but try not to let it bother you.

Charts like this are most likely to be generated by the producer or project manager who is tracking the entire project in detail with project management software. They can easily separate out individual parts of the project (such as your parts) and print them out. If you know someone is tracking the project in this detail and they don't give you a copy of your part of the project, ask for it.

Establish the Reader

Now you know where you'll be working and with whom, and what you have to do by when. But who are you writing all this for? Who are the audiences for the product and the manual? Are they the same?

To find this out, you'll want to talk to the producer, plus any or all of the following: other writers, editors, people from marketing, customer service, and technical support. It is very possible that the marketing department has a complete customer analysis for this product, but they probably won't think to give you a copy. Ask for one.

After exhaustive research, you think you know your customers.

The product creates and prints reading material for young children—this particular product, the first-grade edition, will be targeted at five- to seven-year olds. But it will be the parents or teachers who will be using the program itself—and reading the manual.

But there's a slight complication. Since there will be multiple editions of this program ranging from first through sixth grade, you are expected to make this manual the template for all the rest. The manual (and help system) for this product will be adapted—with as little additional work as possible—for the next few versions, which will be made for older and older children in steps. As the age level rises, the kids will start controlling the program—and reading the manual.

Therefore, you know:

- The audience is definitely consumers—kids, parents and teachers—not high-tech workers.
- You have to keep it simple enough for kids, say 9 to 12, to read.
- You can't "write down" to them too much or it'll insult or annoy the parents and teachers.

One final thing you may want to do is put together a reader profile sheet, also known as a customer fact sheet. It will help you define and remember who you're writing for. Put the sheet up near your computer and look at it every so often as you write.

On the next page is a sample reader profile sheet. If there are other points of information you want on your sheet for your product, add them. If some of these points don't fit your product, delete them.

Reader Profile Sheet

Project:	Personal Newspaper, 1st Grade Edition
Average age:	n/a
Age distribution:	Kids: 9–12, parents: mid-20s to late-40s, teachers: various
Gender distribution:	Assume equal distribution
Technical expertise level:	Kids and consumer parents, some elementary teachers—treat as new to computers
Education level distribution:	Range: second grade through education degrees
% repeat customers:	n/a (new product)
Professional field:	Mixed, some in education
Other special attributes:	Definitely not a homogeneous group.

Picture of kids

Name _____

Picture of teachers

Name _____

Picture of young parents

Name _____

Picture of older parents

Name _____

Your Tools

Next, you have to identify and gather your tools.

First and foremost, you need whatever computer is standard at that company, equipped to run the company-standard word processor. If the computer and word processor aren't your personal favorites, try to live with them. Don't expect a whole company to change their ways to suit your personal preferences. Learn to use what they use.

Contractor Tip

If you're a contractor and don't have the company's standard machine and word processor, then it's a good idea to negotiate into your contract that the company provide you with them for the term of the contract. If they won't go for it, then one of the first things you must do is make sure you can trade files compatibly with the producer and the graphic artists.

Other than a word processor, you'll need a way to capture and edit—at least crop, if not do a lot more touch-up to—screenshots. And you'll probably find a spreadsheet to be a handy tool for lists and planning, if not for actually producing content for the manual. Some sort of flowcharting program often comes in handy for showing processes.

Email is of course necessary. So is access to the company network, with knowledge of where you can get information and where you should put your finished work.

For this project, we'll assume that the company supplied a computer with a complete office suite of software including word processor (with built-in limited flowcharting), spreadsheet, email, and a basic image-editing program.

Software you won't need on this project includes programs for page layout (graphic arts will take care of that), help-system compilation (an engineer will take care of that), web publishing, or prototyping (the project's already too far along).

Beyond software, tools that you'll want to have handy are:

- A small tape recorder
- Paper and pencil
- Calendar (on or off computer)
- Whiteboard
- Reference books—at least a dictionary, and a couple of your favorite references on grammar and punctuation.

One more possibility: for the ultimate luxury, you'll want an extra computer.

You'll be writing about an unfinished program. You'll be using every function, button and control of a pre-beta version. You'll be crashing the computer a lot.

If you're running a program through its paces and writing about it on the same computer, you're bound to lose data. If you run the program on one computer and write about it on another, then you lose only a little time with each crash.

Of course, most companies don't like supplying writers with multiple computers. You may have to bring in one from home. You may be able to check out an old laptop or outmoded computer that isn't in use anymore, but can run your word processor.

The best likelihood for getting two computers is if the company makes versions of the product for more than one platform. For instance, if your company produces versions of products for both Mac and PC, then run the Mac version on the Mac and write about it on the PC, and run the PC version on the PC and write about it on the Mac.[12]

Problems and Solutions

Problems that you might run into during this stage—and their solutions—are:

 • **You may be expected to get right to work and start cranking out pages without first taking a few hours to learn the system and get set up.**

First try logic: explain that if you get some questions answered first, you'll be able to work faster, with fewer interruptions later. If logic doesn't work, or the project is in such a panic that you don't even want to try reasoning, then do your best to start the project, and establish the system and setup over a period of days, whenever you can get away from your desk without raising suspicion.

 • **You have multiple people who think they're your boss, who make conflicting demands, and don't talk to each other.**

This is a tough one, and the solution—or as close to it as you can get—is more a matter of politics than writing or software development. There are three approaches to tackle this:

First, the bottom-up approach. Talk to others on the project to find out what they would do in this situation. How do they handle this conflict? Who do they listen to? Who do they think *really* has the power? Who do you least want to be mad at you?

---

[12] *This was our setup for many years at Maxis. It worked well, especially because the word processor we used was available for both platforms, and there was no problem moving files between the two computers.*

Next, the straightforward, but gentle, approach. Put together a list of items where the two (or more) potential bosses differ in opinion. Not a list of complaints, peeves, personality issues or minor confusions. The list has to be specific to your work. A typical item may be that one person has told you in no uncertain terms that your manual can be no more than 40 pages, while another has said that 60 is OK. (Of course, if you only need 40 pages, then don't worry about it. Only mention it if it's actually important to your ability to do a good job.) Send email to all concerned parties. Word it so that you are not placing blame or being blatant about the problem.

Say something to the effect that you think you've been given mixed messages and don't understand exactly what you need to do. List the items in contention. Invite all concerned to a quick meeting to decide once and for all what you'll be doing. If you absolutely don't want to be in a room with both (or all) of these people at the same time, then ask that they work out the answers and present them to you—in writing. This is a cop-out, and eliminates your ability to influence the answers, but it may be the best thing if these people really don't like each other.

Lastly, the overhead approach. Find out who your multiple bosses report to, and present the list. Say that you can't get consensus on these issues from the parties in question, and need answers to move forward. At this point, the boss' boss will make the decisions or force one out of the warring parties. Save this approach for last. It's never a good political move to go over someone's head.

• **There is no editor.**

If there is no staff editor or writing manager, then you have to find someone to edit your work—at least for the copy edit, if not the structural edit. There are professional editors all over the country that will do a great job for a reasonable hourly rate. Some will even do it via email, so there's no time wasted with travel.

If you can't get a budget for an editor, then search the company for a reasonable substitute. There's usually someone around who was an English major, and would be glad to edit your work. They may not be as good an editor as you are, but they are a fresh set of eyes, and will catch mistakes that you won't. Run it by two people if you can. Have them make their edits on paper, then you input the actual edits that you agree with into the file.

Another option is if you have a friend who is an editor. Work out a barter deal. See if they'll donate some editing time in trade for some writing time they may need in the future. Be creative.

- **You're not given the tools you need.**

Any truly professional organization will supply its employees with the tools they need to do the job. Unfortunately, many software companies aren't truly professional organizations. And some that are, are less than cooperative with contractors.

In this case, it's up to you to be the professional. Bring in your own reference books, software, even your computer from home—but make sure that they are marked with "Property of *Your Name.*"

If you need tools that you don't already own, buy them if they aren't too expensive. If you need tools that are more expensive than you want to spend, then maybe the job isn't worth doing.

Complications and Opportunities

Here are some likely complications for this stage, and opportunities to help, learn or have fun:

- **You have a very disorganized, confusing first day.**

This is actually very typical for new employees, temps and contractors. Unless the company has their act together—usually through the urging of the human resources department—you are unlikely to show up your first day (on the job or on a new project) and have your computer waiting with all the software and network connections you'll need, a working phone, a list of the project members, a project schedule and all the information you'll need to do your work (or at least the location of that information). I've seen people wander around for a week waiting for a desk, then sit there for another week waiting for a computer.

What you can do for yourself is show up with your list of everything you'll need—basically what's covered in this subchapter. That'll help you get going and organized quicker.

A sample of a list like this can be found in the Exhibits section, under New Employee/Onsite Contractor Checklist.

If you want to take it a step farther, you can pass this list on to your local human resources representative, once you've modified it to suit the particular company. They may thank you. Or ignore you.

- **Nobody knows what the development lifecycle is.**

You may find during your initial investigations that the producers or project managers don't know much about the theory of project management—even if they're doing a fairly good job.

If it seems appropriate, then you might suggest a few books from the recommended reading appendix. If it doesn't seem appropriate, then you might keep one of the books on your desk, where someone just may notice it and ask about it.

Then again, if the producer isn't doing a very good job, and you understand the development process and have been through a few projects from beginning to end, you might want to apply for a job as a producer for the next project.

• Marketing has no team representation.

In many companies there is a state of war between marketing and product development. It stems from the fact that the two groups usually know very little about what the other does.

As a writer, you straddle the two groups. You may officially report to either one, but you'll most likely work closely with people from both groups. Also as a writer, you can be a go-between for the two departments. As much as they may dislike each other, they need each other.

Keep the project's product manager informed of the state of the documentation. Forward any good product descriptions you come up with for your introduction chapter.

You can even help integrate marketing—in a helpful way—into the project. Work with the product manager to set up a small focus group to test your tutorial (if there's time). Encourage the producer to realize (all on his own) that a similar focus group could help identify the rough spots of the interface.[13]

Once again, knowing about more than the actual mechanics of writing manuals is useful.

---

[13] By no means are focus groups the answer to all questions, to all design issues and to all concept approvals. I've seen good projects ruined and scrapped because focus-group input was taken too seriously. What they are definitely good for is to find the rough spots in an interface or in a tutorial. They're good for more than that, but only if they're run well, and the information gained from the group is interpreted well.

Stage 2: Learning the Product—Research

This chapter covers your actual start on the project itself. Time to learn everything you can about the product that you're going to write about.

The sections are:

- Research
- Problems and Solutions
- Complications and Opportunities

Research

Your goal in your research is to find out everything you can about the product and its interface, especially everything that might confuse the new user.

As you do your research, write down notes on what you learn. You might even start a preliminary manual outline now.

Preliminary Things to Establish During Research

While the main goal of your research is to find out everything you possibly can about the product, you need to find out more about your sources first.

What are your sources?

The sources are people, on the team and off the team, design documents, the product itself and marketing documents.

How reliable are each of the sources and the documents?

You'll need to use your own judgement on how reliable and accurate each person is. Take into account what their personal agenda may be. Always, always, *always* verify everything you see in a design doc with the actual product before you put it into the manual. Design docs can be very useful for you, or they can be complete fiction. Even the best will have some variance from the product, if only a small error or a last-minute change.

Who's REALLY in charge? Of the design, of the project, of you?

On this project, the producer is in control of the project. He has done the design and the design docs, and makes the final decisions on almost everything. From talking to others on the team, you find that he will listen to suggestions, and sometimes takes them—if you can back up your suggestion with a good reason. Of course, as mentioned before, he most likely won't be expecting or wanting you to take over the design, but if you handle it right, you can contribute.

Questions to Ask Your Human Sources

Once you have your list of people to talk to, ask them each some or all of these questions:

- Who on the team knows and does what on the project? (Ask everyone about everyone else's areas of specialty.)
- Specifically, what are your areas of responsibility and expertise?
- What questions should I bring to you?
- Could you describe what this product is, in your own words?
- What docs do you have that describe the product or any part of the product?
- What do think will be the product's most confusing operations or the most difficult concepts for the user to master?
- Where is the latest version of the product, and how final is it?
- What is missing or is going to change?
- Where, how and how often can I get updates?

Why Writers Should Contribute to Interface Design

You may have noticed that I've repeatedly hit on the subject of writers getting involved with interface design, or at least making design suggestions. I've touched on the politics of design ownership, and suggested ways to subtly influence the project.

Why deal with topics that aren't usually mentioned as part of a technical writing job?

It's not a matter of ego, of trying to do other people's jobs or of positioning yourself for another job. It's a matter of making your work easier and being able to do your job better. More importantly, it makes the customer's life easier.

Here's a rule of thumb:

The easier something is for you to explain, the easier it is for the customer to understand and use.

If you find something that's very difficult for you to explain, then you know the customer will have problems, too. Most experienced technical writers have been in the situation where they've had to spend many hours and many pages describing a function or control that, if designed better, would need little explanation at all. And more often than not,

continued on page 114

Source Documents

What you find for this project is that there are few source documents:

- The original project proposal,
- An initial design document, and
- Earlier company manuals.

There is no detailed design document, and the initial design hasn't been updated—or looked at—in at least six months.

You get copies of these documents, and read them carefully. Your conclusion is that they are good for a general understanding of what the product is, but you won't be able to directly incorporate any of them into the manual.

The biggest, most noticeable difference between the design document and the program as it exists is that at least one screen has been eliminated from the program. You expect there to be more changes.

Copies of the proposal and initial design document can be found in the Exhibits section, later in this book.

From the earlier manuals, you get a feel for what has been done before, and can see how they are organized. You know you have to do at least as good a job on your manual as has been done on any of the others.

Marketing Documents, Etc.

The marketing documents you can locate are:

- Product description (based on the proposal), and
- Market analysis (with a good customer description).

At this point, marketing is just beginning to work on the package concept and manual design. You find out who to check with every so often to stay in the loop. Knowing what the package and manual will look like will give you a good guide for the tone of your writing.

The Program Itself

The majority of your research time will be spent with the product itself. Try to approach it from the point of view of the new user, which you usually are, at least at first.

Play it. Take notes. Draw up flowcharts of the interface, for your own understanding, if not for inclusion in the manual.

Write down any questions you have, anything that confuses you the first time you see it.

An important thing to do now is to carefully read all the screen text—down to the last word. Is it consistent? Are windows, functions, buttons or anything else ever referred to by more than one name? Is anything given a name or label that is more geared toward a programmer's vocabulary or mental model than the customer's vocabulary or mental model? Make suggestions for consistency and improvement.

Also note any places where text is missing or incomplete.

Decide what you think the tone of the product is. Serious? Playful? Silly? Think about how your writing can reflect and reinforce that tone.

At this stage, the program probably won't have the final installation process in place, so reserve judgement on that part of the customer experience.

If and when the program is far enough along, sit and watch others use it for the first time or three. Ask them to think out loud. Record or write down all their questions and confusions.

Research Results

After a week or so of research (on this project, anyway[14]), you should have a good grasp of the situation. You've covered all the people, documents and subjects mentioned in the previous few pages.

If you're a copious note-taker, you may have dozens of pages; if you're not a

---

[14] For a very simple program, you may only need a day for research. On a large, complex program, it may take many weeks before you know the program well enough to move on to the next step.

continued from page 112

they can see a better way to do it. After all, they've spent so much time thinking about what it does, how it works, and how the customer will think it works.

What gives writers the right to mess with the design?

A technical writer's job is mostly dissecting and describing interfaces. A technical writer is the customer's interface to the interface. An experienced writer has dissected and described dozens if not scores of interfaces, and can become very knowledgeable in the subject without even trying. With a little extra reading and study, a writer can become an expert.

In summary, I'm not saying that writers should be the designers, but if our knowledge and suggestions can make the product better—and easier for the customer to use—then we should contribute. Even if we have to be very subtle—even sneaky—to do it.

But make sure you know what you're doing before you speak up. A novice writer trying to tell experienced developers what to do isn't going to be taken seriously. Once you've been through a number of projects, have analyzed many interfaces and can bring examples and facts to the table—not just opinions—then it's time to speak up.

note-taker, you may have only a page or three of the most important points that you don't want to forget.

These notes are for you, so there's no need to edit them or make them pretty. But be aware that others may read them, even if they're never printed out, so don't say anything insulting in them, even if somebody you work with really is full of bull.

At this time, you should present your list of screen-text problems and solutions. You might first want to talk it over with the producer/designer, to make sure that he didn't have something else in mind, then give it to whoever is currently collecting the list of bugs and other items to be fixed.

Problems and Solutions

Problems that you might run into during this stage—and their solutions—are:

• **The design docs may be nonexistent or very different from the actual program.**

This isn't surprising in a small company, especially with a new product. And even in larger, more organized companies, earlier design docs tend to describe a bigger, better, fancier product than actually gets made. This is partly because the team is trying the sell the idea to the management team to get support and funding, and partly because the team really wants to make a bigger, better, fancier product.

Once a budget starts to run low and time starts to run out, features are dropped.

In an extremely organized (possibly regimented) company, the design docs would be carefully scrutinized by experienced managers who will help the team pare down the features so the product will still be good, but will also be doable within the allotted time and budget.

In any event, you are documenting the product itself, not the design docs. Even if the docs almost perfectly match the program, you still need to check each and every feature, control and button in the actual program.

• **Other team members are too busy to help or answer questions.**

Often by the time a writer is brought into a project, deadlines are looming, and everyone else is far more concerned with finishing their jobs on time than helping you finish yours.

You have to remind them that the product isn't done until the manual is done, and explain your deadlines. But you also have to be as efficient as possible—and considerate—with other people's time.

Here also is an opportunity for mutual back-scratching. You may be able to find ways to help other team members save time and energy on their jobs to free up some time to help you. This doesn't mean to start programming or creating art, but it could mean spending some extra time testing a particular program function, helping edit or organize a graphics list, or even a little secretarial busywork. Usually, if you can find anything to help with, it'll be part of your job (or close to it) anyway.

Another very effective approach here is bribery. When someone is very busy and stressed, a cup of good coffee, some chocolate, homemade cookies or other treats can convince them to take a short break and answer some of your questions.

• **Someone keeps popping in and asking why you're not writing.**

Some people just don't realize that writing is a matter of learning, then thinking—then typing. They expect to hear that keyboard clicking from day one.

If this pest has been around software for a while, they'll realize that this is true for programmers—some of the best programmers spend a lot of time staring out a window or off into space between fits of typing—so it might also be true of writers. Draw the parallel for them.

If that doesn't work, and the person isn't someone you can just ignore, then put on an act—take a few extra notes when that person is around. If you are a person who likes to write pages and pages of notes, give the person a copy of your notes (with lots of extra padding) and ask if they'd look them over

Product-driven and Market-driven Companies

The difference between product-driven and market-driven is how you approach choosing and designing products.

For instance, with a word processor—a well-understood product with a lot of competition—you would look first to the market. You'd estimate the size of the market, your potential market share, what the competition is selling, and what features the customers really want and need. You would then design your product based on this market information. This is market-driven.

A new type of product with no existing market to analyze, or an entertainment product that can't be analyzed, quantified and evaluated based on numbers of features would first look to the product. You'd want to make the best product you can, then find the market to sell it to. This is product-driven.

Of course, most market-driven companies also think about the product up front, and most product-driven companies think about the market up front as well. It's a matter of priority, and where and when you put the most energy and place the most importance.

and comment on them. If you ask that they get back to you within three days with their contribution, you won't see that person for at least five days.

Complications and Opportunities

Here are some likely complications for this stage, and opportunities to help, learn or have fun:

• **There may be little communication between marketing and product development.**

An important aspect of package and manual design is that they should reflect the tone of the product. Or the product should reflect the tone of the packaging, in the case of market-driven products or companies. You may find yourself the link between the development team and marketing.

It may be up to you to keep marketing informed about how the program may be diverting from the original design documents.

• **Finding features that fell through the cracks.**

As you review the design docs, look for features that may have been dropped by accident. There will always be differences between the design doc and the final product, but you may find some features that weren't intentionally dropped, and may be easy to add in. Put together a short list and show it to the producer.

Of course, if you join the project so late that everything is in a total rush, you may not even want to think about bringing up additional features.

• **Design document work.**

If the company takes their design documents seriously, you join the project early enough, and have the time, you may be able to (or be forced to) update the design document.

Don't complain about being given extra work. The research you'll have to do to update the doc to the actual product will be much the same that you'd do for the manual, except a little more technical, with more behind-the-interface explanations. And you'll be able to reuse much of your work in the actual manual. You'll also have the opportunity to work closely with the designer. If the designer is experienced or inspired, you could learn a lot.

Stage 3: Organizing the Information—The Outline and the Structural Edit

This chapter covers writing the outline and the structural edit—your first real feedback from your editor.

The sections are:

- Thinking and Preparing
- Writing the Outline
- Pre-edit Feedback
- The Structural Edit
- The Finished Outline
- Problems and Solutions
- Complications and Opportunities

Thinking and Preparing

By now you should have a good idea of what the program is and what you want to write. You've also talked with the producer and product manager about what they expect from the manual.

You know that you want a complete tutorial that covers most, if not all, of the program's functions, and a complete reference.

You know that the onscreen help will be text-only, so you'll need good graphics with examples in the manual. And you know that you want people to be able to read the manual away from the computer and understand what the program is about.

Because of time and space limitations—and because it really won't be helpful for the customer—you are discouraged from writing an extensive background section on real newspapers, but because the company may want to make a special educational version of the product, they would like to see an appendix on The Personal Newspaper in Education, covering topics for parents, and mentioning a teacher's guide that will be available later.

Writing the Outline

Just how much detail you put into an outline is up to you and your editor. You may just want to establish a loose framework, adding detail as you write the actual text, or you may want to nail down the entire structure now.

It never hurts to put in as much detail as you can—or as much as you can be sure about. With pre-beta software, that might be less than you'd think.

One way to approach it is to list—or print screenshots of—each window and dialog box, and organize them in an order that makes sense to you, then write about them in that order.

Use the Parts of the Manual Checklist in the Exhibits section of this book as a guide.

Pre-edit Feedback

Before turning your outline over to your editor, you'll probably want to show it to a couple of other people. At a minimum, check with the producer to see if there's anything else or anything special to be added. Check with the testers to see if they see any potential problems or omissions. And if there are any other staff writers around, ask them to look at it and comment.

After you get this feedback and update the outline, it's time to turn it in.

The Structural Edit

The structural edit is done by an editor who may be a staff editor, a contracted editor (hopefully familiar with the company's products and style), the head of the writing group, another writer, or a number of other people.

The purpose of the structural edit is to make sure that the outline is complete and properly organized. The better the outline, the easier and faster the writing.

The main things the editor will look for at this stage of the project are:

- Does it make sense?
- Is it well-organized?
- Is it clear?
- Is it consistent with other company manuals?
- Is it consistent within itself?

- Is everything there that needs to be there?
- Is there anything that should be cut?
- Does the tutorial cover enough for beginners and the target age groups?

The Finished Outline

On a real project, your outline will be mainly based on the actual pre-alpha version of the software. Since this program doesn't really exist, it is based on an imaginary pre-alpha that is very close to the program described in the Initial Design Document in the Exhibits section. Look over the design doc as you analyze this outline.

Here's the finished outline for The Personal Newspaper after incorporating the edits from the structural edit:

Manual Outline—The Personal Newspaper

Title Page

License Page

Credits

Table of Contents

Introduction

- Welcome
- Product Description
- Product Line Description
- Mention Future Add-ons
- About the Manual
- Reg. Card Plea
- Getting Started
  - Refer to Quick-Start guide for Installation and Starting Instructions

Tutorials

Tutorial Introduction

- Welcome
- What you will do in these two tutorials

Tutorial I—The Basics

- Have your printer hooked up and turned on
- Refer to Quick-Start guide for Installation and Starting Instructions

Part 1—A Tour of Your Personal Newspaper Office

- What we'll do in this part
- The opening splash screens
- Brief description of Main Menu screen
- Mention Help

Part 2—The Reader Department

- What we'll do in this part
- Once-over of the department options
- Add a new reader
- Print a blank reader survey

- Fill out the blank survey—just what's necessary to print the tutorial newspaper
- Update the reader survey on the computer
- Mention the available help

Part 3—The Editorial Department

- What we'll do in this part
- Create a new newspaper (for the new reader)
- Mention but skip printing blank newspaper profile
- Update the Newspaper Profile
- Mention available help

Part 4—The Print Department

- What we'll do in this part
- Preview a newspaper
- Print a newspaper (the tutorial special one-pager)
- Mention the available help

Part 5—The Help Department

- What we'll do in this part
- Look at program overview
- Look at the help index
- Look at the How Do I ... index
- Look at the What Now? page

Tutorial I Summary

- Review what they did
- Invite to repeat the tutorial any time
- Remind about help
- Tell them they now know all they'll need to use the program's basic functions
- Invite to continue to the next tutorial for the advanced features

Tutorial II—Advanced Features

- If continuing from Tutorial I, skip to page XX.
- If starting fresh, have your printer hooked up and turned on
- Start the program
- Refer to Quick-Start guide for Installation and Starting Instructions

Part 1—The Story Department

- What we'll do in this part
- Write a story
- Edit a story
- Import a story

- Mention available help

Part 2—The Art Department

[note: The drawing screen has been eliminated from the program since the design doc, so there will be no creating or editing pictures.]
- What we'll do in this part
- Import a picture
- Mention available help

Part 3—Back to Editorial

- What we'll do in this part
- Update the newspaper for a single day
- Add two stories
- Add a picture

Part 4—Back to the Print Department

- What we'll do in this part
- Print the tutorial newspaper

Part 5—Clean-up

- What we'll do in this part
- Go to Art Department, delete picture
- Go to Story Department, delete stories
- Go to Reader Department, delete reader
- Show message that if you delete a reader, you auto-delete the newspaper

Tutorial II Summary

- What you've done
- What you can do—the possibilities
- Repeat either tutorial any time
- Mention available help once again
- Send them off to publish their own newspapers

Reference

Introduction

- What's in this reference
- How it's organized

The Basics

- Program Overview
- Main Screen
- Getting Help

The Departments
- Reader Department
- Editorial Department
- Print Department
- Story Department
- Art Department
- Help Department

Screens and Dialogs
- Reader Survey screen
- Newspaper Profile screen
- Print Preview screen
- Special Edition screen
- Story Writing screen
- Survey of dialogs, give generic instructions for all

Appendix 1—Troubleshooting

Appendix 2—Support Information

Appendix 3—The Personal Newspaper and Education

Glossary (if necessary, probably not)

Index

Problems and Solutions

Problems that you might run into during this stage—and their solutions—are:

- **There isn't an editor.**

If there's no "official" editor around, find someone to look the outline over and comment. While an experienced editor who knows the company, the company's style and the company's products is the best, almost anyone is better than no one. It could be a friend, another writer, a tester, or an administrative assistant.

One of the biggest mistakes you can make—and even very experienced writers can make—is to finish a project without running it by others for comment. Not only will the fresh sets of eyes find mistakes and omissions, they will give you a wider perspective. If you're writing only for yourself, then you only have to show it to yourself. If you're writing for thousands of different people, then you should show it to at least a few people along the way.

Find someone.

- **The program isn't far enough along to outline the tutorial.**

You'll often start working on a manual before the program is far enough along to actually write the tutorial. Expect it. You often have to write the tutorial last. If you can't even loosely outline the tutorial to the level of the sample above, then the program has a very long way to go.

Make your best guess, but be ready to revamp the outline a time or two before the program is finalized and it's time to write the tutorial.

Complications and Opportunities

Here are some likely complications for this stage, and opportunities to help, learn or have fun:

- **Things are always more complicated than they first appear.**

If you hadn't noticed before you wrote the outline, you should have by the time you finished it: even a simple program like this isn't that simple.

All this program really does is ask for some names, dates, etc., automatically generate a report, then print. Yet it has over 20 screens and dialogs, plus numerous message boxes, and will take a lot of work and quite a few pages to create a good manual for it.

Stage 4: Writing the Manual—The First Draft

This chapter covers writing the first complete draft of the manual.

The sections are:

- Time to Write
- Format and Presentation
- The First Draft
- Problems and Solutions
- Complications and Opportunities

Time to Write

Now that the outline is done and approved, you know what you're going to write. So it's time to start the actual writing.

You may want to start at the beginning and plow through the whole manual. You may need to write everything but the tutorial first, and wait for the program to be finished before writing the tutorial. You may have to delay the introduction until marketing supplies some product-description text.

At this stage, you don't need to detail out the title page, license page or credits. What you need to concentrate on now is the actual product. You need to concentrate on and put down in writing everything the user will need to know.

Parts of the manual will not yet be totally complete. At this stage of the program, you won't have or be able to get all the answers. All parts and sections of the manual will be there, but they won't all be finished. Anything that isn't complete should be marked with either notes to programmers, producers, designers or testers to check things out and fill in the missing info, or notes to yourself to find out more when you can.

Once you're through with your first draft, go back over it again, and possibly again. Make sure you've covered everything. And run your spell checker.

Format and Presentation

As mentioned earlier, you will be using the company's standard word processor, and will deliver the text in that format. You will assign styles to the headings and a few other parts of the text.

If the graphic artist prefers that you don't assign any styles, or can't import them, then you'll have to put tags in to mark the styles, for example:

[H1] This is a heading level 1.

[H2] This is a heading level 2.

[Instr] This paragraph is formatted as an instruction.

Whenever possible, assigning styles is the preferred route. You can make your headings big and bold, with easily visible differences in size so they can be visibly distinguished by the reader.

The sample document has styles assigned, and all the heading styles are marked, as well, to make it easier for readers of this book to see the structure of the sample manual.

One more reason to assign styles is that you can make the draft look better. It's often difficult to get people (other than editors) to read drafts. They'd much prefer to wait until it's printed in a manual. But you need them to read it before it goes into the manual.

A dozen or 50 or 100 pages of solid text all the same size and shape is pure and simple, but very uninviting. It looks like one long, boring read. Breaking up the pages with large headings and possibly a few other styles lets the reader easily see that the long document is made up of many small parts, making it more inviting. This refers back to an earlier chapter that mentioned writing *and presenting* information in bite-sized chunks, and using lots of headings and subheadings.

Check with your editor to see whether you should single or double-space your document when you send it out. If you use 12-point type, leave reasonable margins, keep paragraphs short, and leave space between paragraphs, you may be able to get away with single spacing, and save a few trees.

Also, while you'll want to eliminate any extra spacing and returns in the document before you turn it in for layout, adding some extra space here and there is fine in this draft if it makes the pages easier to read.

The example in this book is single-spaced.

The First Draft

Here's the first draft of the entire manual for The Personal Newspaper.

Notice the notes and unfinished spots. Also notice that the headings and contents listings aren't identical to the outline. All the information that was called for in the outline is still there, but in arranging and organizing the information, some headings changed.

The table of contents isn't the final one—that one will be generated during the layout process. But you should include a table of contents, temporary though it may be, especially since there's no index yet. It'll help your editors understand the structure of the document, and zero in on their areas of expertise.

Throughout the document, there are a few text boxes containing comments on the draft. These aren't part of the document, and won't be included during an editing stage. They're there to show you some of the typical thought processes and decisions that are part of writing a manual.

The Personal Newspaper

User Manual (Editor-in-Chief's Handbook)

Draft 1, 7/24/2001

[H1]Title Page [next draft]

[H1]License [next draft]

[H1]Credits [next draft]

[H1]Table of Contents

Introduction **4**

    Welcome 4

    What Can You Do with The Personal Newspaper? 4

    Why The Personal Newspaper? 4

    The Personal Newspaper Product Line 5

    Registering The Personal Newspaper 5

    About This Manual 5

    Getting Started 5

Tutorials **6**

    Introduction to the Tutorials 6

    Tutorial I—The Basics 6

        Before You Begin.. 6

        Part 1—A Tour of Your Personal Newspaper Office 6

        Part 2—The Reader Department 8

        Part 3—The Editorial Department 10

        Part 4—The Print Department.. 11

        Part 5—The Help Department.. 13

        Tutorial I Summary 13

Tutorial II—Advanced Features 15
    Before You Begin.. 15
    Part 1—The Story Department.. 15
    Part 2—The Art Department 17
    Part 3—Special Edition 18
    Tutorial II Summary.. 20

Reference **21**
  Introduction... 21
  The Basics... 21
    Program Overview 21
    Main Menu Screen 22
    Getting Help 22
  The Departments.. 23
    Reader Department... 23
    Editorial Department 23
    Print Department 24
    Story Department 24
    Art Department.. 25
    Help Department 25
  Screens and Dialogs 26
    Reader Survey Screen 26
    Newspaper Profile Screen 26
    Print Preview Screen 27
    Story Writing Screen 28
    Special Edition Screen 28
    Dialog Boxes.. 29
  Hints and Tips 31
    Standard Formats and Parts of the Newspaper............................... 31
    Suggested Lengths of Stories for the Different Parts of the Paper............ 31
    Adding Pictures 31
    Adding Stories.. 32
    Your Hints and Tips 33

Appendices **34**

    Appendix 1—Troubleshooting 34

    Appendix 2—Support and Contact Information 34

    Appendix 3—For Parents and Teachers 34

Index **35**

[H1]Introduction

[H2]Welcome …

… to The Personal Newspaper, First Grade Edition.

We trust—in fact, we guarantee—that you will find this product both useful and fun.

[H2]What Can You Do with The Personal Newspaper?

As owner and Editor-in-Chief of this program, you can create and print daily personalized newspapers for the early readers in your family—every day for a year.

These newspapers will feature stories about the readers, their families, friends, pets and hobbies. It also features jokes, date countdowns and exciting cliffhanger stories that will have kids wanting to read tomorrow's paper today.

Newspapers can be customized to the individual's taste—if the readers love sports, they'll get a lot of sports stories; if they don't like sports, but love cute animals, they'll get cute animal stories.

And beyond that, you can replace any day's automatic stories, jokes and pictures with your own stories, jokes and pictures. This lets you make special editions to announce or commemorate special family outings and events.

[H2]*Why* The Personal Newspaper?

We'll let our company president field this question:

"We believe that good reading skills are the foundation of a good education. We also believe that people who enjoy reading read more and gain more skills faster.

We created The Personal Newspaper to provide every child with daily reading material that they will enjoy."

> — The company president

[marketing: can we get the president to OK and sign this quote? If so, might it be useful for the package?]

Let's face it: when it comes to interesting subjects to read about, nothing beats ourselves. We make your child the star of a daily newspaper, so even reluctant readers will want to read—every day.

[H2]The Personal Newspaper Product Line

The Personal Newspaper comes in editions for first through sixth grades. Plus, there are Personal Newspaper Add-on Packs of specialty stories that let you customize the paper even more perfectly to your child's reading interests.

[H2]Registering The Personal Newspaper

Now would be a good time to fill out the registration card. Registering provides you with extended technical support. And we keep registered owners notified of new products and add-ons, updates, upgrades and special events like story contests.

[H2]About This Manual

This manual is short and simple—and very useful.

It has two tutorials—one basic and one advanced—that will guide you through every step of creating and printing newspapers.

It also has a reference section that explains all the menus, screens, windows and dialog boxes.

At the end of the manual, you'll find:

- some troubleshooting tips—just in case,

- contact information if you have questions or need support, and

- useful information for parents and teachers on getting the most educational value from The Personal Newspaper.

[H2]Getting Started

The Personal Newspaper is available for different computer systems. Refer to the Quick-Start guide for installation and starting instructions for your computer.

> Even with the installation and starting instructions covered in a separate Quick-Start guide, you may want to duplicate the information here. It's up to you, your editor, and the space available.

[H1]Tutorials

[H2]Introduction to the Tutorials

Welcome to The Personal Newspaper Tutorials.

In Tutorial I, you will learn the basics of the program, and actually create and print a sample newspaper.

In Tutorial II, you will learn about the advanced features:

- writing, editing and importing stories,
- importing pictures, and
- using these stories and pictures in a newspaper.

One last point before you begin:

While reading this tutorial, when you see text that looks like this, it is an instruction for you to follow.

Any other text is an explanation.

Relax and enjoy yourself. You've just been put in charge of a newspaper.

[H2]Tutorial I—The Basics

[H3]Before You Begin

Make sure your computer is on and your printer is hooked up, loaded with paper and turned on.

Start The Personal Newspaper.

If you haven't already installed the program, please refer to the Quick-Start guide for installation and starting instructions.

[H3]Part 1—A Tour of Your Personal Newspaper Office

[H4]What We'll Do:

1. Take a quick tour through the opening screens.
2. Get acquainted with the Main Menu screen.

From the top through a certain level of heading (H3 in this document), it is important for the headings to be absolutely clear and descriptive. Even if these headings don't appear in the table of contents, readers are likely to use them to re-find their place between sessions or to locate particular instructions if they come back for a refresher.

Each part of the tutorial begins with this "What we'll do:" list. It helps the reader find the exact spot or activity that they want to find. It also helps "wet the sponge."

[H4]Make a Splash

As the program starts, you will be entertained by the appearance and disappearance of a couple of "splash screens." These are screens that let you know what company made this product (UnTechnical Press) and announce the product itself (The Personal Newspaper).

At a certain level of heading (H4 in this document), it's OK to sacrifice absolute clarity for fun. Humor, as long as it doesn't interfere with or delay the workflow, is important in tutorials. People who work through tutorials are dealing with something that is totally new, possibly confusing, sometimes intimidating and always boring. Don't get too far from the point, but if you can coax a chuckle or groan from the reader, then you've done them a service.

Once those screens have passed, we begin the actual program at the Main Menu screen.

Something to establish early with your editor and the keepers of style at the company is how to handle initial capitalizations of items in the program. Initial-capping important words or names of screens, buttons, etc., makes them stand out. But if you overuse it, it loses its impact. For this manual, the convention will be that the actual names of screens, menus, buttons, etc., will be initial-capped, but the words "screen," "menu," "button," etc., won't be. In the case of the Main Menu screen, the word "menu" is initial-capped because it is part of the name of the screen.

[H4]What's on the Menu?

The Main Menu screen is the heart of The Personal Newspaper.

[g of Main Menu screen, large, with callouts for Button Bar, Departments and Help]

Think of yourself as the Editor-in-Chief of a local newspaper. Any time you want anything done, just click. (Of course, as Editor-in-Chief you have every right to yell your orders while you click.)

The Main Menu screen is divided into six departments and a Button bar.

Everything you can do—and could ever want to do—with this program is done through one of the six departments. There's even a whole department dedicated to helping you run the program and the newspaper.

Each department has a picture showing what goes on there, plus a list of all the different tasks that that department handles. When you want to carry out a task, you just click on it—*but don't click yet.* We want to finish looking around first.

At the bottom of the screen is the Button bar. It lets you quit (not now, of course) and find out who made this program (About …).

One last thing before we move on—notice that at the bottom-right corner of each department is a help button for that department. You can click on it for a complete explanation of all of that department's tasks.

Now let's take a look at the Reader Department.

[g of xxx] is a typical way to indicate that a graphic such as a screenshot should be inserted here during layout. The "g" stands for graphic, so you can tell this graphic call from notes or questions. It should contain a description of the graphic, plus any callouts or captions. Callouts and captions should be typed in exactly as you want them, capitalization and all, so the graphic artist can copy and paste them without retyping. Don't name or number the graphics until you're ready to start actually preparing the graphics.

[H3]Part 2—The Reader Department

[H4]What We'll Do:

1. Look over the Reader Department tasks.

2. Add a new Reader.

3. Input information about the new Reader.

[H4]What Goes on Here?

Take a look at the Reader Department.

[g of Reader Department. Callouts: Tasks, Help.]

Notice that there are five different tasks that can be performed in this department—plus a way to get help.

Let's start at the beginning, and add a new Reader.

[H4]Increasing Circulation

Click on "Add a New Reader."

The Add a New Reader dialog opens.

[g of Add a New Reader dialog]

For this tutorial, go ahead and use your own name.

Click in the box next to "First Name:" and type in your first name.

Click in the box next to "Last Name:" and type in your last name.

Click OK.

This is the first time the reader comes across an instruction to actually manipulate the program. Make sure it stands out from the explanatory text.

The Add a New Reader dialog disappears and you are back at the Main Menu screen.

[H4]Drawing a Blank

We could go ahead and start filling in the information about the new reader right now by clicking on Update Reader Survey—but we won't.

First, we'll print out a blank reader survey to look over.

When gathering information about a reader other than yourself, you may want to sit with that person and the blank survey and talk it over away from the computer. You can fill out the survey by hand, then come back to the computer later and enter the information.

Click on "Print Blank Reader Survey."

Depending on your computer and printer this may take a few minutes. You may want to take this time to practice saying, "And don't call me chief!" in your gruffest voice.

Once the reader survey is printed, look it over. All the information on the survey will be used in various newspaper stories about the Reader.

For the purposes of this tutorial, you won't need to fill in all the information. The special tutorial newspaper that we'll be printing later only uses a few bits of information.

On the blank reader survey form, fill out:

- **Your first and last name**
- **Your city**
- **Your state**
- **Your gender (boy or girl)**
- **Your birthday**
- **Your favorite holiday (or two)**

Now, we'll go back to the computer and the Reader Department.

Click on "Update Reader Survey."

The Choose Reader dialog will appear.

[g of Choose Reader Dialog]

This dialog box displays all the Readers that have been entered. Your name may be the only one there.

Click on your name in the name list.

Click OK.

The dialog disappears, and is replaced by an onscreen version of the Reader survey.

[g of reader survey screen. Callouts: scroll bars]

Your first and last name are already filled out for you. As you enter the rest of your information, you may need to use the scroll bar to scroll the screen down to find all of the information blanks.

Click in the box next to "City:" and type the name of your city.

Click in the box next to "State:" and type the name or abbreviation of your state.

Check the checkbox next to either Boy or Girl.

Click in the box next to "Birthday:" and type in your birthday (mm/dd/yyyy).

Check the checkbox next to your favorite holiday or two.

Click OK.

The Reader Survey screen will close and the Main Menu screen will reappear.

Before we move on to the next department, take a look at the other Reader Department tasks:

- **Print Existing Reader Survey** lets you print out Reader information that you've already entered, in case you want to review it for changes or updates.
- **Delete a Reader** lets you remove a Reader that you've entered.

- And **Reader Department Help** shows an onscreen explanation of all the Reader Department tasks.

OK, now it's time to visit the Editorial Department.

[H3]Part 3—The Editorial Department

[H4]What We'll Do:

1. Create a New Newspaper (for you).
2. Update the Newspaper Profile.

[H4]New News Is Good News(paper)

Take a look at the Editorial Department.

[g of Editorial Department. Callouts: Tasks, Help]

We have a Reader; now we need to create and customize a newspaper for that Reader.

Click on "Create a New Newspaper."

The Create a New Newspaper dialog will open.

[g of Create a New Newspaper dialog]

Click on your name.

Click OK.

That was odd. You're supposed to be creating a newspaper, but you chose your name from a list. Why?

Because The Personal Newspaper is, after all, personal—it is created for one and only one Reader. The first thing the program needs to know is who the newspaper is for. The newspaper you create will be linked to the information in that one Reader's Reader survey.

Now let's deal with the newspaper itself.

> This is an attempt to forestall potential confusion.

[H4]File That Profile

The way to customize a newspaper is by filling out its Newspaper Profile. As with the reader survey, you have the option of printing it out first and talking it over with the reader, but we'll skip that step, and go right to filling out the profile.

Click on "Update a Newspaper Profile."

The Choose a Newspaper dialog will open.

[g of Choose a Newspaper dialog]

Click on the Unnamed Newspaper created for you (as Reader).

Click OK.

The Choose a Newspaper dialog will close, and the Newspaper Profile screen will appear.

[g of Newspaper Profile screen]

You can name the newspaper anything you want, up to 24 characters. If you need some help coming up with a name, some possibilities are Tutorial Times, Your Name Gazette, or Your Family News.

Click in the box next to "Name:" and enter a name for the newspaper.

Each newspaper has to have a start date. This lets the program track stories, birthdays and holidays, and allows for special editions without losing days on the continuing stories. The default start date is today.

Make sure that "Today" is selected.

The newspapers can be presented in a number of different styles to suit almost any reader. For this tutorial, pick the tutorial style.

Click on and highlight the "Tutorial Style" newspaper.

Click OK.

> Notice how the explanation is given in steps, between the instructions that the readers will execute.
>
> This lets them concentrate on, understand, and perform one thing at a time.

The Update a Newspaper Profile screen closes, and we're back at the Main Menu screen.

Before moving on, take a last look at the Editorial Department. Note that here you can also:

- **Create a Special Edition**—we'll do that in the advanced tutorial.
- **Delete a Newspaper.**
- View the **Editorial Department Help.**

Time to print!

[H3]Part 4—The Print Department

[H4]What We'll Do:

1. Preview a newspaper.
2. Print a newspaper.

[H4]Hold the Presses

Take a look at the Print Department.

[g of Print Department. Callouts: Tasks, Help]

Like the other departments we've visited, it consists of tasks and help.

Now let's take a preview look at our newspaper.

Click on "Preview Newspaper."

The Choose Newspaper dialog appears.

[g of Choose Newspaper dialog]

Choose the newspaper we've been working on. Only you know its name.

Click on the newspaper you just profiled.

Click OK.

Now the Choose Dates dialog opens.

[g of Choose Dates dialog]

We're only going to print one day's newspaper—today's—so make sure that Today is selected in both the From: and To: columns.

Click on the radio buttons next to Today in both the "From:" and "To:" columns.

Notice that you can preview (and print) many days at a time—even the whole year at once. You can also input special days or periods of time. If you enter a date that isn't within a year from the start date, you'll get an error message.

Click OK.

The Choose Dates dialog will close and the Print Preview screen will appear.

[g of Print Preview screen. Callouts: Page Size buttons, Scroll Bars, Previous/Next Day buttons, Print buttons, Close button]

The newspaper is shown, just as it will print, except that it is shrunk down to fit in the window. You can expand the paper to full size by clicking on the Full Size button. While full size, the whole paper probably won't fit in the window. To see it all, you can either use the scroll bars, or just click and drag the paper itself to move it around the screen.

Click on the Full Size button.

Move the page around on the screen with the scroll bars.

Move the page around on the screen by clicking and dragging the page.

[H4]Roll the Presses

We can print the newspaper from here, or go back to the Main Menu screen and print from there. Since we're ready to go, we might as well print here and now.

Make sure the Personal Newspaper CD is in your CD-ROM drive.

Click on the Print button.

A standard Print dialog will open.

Click OK.

The Print dialog will close and the printing process will begin.

While we're waiting for the printer, let's return to the Main Menu screen.

Click the Close button.

As we take a last look at the Print Department, be sure to note the **Print Department Help** in the lower-right corner.

When the paper has been printed, take a look at it. You'll notice that it has a banner, a feature story—about you—with a picture, a joke, a date countdown, and the first installment of a cliffhanger story.

[g of sample newspaper, with callouts: Feature Story, Feature Picture, Joke, Date Countdown, Cliffhanger]

You'll also notice that the picture isn't very flattering and the joke isn't very funny. We did that on purpose, so you can make a special edition of this paper—with a better picture and joke—in Tutorial II.

Let's take a quick look at the Help Department to close out Tutorial I.

[H3]Part 5—The Help Department

[H4]What We'll Do:

- Explore the Help Department.
- Look at the How Do I … help system.

[H4]Help Is on the Way

Take a look at the Help Department.

[g of Help Department. Callouts: Tasks, Help on Help]

This department exists only to serve. It has three tasks that it can perform for you:

1. Program Overview gives a general description of the program.
2. Hints and Tips gives suggestions on how to run your newspaper more easily.
3. How Do I … opens a listing of all the different tasks you can perform with The Personal Newspaper, and let's you jump right to them.

If you wish, you can play around with the Help Department tasks. Otherwise, just move on to the Tutorial I summary—you've finished!

[H3]Tutorial I Summary

Congratulations! You've finished Tutorial I.

You now know all the basics you need to know to use The Personal Newspaper. In the last 15 minutes, you:

Went to the Reader Department and …

1. Added a new Reader,
2. Printed and filled out a Reader survey form, and
3. Entered the data in an onscreen Reader survey form.

Went to the Editorial Department and …

1. Created a new newspaper, and

2. Updated the newspaper's profile.

Went to the Print Department and …

1. Previewed your newspaper, and

2. Printed it.

And last but not least, you took a look at the Help Department.

Now you can:

1. Quit the program and call it a day,

2. Start using the program to create newspapers for the early reader in your home, or

3. Move on to the next tutorial to learn how to add custom stories and pictures to newspapers.

For more details on any part of this program, see the reference section of this manual.

And, of course, you may repeat this tutorial any time you want a refresher course.

[H2]Tutorial II—Advanced Features

[H3]Before You Begin

If you're coming directly from Tutorial I, then jump ahead to Part 1—The Story Department.

If you haven't already been through Tutorial I, it's a good idea to turn back a few pages and start at the beginning.

If you're ready to move on, then make sure your computer is on and your printer is hooked up, loaded with paper and turned on.

As a reminder:

Text that looks like this is an instruction for you to follow.

Any other text is an explanation.

Here we go:

Start The Personal Newspaper.

If you need a reminder on starting the program, see the Quick-Start guide.

[H3]Part 1—The Story Department

[H4]What We'll Do:

1. Write a story.

2. Import a story.

3. Edit a story.

[H4]Story Time

Take a look at the Story Department on the Main Menu screen. (If you're just starting the program, you may have to wait for the splash screens to clear.)

[g of Story Department. Callouts: Tasks, Help]

We're going to write a story with The Personal Newspaper's internal text editor. Don't worry—in The Personal Newspaper, stories can be very short. We even count jokes and riddles as stories.

Click on "Write a Story."

The Story Writing screen appears.

[g of Story Writing screen]

This screen looks and works like a very simple text editor.

[Note: This screen isn't in the program yet, so I can't describe it here. I've heard a rumor that it might be eliminated. If it survives, I'll have them type in a joke and

save it, then close the window. If it doesn't make it, then I'll have to explain how to use NotePad for Windows and SimpleText for Mac.]

[Note to anyone: will there be a Story Writing screen? If so, when? And if it's not right away, then when can I get the exact specs?]

Click on the Close button.

The Story Writing screen closes, and we're back at the Main Menu screen.

You may prefer to use another computer or word processor to write stories. That's OK. The Personal Newspaper can import stories from other programs, as long as they're plain text, or .RTF format. Any text editor, like TeachText or SimpleText on the Mac and Notepad on Windows creates plain text. Most word processors, even the fanciest ones, can save files in text or .RTF format.

Let's try importing a story.

[H4]*Import*-ant Information

We'll import a story from the Personal Newspaper CD.

[Note: the importing function isn't working yet, so this is my best guess at how it will work. Design: can you look this over carefully and let me know how close I am? Engineering/Testing: please let me know when this function is in a build so I can see it in action.]

Put the Personal Newspaper CD in your CD-ROM drive.

Click "Import a Story."

The Import a Story dialog opens.

[g of Import a Story dialog. Callouts: Drive Selector, List box, Destination Selector]

There are two parts to importing a story:

1. Finding the story you want to import, and
2. Telling the program where you want the story to go.

[Note: this seems a bit awkward and complex. Is there any way to simplify or automate some of this so the user only has to find the story and not tell it where to go?]

First, we'll find the story. We want to import the story called Chicken Joke.

Click on the down-arrow under the word "Drive:" and select the drive with the Personal Newspaper CD in it.

In the list box, double-click on the "Tutorial directory."

Click on the file named "Chicken Joke."

Now we tell the program where to put the story. When The Personal Newspaper is installed, it automatically sets up directories for different types of stories to make it easier for you to find them when you need them.

The four directories are:

1. Features for the big, main story,

2. Reviews for book and movie reviews,

3. Jokes for jokes, and

4. Other for everything else.

Since Chicken Joke is a joke, let's store it in the Joke directory.

Click on the checkbox next to "Jokes."

Click OK.

The story will now be imported and stored on your hard drive, ready to be inserted in a special edition.

[H4]A Word Here and a Word There

[Note: If there's no Story Writing screen, then there will be no editing within the program, and this section will be eliminated. If there is a Story Writing screen, then this section will tell how to load a story, change a couple of words, and save it under a different name.]

That's it for the Story Department for now, but before we move on, take a last look. Note that you can also delete stories that you don't need any more.

And, as with all the other departments, the Story Department has a help option in the lower-right corner.

[H3]Part 2—The Art Department

[H4]What We'll Do:

1. Import a picture.

[H4]Picture Perfect

Take a look at the Art Department on the Main Menu screen.

[g of Art Department. Callouts: Tasks, Help]

We're now going to import a picture. We're assuming that the picture we supplied for the tutorial newspaper feature story didn't quite meet your personal standards, so you get to replace it. It's on the same CD, in the same directory as the joke we imported.

Click on "Import a Picture."

The Import a Picture dialog opens. It looks very much like the Import a Story dialog.

[g of Import a Picture dialog. Callouts: Drive Selector, List Box, Destination Selector]

Let's get the picture.

[Note: again, this is just my best guess, since this function isn't in and working yet.]

Click on the down-arrow under the word "Drive:" and select the drive with the Personal Newspaper CD in it.

In the list box, double-click on the Tutorial directory.

Click on the file named "Editor-male" if you are male, or "Editor-female" if you are female.

The Personal Newspaper creates two directories on your hard drive for storing pictures:

1. Features for the big pictures that go along with feature stories,

2. Other for anything else.

Click on the checkbox next to "Features."

Click OK.

The picture will now be imported and stored on your hard drive, ready to be inserted in a special edition.

We have a story and a picture, so we're ready to make a special edition.

[H3]Part 3—Special Edition

[H4]What We'll Do:

1. Make today's newspaper into a special edition by inserting our imported joke and picture.

[H4]You're Special

Look at the Editorial Department on the Main Menu screen again.

[g of Editorial Department. Callouts: Tasks, Help]

Let's remake the newspaper we created in Tutorial I into a special edition, by replacing the picture and joke.

Click on "Create a Special Edition."

The Choose Newspaper dialog appears.

[g of Choose Newspaper dialog]

Choose the same newspaper we made in Tutorial I.

Click on the newspaper you made.

Click OK.

Now the Choose Dates dialog opens.

[g of Choose Dates dialog]

This Choose Dates dialog is just like the Choose Dates dialog we saw when we previewed the newspaper earlier.

Once again, we're only going to print one day's newspaper—today's—so make sure that Today is selected in both the From: and To: columns.

Click on the radio buttons next to "Today" in both the "From:" and "To:" columns.

Click OK.

The Choose Newspaper dialog appears, and the Special Edition screen opens. It looks very much like the Print Preview screen, with a couple of important differences:

1. It allows you to replace some of the parts of the newspaper, and

2. It has a Cancel button, so you can experiment with changes, and then undo them if you don't like them.

The parts of the newspaper that you can customize in the Special Edition screen are:

1. The feature story,

2. The feature picture, and

3. The joke.

The banner, the date countdown and the cliffhanger story cannot be changed in this screen. But they can be changed in the Reader Survey.

[Note: the following section is again just a guess. Let me know when this function is in a build that I can work from.]

To change a story or picture, double-click on it.

Double-click on the feature picture.

The Change a Story or Picture dialog opens.

[g of Change a Story or Picture dialog. Callouts: Drive Selector, List box]

The drive selector by default shows the drive where you installed The Personal Newspaper, so you shouldn't have to mess with it.

The list box defaults to the directory where you installed The Personal Newspaper. It will display a number of directories, including Stories and Pictures.

Double-click on "Pictures" in the list box.

The list box now displays the contents of the Pictures directory, which will be the file you imported: either Editor-male or Editor-female.

Click on the file you imported.

Click OK.

The Change a Story or Picture dialog will disappear.

The new feature picture will be shown in the Special Edition screen. A little better than the other one?

Now let's change the joke.

Double-click on the joke.

The Change a Story or Picture dialog opens.

Double-click on "Stories" in the list box.

Click on "Chicken Joke."

Click OK.

The Change a Story or Picture dialog will disappear and the new joke will be shown in the Special Edition screen.

It's that easy.

Now you get to make a decision. You can:

1. Click the **Cancel** button if you really like the original picture and joke better.

2. Click the **Close** button to save your changes, in case you want to print later, or

3. Print the special edition now by clicking the **Print** button, clicking **OK** on the Print dialog, and then clicking **Close** on the Special Edition screen.

Once you've decided, and are done with any one of the above three choices, you can congratulate yourself again. You've finished Tutorial II.

[H3]Tutorial II Summary

You now know not only the basics but the advanced features of The Personal Newspaper.

You've learned how to import pictures and stories, and place them into a special edition.

If you ever want more details on any of this program's features, see the reference section of this manual.

And, of course, you may repeat either tutorial any time you want a refresher course.

Now, go forth and publish newspapers! (Or take a break and do it tomorrow.)

[H1]Reference

[H2]Introduction

Welcome to the complete reference to The Personal Newspaper. This reference explains every screen, window, dialog box and control in The Personal Newspaper, First Grade Edition.

If you haven't already installed the program and performed the tutorials, now is the time. Everything in this reference will be easier to absorb after the tutorials.

[H2]The Basics

[H3]Program Overview

The Personal Newspaper, First Grade Edition is a program that prints out a beginning reader's newspaper for every day for a full year.

Personal information about the Reader, including name, birthday, pets' names, friends' names, favorite sports, favorite holidays, etc., will be integrated into the feature story, so every day's paper will be about the Reader.

The words used in the stories are all from published lists of words that kindergartners, first graders and second graders learn. The use of the words is graduated—in the early part of the year, only the simplest words will be used, and as time goes on, the vocabulary expands.

There are five parts to each daily newspaper in this edition:

The Banner—the name of the newspaper, the date and the issue number.

The Feature Story—the main story for the day, customized to be about the Reader.

The Daily Joke—a little humor to make the reading more attractive.

The Date Countdown—a listing of how many days until important events, like birthdays, holidays and the last day of school.

The Cliffhanger—a continuing exciting story that lasts the entire year; each day's installment ends with a cliffhanger that is designed to have the child looking forward to the next day's episode.

[g of a sample newspaper. Callouts: Banner, Feature Story, Feature Picture, Joke, Date Countdown and Cliffhanger]

In Personal Newspaper versions for older children, the type size is reduced, stories are lengthened, and more stories are added. For instance, in the Second Grade Edition, there is a daily media review, describing a book, movie or piece of educational software.

The Personal Newspaper can print out newspapers in a number of different styles, ranging from traditional to modern to cute and cuddly. The Reader can pick the style they like—and change it during the year. And the name of the newspaper is entirely up to the reader as well.

The Personal Newspaper can generate custom newspapers for more than one Reader, and more than one newspaper for each Reader. But if you keep adding papers and Readers, there will eventually be some recycling of the content.

But you and the Reader are not limited to the included content. You can make special editions for any day of the year with your own jokes, feature stories and pictures.

Above all, The Personal Newspaper is simple to use. There are three basic steps:

1. Fill out an onscreen form with information about the Reader (or Readers).

2. Choose the newspaper name and style.

3. Print—for a day, a week or a whole year at once.

[H3]Main Menu Screen

The Main Menu screen is your master control panel for controlling The Personal Newspaper.

> Here, the word Screen is initial-capped, because it is part of a heading with an initial cap style.

[g of Main Menu screen]

It consists of six departments, dividing the different tasks into logical groups.

At the bottom of the Main Menu screen are two buttons:

About … opens a message box that gives the date and version of the program. The message can be scrolled to reveal the complete credits for this product.

Quit ends The Personal Newspaper.

[H3]Getting Help

The Personal Newspaper has a lot of built-in help. Each department has a help screen, plus there's a whole department dedicated to help. All you have to do is ask (well, click).

[H2]The Departments

The Personal Newspaper is divided into six departments, each of which helps you carry out specific tasks.

Each department has a name, a graphic, a list of tasks and help. To perform a task, simply click on the task's name.

[H3]Reader Department

The Reader Department is where you perform all tasks that involve the Readers—the ones for whom the newspapers are printed.

[g of Reader department. Callouts: Name, Tasks, Help]

The tasks that can be performed in this department are:

Add a New Reader—clicking here lets you establish who will read the newspapers. There can be multiple Readers. But eventually, some of the stories will repeat.

Print a Blank Reader Survey—prints out a copy of all the information you can input about each Reader. You don't have to print it out; you can simply enter the information into the computer. But printing it out lets you take your time to talk it over with the Reader, to make sure you have all the names and preferences correct.

Update a Reader Survey—opens the onscreen Reader survey for entering or modifying the information.

Print an Existing Reader Survey—prints out a Reader survey that you've already filled in, completely or partially. This allows you to look at what you have and decide if you want to change anything.

Delete a Reader—removes a Reader from the Reader list.

And you can also get help with the Reader Department by clicking on **Reader Department Help.**

[H3]Editorial Department

The Editorial Department is where you perform all tasks that involve defining and modifying the actual newspapers.

[g of Editorial department. Callouts: Name, Tasks, Help]

The tasks that can be performed in this department are:

Create a New Newspaper—clicking here lets you establish a new newspaper for one of the Readers. There can be multiple newspapers for each Reader. But eventually, some of the stories will repeat.

Print a Blank Newspaper Profile—prints out a copy of all the information you can input about each newspaper. You don't have to print it out; you can simply enter the information into the computer. But printing it out lets you take your time and talk it over with the Reader, to make sure you have the newspaper name and style correct.

Update a Newspaper Profile—opens the onscreen newspaper profile for entering or modifying the information.

Create a Special Edition—lets you customize individual newspapers by replacing the included pictures and stories with your own.

Delete a Newspaper—removes a newspaper from the newspaper list.

And you can also get help with the Editorial Department by clicking on **Editorial Department Help.**

[H3]Print Department

The Print Department is where you preview and print the newspapers.

[g of Print department. Callouts: Name, Tasks, Help]

The tasks that can be performed in this department are:

Preview Newspapers—clicking here lets you view and examine one or more days' newspapers prior to printing.

Print Newspapers—prints out newspapers for the date or dates you want.

> Notice the consistency in the way each department is described. They all follow the same format. The first option of each department always mentions clicking. Each description is written in the active voice, each begins with a verb.

And you can also get help with the Print Department by clicking on **Print Department Help.**

[H3]Story Department

The Story Department is where you can create and import your own stories for use in special editions.

[g of Story department. Callouts: Name, Tasks, Help]

The tasks that can be performed in this department are:

Write a Story—clicking here opens the Story Writing screen, where you can type in your own stories to be used in special editions.

Edit a Story—opens a story you already wrote, started or imported in the Story Writing screen, so you can make changes before using it in a special edition.

Import a Story—lets you import a story that was written with any text editor or word processor—as long as it was saved in either a text format (.TXT) or rich text format (.RTF)—for use in a special edition.

Delete a Story—removes a story that you've written or imported from your hard disk.

And you can also get help with the Story Department by clicking on **Story Department Help.**

[H3]Art Department

The Art Department is where you import your own pictures for use in special editions.

[g of Art department. Callouts: Name, Tasks, Help]

The tasks that can be performed in this department are:

Import a Picture—clicking here lets you import a picture that was scanned or created with any paint or draw program—as long as it was saved in either .JPG, .BMP or PICT (Mac) format—for use in a special edition.

Delete a Picture—removes a picture you've imported from your hard disk.

And you can also get help with the Art Department by clicking on **Art Department Help.**

[H3]Help Department

The Help Department is where you can get help and find out all about The Personal Newspaper.

[g of Help department. Callouts: Name, Tasks, Help]

The tasks that can be performed in this department are:

Program Overview—clicking here opens a screen that gives a general overview of what The Personal Newspaper is, and how to use it.

Hints and Tips—opens a screen with lots of useful information that will let you use The Personal Newspaper better and faster.

And you can also get help with the Help Department by clicking on **Help Department Help.**

[H2]Screens and Dialogs

There are four main screens in The Personal Newspaper where you will spend some time and energy. They are described in detail here.

[H3]Reader Survey Screen

The Reader Survey screen is where you fill in the personal information about a Reader that The Personal Newspaper incorporates into the feature story. The more information you fill in, and the more personal it is, the more the stories will feel tailor-made for the Reader.

You can print out a complete Reader Survey, spend some time with the Reader to answer all the questions, then enter the information into the computer later. Any information you leave out will be filled in with a default value in the stories. You can change information at any time to reflect changes in the Reader and the Reader's friends.

[g of Reader Survey screen. Callouts: text box, number selector, radio button, check boxes—if the screenshot can't cover all of these, then we'll need separate graphics of each one below.]

There are four different ways to fill in blank information in the Reader Survey screen:

Text boxes are the most common, and are used for names and addresses. Just click in a text box and type in the information.

Number selectors are used for dates and some other numbers. Click on the down-arrow to open a submenu of possible answers, then click on the answer you want.

Radio buttons are for selecting either/or choices, like boy or girl, or paper, rock or scissors. No matter how many radio buttons there are, one and only one can be selected at a time. Click on the button next to the answer you want. Anything that was selected before will automatically be unselected.

Check boxes are for selecting items from lists. You may select none, one, many or all of the items in a check-box list. Click in an unchecked check box to check it. Click in a checked check box to uncheck it,

When you are done with the Reader Survey screen, click **OK** to save the changes and close the screen. Click **Cancel** to close the screen without saving the changes.

[Question: anyone think it's necessary to show a copy of the complete Reader Survey and explain each and every entry? I'm leaning against it, since the information is all very basic and they can print it out to think it over. Comments?]

[H3]Newspaper Profile Screen

The Newspaper Profile screen is where you name the newspaper and choose its style.

You get to the Newspaper Profile screen by clicking on **Update a Newspaper Profile** in the Editorial Department, and selecting the newspaper whose profile you want to display in the Choose Newspaper dialog (see below).

You can print out a Newspaper Profile, spend some time with the reader to answer all the questions, then enter the information into the computer later. Any questions you don't answer yourself will be given default values.

[g of Newspaper Profile screen. Callouts: Newspaper Name, Start date, Style selections]

This screen asks for only three pieces of information:

Newspaper name is what you want to appear in the banner of the newspaper. Some suggestions are The *Your Name* Life and Times, The Personal Picayune, or anything with your name or home town and one of the following: Times, Chronicle, Examiner, Tattler or any other newspapery-sounding word. Then again, you could call your newspaper Harvey. It's up to you.

Newspaper names are best limited to 24 characters. If you go beyond 24, the banner won't look very nice. But it's up to you.

Start date lets the program know for which day the first newspaper will be printed. The Personal Newspaper prints out a paper for every day for one year. You have to let it know when to start.

Warning: Don't change the start date once you've started printing newspapers, or you'll get repeated stories right away.

Style is the look of the newspaper. Style won't affect the contents (words or pictures), just the type, the borders and other incidental graphics that give the paper the feel that the Reader wants. You can change the style on a daily basis if you want. To get an idea of what each style looks like, print out the first week with a different style every day.

When you are done with the Newspaper Profile screen, click **OK** to save the changes and close the screen. Click **Cancel** to close the screen without saving the changes.

[question: anyone think it's necessary to show a sample of each newspaper style? I think not. It is easy to print out a sample for each one or change on a daily basis. Also, if we offer additional styles as add-ons or give-aways on the web, they won't be covered. Comments?]

[H3]Print Preview Screen

The Print Preview screen lets you see what the newspapers will look like before you print them.

You get to the Print Preview screen by clicking on **Preview Newspapers** in the Print Department, and selecting a range of dates to display in the Choose Dates dialog (see below).

[g of Print Preview screen. Callouts: scroll bars, control buttons, the newspaper]

The controls for this screen are mostly along the bottom:

Whole Page displays the entire currently previewed newspaper so the whole thing is visible in the Print Preview screen. This is the default setting.

Full Size enlarges the newspaper to approximately full size. Unless you have a very large monitor, the entire full-size newspaper will not be visible. You can move the newspaper on the screen so you can see it all (though not all at once) by using the scroll bars. You can also click and drag the newspaper itself with the mouse to move it around on the screen.

Previous and **Next** change the displayed newspaper to the previous or next day's paper. This is limited to the range of dates you selected in the Choose Dates dialog when you entered the Print Preview screen. The range of selected dates is displayed at the top of the screen.

Print Page sends the currently previewed newspaper to the printer.

Print Range prints the papers for all the days that were selected in the Choose Dates dialog when you entered the Print Preview screen. The range of selected dates is displayed at the top of the screen.

Close closes the Print Preview screen.

[H3]Story Writing Screen

[note: this section won't be written until we're sure this screen will be included in the program and has been designed.]

[H3]Special Edition Screen

The Special Edition screen lets you replace some of the automatic stories and pictures in newspapers with your own stories and pictures.

You get to the Special Edition screen by clicking on **Create a Special Edition** in the Editorial Department, and selecting a range of dates to display in the Choose Dates dialog (see below).

[g of Special Edition screen. Callouts: scroll bars, control buttons, the newspaper]

The controls for this screen are mostly along the bottom:

Whole Page displays the entire currently previewed newspaper so the whole thing is visible in the Print Preview screen. This is the default setting.

Full Size enlarges the newspaper to approximately full size. Unless you have a very large monitor, the entire full-size newspaper will not be visible. You can move the newspaper on the screen so you can see it all (though not all at once) by using the scroll bars and scroll arrows. You can also click and drag the newspaper itself with the mouse to move it around on the screen.

Previous and **Next** change the displayed newspaper to the previous or next day's paper. This is limited to the range of dates you selected in the Choose Dates dialog when you entered the Special Edition screen. The range of selected dates is displayed at the top of the screen.

Print Page sends the currently previewed newspaper to the printer.

Print Range prints the papers for all the days that were selected in the Choose Dates dialog when you entered the Special Edition screen. The range of selected dates is displayed at the top of the screen.

Close closes the Print Preview screen.

The Newspaper itself is what you modify. Double-click on the feature story, the feature picture or the joke to replace them with your own story, picture or joke. The Change a Story or Change a Picture dialog box will open so you can choose the replacement.

The Banner can only be modified in the Editorial Department by selecting **Update a Newspaper Profile.** The Date Count and Cliffhanger can only be modified in the Reader Survey.

[H3]Dialog Boxes

There are various dialog boxes in The Personal Newspaper that will appear and ask you for information. They all work in very similar ways. Here is how to enter information into a dialog:

Text boxes let you type in information like names or addresses. Just click in a text box and type in the information.

Radio buttons let you select either/or choices. No matter how many radio buttons there are, one and only one can be selected at a time. Click on the button next to the answer you want. Anything that was selected before will automatically be unselected.

List boxes let you choose one name or item from a list. Click on the name or item you want to select, then click **OK.** You can also double-click on the name or item in the list and the OK will be taken care of automatically.

Drop-down menus contain all the possible choices. Click on the down-arrow to open the menu, then click on the menu item you want.

All dialog boxes have **Cancel** and **OK** buttons. **OK** accepts your choices or entered information and closes the dialog box. **Cancel** closes the dialog box and ignores your choices or entered information.

Here are the dialog boxes:

[g of Add a New Reader dialog. Callouts: Text Boxes]

[g of Choose a Reader dialog. Callouts: List Box]

[g of Create a New Newspaper dialog. Callouts: List Box]

[g of Choose a Newspaper dialog. Callouts: List Box]

[g of Import a Story dialog. Callouts: List Box, Radio buttons, Drop-down menu]

[g of Import a Picture dialog. Callouts: List Box, Radio buttons, Drop-down menu]

[g of Choose Dates dialog. Callouts: Text Box, Radio buttons]

[g of Choose a Story dialog. Callouts: Drop-down menu, List box]

[g of Choose a Picture dialog. Callouts: Drop-down menu, List box]

[H2]Hints and Tips

[H3]Standard Formats and Parts of the Newspaper

The Personal Newspaper, First Grade Edition creates newspapers that have each of these:

- Banner—The newspaper's name, date and edition.
- Feature story—the main story of the day, which includes some personal information about the reader.
- Feature picture—the picture of the day.
- Joke—a little humor.
- Date countdowns—vital information like how many days until the Reader's next birthday, the last day of school or favorite holidays.
- Cliffhanger—a continuing story that lasts the whole year, designed to make the child eager to see each day's paper to find out what happened.

[H3]Suggested Lengths of Stories for the Different Parts of the Paper

When you import a picture or story into The Personal Newspaper, it will automatically resize the type or graphic to fit the space. If an imported picture is too large, then it will be shrunk so small that it will be hard to see, and a long story might be displayed in type too small to read—especially for a young Reader.

Here are the recommended maximum and absolute maximum sizes for each part of the newspaper:

Part of Paper	Recommended Size	Maximum Size
Banner	24 characters or less	30 (if you really must)
Feature story	100 words or 500 characters	150 words or 750 characters
Feature picture	300w x 400h pixels	600w x 800h pixels
Joke	25 words or 125 characters	40 words or 200 characters

You cannot enter your own cliffhangers or date countdowns. You can choose which dates to count down and which cliffhanger you want in the Reader Survey screen.

[H3]Adding Pictures

The Personal Newspaper allows you to put your own pictures into the newspapers.

These pictures can come from many sources, including:

- Clip art that comes with many programs you may already own,
- Clip art that is free over the Internet,

- Low-cost clip art—CDs full of pictures that can be bought for very little at your local software store,

- Pictures and drawings that you or your child make with a paint or draw program, and

- Your own family photos.

Scanners—computer peripherals that take a digital picture of your photographs (or almost anything that fits into the scanner) so they can be displayed on a computer and inserted into various programs, including The Personal Newspaper—are priced very low these days. If you don't have or want to buy one, you may know someone, possibly at work, who will lend you theirs, or scan some photos for you. If all else fails, there are services that scan your photos and put them onto a CD for a nominal charge.

The Personal Newspaper will import and print any computer graphics files as long as they are in one of the following formats:

- .JPG—a standard format for graphics on the Internet,

- .BMP—a standard format for Windows-based paint and draw programs,

- PICT—a standard format for Mac-based paint and draw programs, or

- .TIF (or .TIFF)—a standard format for both Windows- and Mac-based paint and draw programs.

[question: will any other graphics formats be added?]

[H3]Adding Stories

The Personal Newspaper allows you to replace the automatic feature stories and jokes with your own.

These stories can come from many sources, including:

- Kids' joke sites on the Internet,

- Other interesting sites on the Internet, including news sites, or

- Any word processor—stories and jokes written by you or your child.

The Personal Newspaper will import and print any text as long as it is in one of the following formats:

.TXT—the basic, plain text that is created from programs like NotePad in Windows or TeachText or SimpleText on the Mac. Most word processors—even the big, fancy ones—can save files in .TXT format.

.RTF (rich text format)—this is a standard format that almost all word processors can read and write. It is often used as an intermediary format for getting text from one program to another.

[question: will any other text formats be added?]

If you get stories or jokes from the Internet, they may be in another format, usually HTML or .HTM. You may have to paste these files into a program like NotePad or SimpleText, edit out some of the symbols and garbage (formatting information that you don't need for The Personal Newspaper) and save them as text files before importing them into your newspapers.

> *Important Warning: Material on the Internet may be copyrighted material. Check carefully before you copy. In most cases, if you are allowed to copy, it is still illegal to use jokes or stories you get from the Internet for other than personal use. No selling newspapers.*

[H3]Your Hints and Tips

If you find that you've come up with a good idea that saves time or energy with The Personal Newspaper, share it with others on The Personal Newspaper Discussion Group at (URL).

[help! What other helpful hints are there?]

[H1]Appendices

[H2]Appendix 1—Troubleshooting

[This will mostly be concerned with installation and starting. Since the installer isn't in yet, this part can't be written yet. Can anyone suggest any other troubleshooting tips? Please?]

[H2]Appendix 2—Support and Contact Information

[This will be the standard contact page from previous manuals.

Marketing: have there been any changes to names, numbers, email addresses, web sites, etc., since the last manual?]

[H2]Appendix 3—For Parents and Teachers

The Personal Newspaper, First Grade Edition was designed and created to encourage reading and to make reading fun. It can be used as a home educational aid, and can also be adapted for classroom use.

You can customize the newspapers to the visual style and types of stories that the Reader wants to see and read. And you can change the styles and stories as the child's interest changes.

The vocabulary in the stories is carefully selected and graduated, to begin with very few words and slowly use more and more throughout the year. By the time the child has read a year's worth of personalized newspapers, they will have been exposed to the majority of recommended words that first graders should know, plus a number of words from the second grade list.

When using The Personal Newspaper with your child or student, get them involved in the process. Let *them* fill out the Reader Survey, even if they need a little help. Let *them* choose the paper's name and visual style. Give the child as much control over the process as possible. Make sure they know it's *their* newspaper.

After only a few weeks of reading the papers generated by the program, encourage the child to create their own stories for their newspapers. For the younger ones, let them dictate to you and you can type them (or write them by hand and type them in later) and enter them into special editions. As the children get a little older, they can write—or type—their own stories, and even take over the control of The Personal Newspaper to make their own special editions.

Their stories can be about anything at all: summer vacations, movies they saw, their favorite games, even fights with siblings. The subject doesn't matter nearly as much as the fact that they're creating a story about their own lives.

Check out our website (website educational page URL) for more ways to get educational value out of The Personal Newspaper, and to find out about availability of teacher's guides for this product.

Above all, educational activities that involve The Personal Newspaper should be fun. Please.

[H1]Index

[Note: The Index will be created after the first round of layout.]

Problems and Solutions

Problems that you might run into during this stage—and their solutions—are:

• There isn't enough information.

The program itself isn't far enough along to write many parts, without guessing or trusting old design documents or verbal promises.

All you can do is work on what's ready first, then write the rest based on trust—and be hopeful that the final product will be what's been promised. Make sure you note in the document what parts aren't definite, with a comment to the effect of:

[Note to all: This section was written based on the last known version of the design doc. Please review it carefully, and let me know of any changes.]

You can also ask by name for help or notification:

[Larry: please let me know the minute this part of the program has been implemented. I'll need to update it quickly to meet our deadlines.]

It's a balancing act. You want to show that you trust your teammates, but you don't want to do too much work that'll just be thrown away.

In any event, you have to finish the draft. In the example, there was a lot of guesswork. All the areas that were guesses were marked with notes. Right or wrong, putting it down in writing moves the project forward. Even if you have to go back and rewrite a lot of it, the overall project continues to progress.

• Nobody is willing or able to help.

Often team members will be so busy trying to meet their deadlines that they'll avoid spending time or energy on the manual. Yelling, screaming and whining won't help.

You have to make it as quick and easy as possible for busy people to help you. Find out how they like to work. Some people prefer to be sent questions via email. Others like to meet in person. Others want questions printed on paper. Some like their questions spread out, so they don't have to stop their work for very long. Others prefer to handle all your questions at once and be done with it.

What often works is to make a 15-minute appointment with a person you need to talk with, and show up, on time, at their desk, with all your questions prepared and printed—a copy for each of you. Bring a treat; coffee, tea or chocolate often works. Be prepared to quickly and clearly ask your questions, and write down or record their answers. At the end of the 15 minutes, let them know that time is up. If you haven't finished yet, you can ask if they can possibly keep going or if they'd rather reschedule another time. More often than not, they'll keep going.

Complications and Opportunities

Here are some likely complications for this stage, and opportunities to help, learn or have fun:

● **Refining the designing.**

The first draft serves a purpose beyond being merely a step in the manual writing process. It is actually (whether or not anyone but you realizes it) a detailed design review. The spots in the draft where you have left a blank (and a note) because that feature or screen isn't in yet become a list of all the incomplete portions of the program. All the places where you leave notes with questions asking for a better explanation about a feature become a list of potential design changes or design flaws. (If you look at a feature and play with it for a few minutes and can't understand if and how it works, it's either incomplete or a faulty design.)

You can go through your draft and copy all these notes into a new document, and this document can become (or be added to) a checklist for finishing the product.

● **The power of the written word.**

Sometimes a thing isn't real until it's been written down. Ideas, plans, designs and features can remain as hunches or preferences or assumptions.

Writing it down makes it real. When someone reads what they've promised to deliver, and it's there in black and white, it can sometimes make them really think about what they have to do. It can often make them drop features and back out of promises before it's too late.

Not only the fact that they see it in writing, but the fact that they know that everyone—including their boss and their boss's boss—will see it in writing is a powerful force for reflection.

● **Back up your files.**

One complication you want to avoid is lost data. If your company doesn't have an efficient system to back up all your data on a regular basis, take responsibility. The text for most manuals will fit easily on a single floppy with notes, spreadsheets and other documents. Make yourself a couple of copies, and keep them safe. If you need to back up more than will fit conveniently on a few floppies, find another medium, but *back up your files.*

Stage 5: Validating the Information—Content Editing and Testing

This chapter covers what you do when the first draft is written, and it's time to put it (and yourself) through the ringer.

The sections are:

- Preparing the Draft for Content Editing
- Testing the Tutorial
- Tutorial Test Results
- Mini Design Review
- After the Edit
- Problems and Solutions
- Complications and Opportunities

Preparing the Draft for Content Editing

Once again, the first draft that everyone else sees is not the first draft that you write. Read it over, and work it over *at least* once, and make it as clean and correct as possible. Run the spell-checker before you show your draft to anyone.

At this stage, you want people to correct and comment on the content. If they can't understand what you wrote or are too distracted by mistakes, you won't get the kind of feedback you need.

If you haven't already thought about the page presentation, now is the time. You need a number of people to read this document carefully and put time and thought into it so they can give you good feedback. Other than the "official" editor, nobody really wants to take the time and energy to do this.

If you want people to read it, this draft should be presented so it is as easy to read as possible. It doesn't need to be double-spaced unless your editor requires it. Single-spacing will make the document seem shorter, and use less paper. The shorter it is (or seems), the higher the odds of people actually reading the whole thing carefully. Be sure to leave some space between paragraphs, both so there's room for people to write comments, and also to make the pages more inviting to the reader.

Make the draft easy on people's eyes. Even if your word processor defaults to 10-point type for the normal or body text, raise it to 12. Don't make people squint and suffer to read your work.

Always make sure your draft has page numbers. Papers get dropped and need to be reassembled. Also, when discussing the draft, it's easier to refer to a page number than to a chapter and section name.

Once your draft is prepared, identify who you need to read it.

Your list should include the project's producer, the writing manager or editor, at least one of the team's engineers, at least one tester, the product manager (marketing), and anyone else that asks or whose input you'd like.

For most people, all you'll need to supply is a cover letter and a printout of the whole draft. But some people may need special handling.

If you know someone is very busy, then only ask them to review—and only give them—the sections you really need that person to review. If you give a busy person five or six pages to look over, they'll be more likely to do it than if you give them 50 or 60 pages. You may have to make up special short versions of the draft for a number of busy people.

The cover letter is important. It should contain:

1. The reviewer's name.

2. Date and time it is due—in big, bold type. Leave enough time for a busy person to get it done, but make sure you'll be able to grant a few extra days for "special exceptions," without missing your own deadlines.

3. Where it should be delivered, or who to call for pickup.

4. What the reviewer should be looking for. At this point, it's general content accuracy, answers to questions, and the accuracy of their particular area of expertise. Let them know that if they wish, they can mark typos and errors in grammar, but that it's not really necessary at this stage, since the most important thing right now is the accuracy of the content.

5. Special notes to the individual: "You're welcome to look over the whole thing, and comment on everything, including the grammar, but if time is tight, what I really need is for you to check the accuracy of one or two particular sections." If you know the person is really busy, then only give them the sections you need them to check over.

6. State that many people are editing and reviewing the document, and every comment will be read and appreciated, but not every suggestion will end up in the final document.

7. Thank them in advance.

8. Your name, your phone number and extension, your email address, your location in the office in case they need to find you.

9. Also put the reviewer's name on the draft itself as well as the cover letter, in case the cover letter gets lost. You need to know who the comments come from, if you have questions.

Once the drafts and cover letters are ready, deliver them. If you can, deliver them in person, introduce yourself and explain what you need from them.

Keep a checklist of everyone who has been given a copy of the document.

Send out a reminder, by email and/or in person, enough ahead of the due date so they can actually get it done. Try not to seem like you're nagging while you're nagging. (This may be another good time for bribery.)

While you're waiting for the experts to review the draft, it's time for a preliminary tutorial test.

Testing the Tutorial

Most of the people who have drafts to review will read through the tutorial. Some may even work through it. But all of these people are experts in the program and are very technically inclined. You need to find out how the tutorial flies with potential customers: people who have never seen the program before and who aren't technical professionals.

Your product manager may be able to round up a three- or four-person test group. If not, then ask around the office for volunteers. Various people out of the product development group might be happy to help. Secretaries, administrative assistants, mail-room workers, even those in the accounting department are often thrilled to get involved in a project. Others will do anything to get away from their desk and daily duties for a while.

If they can't get an hour or two off their jobs to test the tutorial, then do it during their lunch. They bring their lunch, you supply the drinks (sodas, coffee, etc.). The company will usually be willing to spring for the drinks. If the company is feeling generous, it may spring for the whole lunch.

If there's nobody around that's willing or suitable, then you and the product manager have to do a little digging. Friends, family members, and people from the office next door all may be potential candidates. If you have to schedule the test for after-hours or a weekend, so be it.

Once you've got your test subjects, sit them down at a computer and give them copies of the manual's introduction and tutorial. Supply graphics to go with the tutorial, if you can. You may want to test one person at a time, or keep them separated, so they don't start working as a group or feel embarrassed about their confusion.

If the program is far enough along and the installer is working, include installation and starting as part of the test. Otherwise, install and start the program for the testers before they begin.

If your test subjects think that they or their abilities or their intelligence are being tested, they'll be less likely to mention every comment and confusion. It is important to tell the test subjects that the *tutorial* is being tested—*not them.* If anything is confusing or doesn't make sense or doesn't work, it's the *program's or tutorial's* fault—*not theirs.* You want—and need—to know every spot, every button, every word that they have trouble with, so you can fix it.

Ask them to read the introduction, and to read and work through the tutorial. Encourage them to think out loud as they go. Encourage them to voice any questions that come to mind, but don't answer any questions unless they get totally stuck. You want to see how far the tutorial can take them without any extra help.

If you have the facilities and inclination, you may want to record the sessions on either audio or video tape. Otherwise, expect to be furiously taking notes.

Tutorial Test Results

You're bound to get two types feedback from your test:

1. Feedback on the tutorial, and
2. Feedback on the program.

In theory, the producer and product manager have already done some customer testing on the program and interface. In reality, it's often skipped.

In the instance of The Personal Newspaper, the main feedback you received about the tutorial was:

1. It seemed complete enough, but there was frustration that they couldn't do a lot of the things in the tutorial because the program wasn't finished.
2. It didn't tell them how to quit the program.

The feedback you received about the program was:

1. Good idea for a program,
2. Fairly clear in concept and operation, though incomplete, and

3. The whole adding stories and pictures part seemed very complicated. Why does it have to be two steps instead of one?

The tutorial feedback was useful, and will be fairly easy to implement.

The program feedback may also be useful. If you have the comments on this section on tape, save it so you can play it for the appropriate team members.

Call a meeting or casually drop by the producer's office to discuss the tutorial feedback—for both the tutorial and the program. Play tapes if necessary. Encourage the producer to take a look at (or have someone else take a look at) the possibility of simplifying the picture and story importing process—especially if there's no Story Writing screen.

Mini Design Review

You've convinced the producer that the picture and story importing interface needs some rethinking. He calls a small meeting of the involved parties: himself as designer, the lead engineer, the lead artist, a tester, and you to review the problem and play the evidence tapes if necessary.

In this case, it turns out that the part of the program called the Art Department was the vestigial remains of the original design that included a Drawing screen. It also turns out that the Writing screen from the Story Department has also been eliminated.

After much discussion, it is decided that both the Story and Art Departments can be eliminated. The import process can be simplified and combined with actual story and picture placement in the Editorial Department.

Going further, it is also decided that the Help Department is too redundant, and can be eliminated as well by adding an extra button or two to the Main Menu screen.

This is good for you—it eliminates many steps from the tutorial, allowing you to easily shorten the tutorial enough that it needn't be broken into two parts.

During the meeting, you take notes on everything that everyone agrees on. After the meeting, you carefully write out all the changes and the new importing process, and email it out to everyone who was at the meeting. Ask that everyone review it and make sure you have everything correct. It's amazing how a group of people can all leave a meeting thinking they are all in total agreement, but later find that they all had different things in mind. Writing down meeting results and having everyone check them for accuracy eliminates a lot of problems down the line.

After the Edit

After a few reminders and bribes, you've finally gotten back all the edited drafts that you're going to get.

Expect a number of people to have few or no comments. Others won't even look at it, especially those in senior management who asked for a copy. They mostly just need to know that progress is being made, and won't have much to contribute.

You may have three, five or even ten reviewed copies with varying amounts of corrections and comments. You now need to combine all those corrections and comments into a single copy, so you can easily use it for the rewrite. This may be something that your editor does, but it is often the writer's responsibility.

Take all the reviewed copies and lay them out on a desk or table. Print out a blank copy.

Turn all the edited copies one page forward, until you find comments or corrections on one or more of the copies. Copy the corrections or comments into your blank master copy.

If you have questions about comments, call, email or visit the commentator in person. If they can't be reached, mark the page and come back to it later.

If there are conflicting suggestions, pick the one that works the best. If you get conflicting information about the product, then search out the absolute authority to make the decision, or call a design conflict-resolution meeting. Get the disagreeing parties together and tell them you don't understand how that part of the program works. Get them to agree on something. Write it down and make them look at what you wrote to be sure you understood what they meant.

Once you have your master correction draft, and all your questions about the comments answered, check through it to make sure all your original questions in the draft were answered. Do you now have information to fill in all the blank spots?

If not, it's time to make up a new list of questions and make the rounds of the team again.

Rarely will you be able to just take the reviewed copies and input the comments and corrections and be done. You'll usually have to resolve conflicting facts and really rewrite the draft. Sometimes more than once.

Problems and Solutions

Problems that you might run into during this stage—and their solutions—are:

- **There are many contradictions and conflicts in the comments you receive.**

If the contradictions and conflicts are about grammar and phrasing, talk it over with your editor. If the contradictions are about what you do and don't cover in the manual, consider the sources. If they're both reliable sources, and you don't want to ignore either of them, then let them know about the conflict, and ask for them to either come to a consensus, or find a third party to pass judgement.

If the conflict and contradictions are about the program itself, then let the producer know. It may be time for a team meeting to go over all the points of conflict and make sure everyone is building the same product.

> • **There still isn't enough information to complete the manual.**

Unless you've got an incredibly uncooperative team—or you've done something to make everyone mad at you—the main reason why you wouldn't have all the information you need at this point is because the information doesn't yet exist. In other words, the program is most likely behind schedule. A program falling behind schedule is generally bad news—but it will allow you more time for the manual.

At this point, to keep the manual moving forward, you have to make another draft using all the information you received, update all the guesses, and do another round of content edit.

Let people know that you'll keep doing more rounds (and bugging them) until you get all the information you need.

Complications and Opportunities

Here are some likely complications for this stage, and opportunities to help, learn or have fun:

> • **Re-refining the designing.**

Sometimes the fact that you write something down and force people to read it can cause them to reevaluate the design. It can be clear or cloudy in their heads, but once it's on paper, it really crystallizes and feels more real.

Also, the fact that you've written a step-by-step tutorial and had a few people work through it, actually using the program, will reveal other design issues.

If you join the project early enough, then be prepared for fairly major changes in both your first draft—especially the tutorial—and the program itself in the last few weeks of development.

Don't worry about throwing out large chunks of what you've written. It's part of the job.

As a consolation, think about how that work that you threw out and rewrote helped crystallize the design and made the program (one hopes) better.

Stage 6: Rewriting and Retesting

This chapter covers the production of the final draft. By now, you've been through one (if you're working on a very organized project) to four or more draft and content edit (or review) cycles, and you should have all the information you need to write a final draft.

The sections are:

- Summary of Changes
- Rewriting
- Numbering the Graphics
- Retesting
- Final Draft
- Problems and Solutions
- Complications and Opportunities

Summary of Changes

Including what you learned through the tutorial testing and from the design meeting, you've received the following feedback from the content edit reviewers:

Title Page

- OK to call it The Editor-in-Chief's Handbook instead of User Manual.

Contents

- No need for a glossary, shorten to match shortened tutorial and reference.

Introduction

- Marketing wants more of what you have in the reference-section program description put into the manual introduction. Expand the "What can you do with The Personal Newspaper" section a little.
- President *will* sign the quote.

- Getting Started: The latest news is that there may not be versions of The Personal Newspaper for more than one computer platform. Include all the installation and starting instructions in the manual, and kill the plans for an addendum. If a second version comes out, then we'll add an addendum to cover the new platform.

Tutorial

- Kill Help, Story and Art departments.
- Use new importing instructions.
- Shorten tutorial to one session.

Reference

- No more text formats will be added.
- .WMF and .CLP graphic formats *will* be added.
- General agreement that there's no need to show and explain a complete Reader Survey.
- General agreement that there's no need to show a sample of each newspaper style.
- Suggestions for hints and tips include more on newspaper names.

Appendix 1—Troubleshooting

- Cover installation and starting.
- Mention the help, Readme and website for more info.

Appendix 2—Support and Contact Information

Marketing reports no changes.

Appendix 3—For Parents and Teachers

Half the comments think you should expand it to include and describe a number of activities for individuals and groups at home and in school. The other half of the comments think a separate teacher's guide would be better. (Because of time limits, you let people know that you can't add much to this section without missing your current deadlines. You suggest a separate teacher's guide be prepared after the manual goes to print—unless someone wants to sign something that says they insist that the product be delayed.) Your suggestion has been accepted. Appendix 3 stands as is.

Rewriting

Before actually beginning the final draft, try to take a fresh look at what you wrote:

- Will it serve the rare person who reads the manual through from front to back?
- Will it work for the person who reads the intro and works through the tutorial and seldom, if ever looks at the reference?
- Is it good for a first-time computer user?
- Will it work for the person who reads through the tutorial away from the computer (enough screenshots)?
- Will it work for the person who only reads the reference and ignores the tutorial?
- Are there enough headings so that people can easily find exactly what they want?

While you rewrite, incorporate all the new information from the reviewers and all other sources. More than that, recheck all the facts with the actual program. Recheck every dialog box, every button. A lot can change while you're off testing tutorials and compiling reviews.

In this draft, you'll also want to fill in all of the blanks you left in the earlier draft. Put in the credits now, so people have a chance to check the spelling of their names. Put in the title page, etc. You won't be able to include the index yet, and you probably won't need to include the license information. The graphic artist will drop in an already formatted license blurb, and you can just mark up a few changes, such as title, copyright date and ISBN number.

Numbering the Graphics

One last thing to do is to go through the draft from the first to the last page and number, or name, each graphic in order. Just add the number after each "g" in the beginning of a bracket. If there are less than 100 graphics, add a zero to the names of the first nine so all the names will be two digits: 01, 02 … 10. If there are more than 100 and less than 1,000 use one or two zeros as needed to make all the names three digits: 001, 002 … 099, 100.

This naming scheme keeps all the graphics in numerical order when the computer alphabetizes[15] them, making it easier for the graphic artist to find the graphics to place. Otherwise, the graphics would be listed: 1, 10, 11, 12, 13, 14, 15, 16, 17, 18, 19, 2, 20, etc.

You'll often find that graphics are moved, removed or added during the various drafts of the manual. In general, the longer you wait to number them, the less changes there will be, but you need to number them before you start to take the screenshots.

One way to deal with these changes is to renumber every graphic at each draft. This keeps it looking clean, but if graphic creation has begun, you could have a lot of file names to change and lists to update.

It's generally easier to just leave some numbers blank and add new graphics with an "a" or "b" appended to their names. For instance, if you add a new graphic between the existing 19 and 20, name it 19a.

Retesting

So, you've written what you think is a final draft. Maybe. But maybe not.

Once more, it's time to test your work with typical readers/customers. Test the tutorial again, this time with the full installation instructions.

Have people read through the whole thing and point out any words, phrases, paragraphs etc., that they don't understand.

Final Draft

Here it is: the final, post-testing draft, ready for the line edit. The heading markings have been removed.

My notes and comments on how and why I did things will be in text boxes as in the previous draft.

---

[15] *When computers display folder or directory contents, they generally alphabetize the files, and don't take actual numerical value into account. 3 would be displayed after 299 and before 30. The numbering scheme with leading zeros, as shown above, compensates for this.*

[Title Page]

The Personal Newspaper

Editor-in-Chief's Handbook

Designed and Produced by Chris Orny

Handbook written by Michael Bremer

UnTechnical Press

[add company logo]

[License Page]

License

[Richard: insert standard license here. We'll update it in the next round of edits.]

Credits

The Program

Designed and produced by: Chris Orny

Lead Engineer: Brian Ranier

Engineer: Joe Okenso

Lead Artist: Sue Topper

Artist: Kevin Kraus

Lead Tester: Dan Amity

Testers: Crash N. Berns

Sound: The Noise Boys

Product Manager: Horace Ecksley

Contributing Story Writers: Bob Smith, Debbie Jones, Laura White, Steve Black.

> FYI: Most of the names in these credits are the made-up ones from stage one of the project, and to the best of our knowledge, don't exist.
>
> The exceptions are: Kevin Kraus created the screenshots that will appear in the final manual and in the demo program; Richard Bagel designed and laid out the final manual, as well as the whole book; Tom Bentley line-edited the manual and the whole book. Oh, and Michael Bremer is real, too.

The Manual

Written by: Michael Bremer

Design and Layout: Richard Bagel

Editor: Tom Bentley

Writing Manager: William Ordyss

Personal Newspaper Manual Draft 3 (final)   8/10/2001   1

The Package

Package Design: Package Design, Inc.

Package Illustration: Illustrators Anonymous (We put the "ill" in illustration.)

Special Thanks To:

Company President: C. P. Resident

VP Product Development: Barry Eeren

VP Marketing: Della Fenster

Manufacturing: Fred Osilin

Graphic Arts Manager: Linda Earnest

And Bob's cat.

Table of Contents

Introduction **5**

Welcome 5

What Can You Do with The Personal Newspaper? 5

Why The Personal Newspaper? 5

The Personal Newspaper Product Line 5

Registering The Personal Newspaper 6

About This Manual 6

Getting Started 6

System Requirements 6

Installing The Personal Newspaper 7

Starting The Personal Newspaper 8

Tutorial **9**

Introduction to the Tutorial 9

Before You Begin 9

A Tour of Your Personal Newspaper Office 9

The Reader Department 10

The Editorial Department 13

The Print Department 14

Special Edition 16

Tutorial Summary 19

Reference **20**

Introduction 20

The Basics 20

Program Overview 20

Main Menu Screen 21

Getting Help 21

The Departments 22

Reader Department 22

Editorial Department 22

Print Department 23

Screens and Dialogs 24

Reader Survey Screen 24

Newspaper Profile Screen 24

Print Preview Screen 25

Special Edition Screen 26

Dialog Boxes.. 27

Hints and Tips 28

Standard Formats and Parts of the Newspaper... 28

Suggested Lengths of Stories for the Different Parts of the Paper............. 28

Adding Pictures 28

Adding Stories.. 29

Your Hints and Tips 30

Appendices **31**

Appendix 1—Troubleshooting 31

Appendix 2—Support and Contact Information 32

Appendix 3—For Parents and Teachers 32

Index.. 33

Introduction

Welcome …

… to The Personal Newspaper, First Grade Edition, the program that prints out customized, personalized newspapers for early readers.

We trust—in fact, we guarantee—that you will find this product both useful and fun.

What Can You Do with The Personal Newspaper?

As owner and Editor-in-Chief of this program, you can create and print daily personalized newspapers for the early readers in your family—for every day for a whole year.

These newspapers feature stories about the Readers, their families, friends, pets and hobbies. It also features jokes, important date countdowns and exciting cliffhanger stories that will have kids wanting to read tomorrow's paper today.

Newspapers can be customized to the individual Readers' tastes—if the Readers love sports, they'll get a lot of sports stories; if they don't like sports, but love cute animals, they'll get cute animal stories.

And beyond that, you can replace any day's automatic stories, jokes and pictures with your own stories, jokes and pictures, allowing you to make special editions to announce or commemorate special family outings and events.

Why The Personal Newspaper?

We'll let our company president field this question:

"We believe that good reading skills are the foundation of a good education.

We also believe that people who enjoy reading read more and gain more skills faster.

We created The Personal Newspaper to provide every child with daily reading material that they will enjoy."

> — C. P. Resident, Company President

Let's face it: when it comes to interesting subjects to read about, nothing beats ourselves. We make your child the star of a daily newspaper, so even reluctant Readers will want to read—every day.

The Personal Newspaper Product Line

The Personal Newspaper comes in editions for first through sixth grades. Plus, there are separately available Personal Newspaper Add-on Packs of specialty stories that let you customize the paper even more perfectly to your child's reading interests.

Registering The Personal Newspaper

Now would be a good time to fill out the registration card. Registering provides you with extended technical support. And we keep registered owners notified of new products and add-ons, updates, upgrades and special events like story contests.

About This Manual

This manual is short and simple—and very useful.

It has a tutorial that will guide you through every step of creating and printing newspapers.

It also has a reference section that explains all the menus, screens, windows and dialog boxes.

At the end of the manual, you'll find:

- some troubleshooting tips—just in case,
- contact information if you have questions or need support, and
- useful information for parents and teachers on getting the most educational value from The Personal Newspaper.

Getting Started

Installing and starting The Personal Newspaper for Windows 95 or later is easy. Just follow the instructions below.

Note: If you have The Personal Newspaper for another operating system, then refer to the Quick-Start guide for installation and starting instructions for your computer.

> This note is a compromise that both eliminates the need for a Quick-Start guide and eliminates updating the manual if and when a new version is released.

System Requirements

This program will run on any PC-compatible computer running Windows 95 or later, with:

- 16 MB RAM
- Hard disk with at least 10 MB free (120 MB for full installation so you can run it without the CD)
- CD-ROM drive
- Any printer supported by Windows

> System Requirements are printed on the box, but software is often bundled without boxes, so it's worth putting here as well.

A color monitor and a sound card with speakers are nice, but not absolutely necessary.

Installing The Personal Newspaper

The Personal Newspaper must be installed before it can be used. To install:

1. Make sure your computer meets the system requirements above.

2. Start your computer and put the Personal Newspaper CD into your CD-ROM drive.

> Notice the level of detail: don't forget to tell them to start the computer.

3. If AutoPlay works on your computer, **click on Install The Personal Newspaper** when the AutoPlay screen opens, then skip to step 6.

   If AutoPlay doesn't work (nothing happens after you've put in the CD and waited a minute or two), then **open (click on) the Start menu** in the lower-left corner of your screen, and **select Run.**

> Don't count on AutoPlay. It just doesn't work on older machines with older CD-ROM drives. Cover manual installation or expect a lot of tech-support calls.

4. When the Run dialog box opens, **type "D:\setup"** in the little box in the middle, then **click OK.** (D is the usual designation for the CD-ROM drive. If your CD-ROM drive has a different letter, type that one instead of D.)

[g01 of run dialog w/D:\setup typed in]

5. Installation will now begin. Just answer the questions, and the computer will take care of all the work.

> The possibility of the CD having a drive designation other than "D" is an important detail to cover. Use a picture when you think it might help.

You'll only have two questions to answer:

Where would you like The Personal Newspaper to be installed?

Unless you have a preference, just **click OK** to accept the default location:

C:\Program Files\Personal Newspaper.

Would you like the minimum installation or the full installation?

The minimum installation only takes up 10 MB of your hard drive, but requires that you always have the Personal Newspaper CD in your CD-ROM drive whenever you print from the program.

The full installation takes up 120 MB of your hard drive, but can perform almost any task without the CD in the drive.

The choice is between space and convenience. If you're not sure, just **click OK** to accept the default minimum installation.

6. Once the installation is complete, it's time to start The Personal Newspaper.

> This might not be necessary here. You might be able to get away with just saying to follow the directions on the screen—if you're sure that the explanation on the screen is clear and complete. If you have the space, it's worth covering this in the manual or Quick-Start guide. In general, try to keep the whole installation explanation to only one page. If it looks longer than that, it'll look too complicated or annoying.

Starting The Personal Newspaper

For your convenience a Personal Newspaper icon has been added to your desktop.

[g02 of Icon] Double-click on this icon to start the program.

Note: if you don't want the icon on your desktop, just drag it to the Recycle Bin. You can start the program by opening the Start menu, then selecting Program Files, then Personal Newspaper then Personal Newspaper again.

Turn the page to begin a quick tutorial that will teach you everything you need to know to use The Personal Newspaper.

Tutorial

Introduction to the Tutorial

Welcome to The Personal Newspaper tutorial.

In this tutorial, you will learn how to create, view, customize and print a sample newspaper.

One point before you begin:

While reading this tutorial, when you see text that looks like this, it is an instruction for you to follow.

Relax and enjoy yourself. You've just been put in charge of a newspaper.

Before You Begin

Make sure your computer is on and your printer is hooked up, loaded with paper and turned on.

Start The Personal Newspaper.

If you haven't already installed the program, please refer to Getting Started in the Introduction chapter (or Quick-Start guide, if your version of The Personal Newspaper is for a computer other than Windows) for installation and starting instructions.

This might be a place where putting a reference to a page might be used instead of a chapter reference. Page references are often a pain to keep accurate. Pages change during layout, sometimes more than once. A wrong page reference is worse than none at all. If you use them, keep a list of all of them, so you and your editor can easily find them all and check them.

If the layout program has the capability to automatically update references, make sure the graphic artist knows how to use it and updates it every draft. In this instance, the Introduction chapter is so close and so short, that it won't be hard for the user to find.

A Tour of Your Personal Newspaper Office

What We'll Do:

1. Take a quick look at the opening screens.

2. Get acquainted with the Main Menu screen.

Make a Splash

As the program starts, you will be entertained by the appearance and disappearance of a couple of "splash screens." These are screens that let you know what company made this product (UnTechnical Press), and announce the product itself (The Personal Newspaper).

Once those screen have passed, we begin the actual program at the Main Menu screen.

What's on the Menu?

The Main Menu screen is the heart of The Personal Newspaper.

[g03 of Main Menu screen, large, with callouts for Departments, Help, other buttons, tbd]

Think of yourself as the Editor-in-Chief of a local newspaper. You are in a big office, overlooking the entire company. This screen is your office building, filled with your eager-to-please employees. Anytime you want anything done, just click. (Of course, as editor-in-chief you have every right to yell orders in a gruff voice while you click.)

The Main Menu screen is divided into three departments and a Button bar.

Everything you can do—and could ever want to do—with this program is done through one of the three departments.

> Reminder: the department count has been lowered from 6 to 3, and Help has become a button on the button bar.

Each department has a picture showing what goes on there, plus a list of all the different tasks that that department handles. When you want to carry out a task, you just click on it—*but don't click yet.* We want to finish looking around first.

At the bottom of the screen is the Button bar. It lets you quit (not now, of course), find out who made this program (About …), and get an overview description of this program whenever you want.

One last thing before we move on—notice that at the bottom of each department is a way to access help for that department. Click on each department's help for a complete explanation of all of that department's tasks.

Now let's take a look at the Reader Department.

The Reader Department

What We'll Do:

1. Look over the Reader Department tasks.

2. Add a new Reader.

3. Input information about the new Reader.

What Goes on Here?

Take a look at the Reader Department.

[g04 of Reader Department. Callouts: Tasks, Help.]

Notice that there are five different tasks that can be performed in this department—plus a way to get help.

Let's start at the beginning, and add a new Reader.

Increasing Circulation

Click on "Add a New Reader."

The Add a New Reader dialog opens.

[g05 of Add a New Reader dialog]

For this tutorial, go ahead and use your own name.

Click in the box next to "First Name:" and type in your first name.

Click in the box next to "Last Name:" and type in your last name.

Click OK.

The Add a New Reader dialog disappears and you are back at the Main Menu screen.

Drawing a Blank

We could go ahead and start filling in the information about the new Reader right now by clicking on Update Reader Survey. But we won't.

First, we'll print out a blank Reader survey to look over.

When gathering information about a Reader other than yourself, you may want to sit with that person and the blank survey and talk it over away from the computer. You can fill out the survey by hand, then come back to the computer later and enter the information.

Click on "Print Blank Reader Survey."

Depending on your computer and printer this may take a few minutes. You may want to take this time to practice yelling, "And don't call me chief!" in your gruffest voice.

Once the Reader survey is printed, look it over. All the information on the survey will be used in various newspaper stories about the Reader.

For the purposes of this tutorial, you won't need to fill in all the information. The special tutorial newspaper that we'll be printing later only uses a few bits of information.

On the blank Reader survey form, fill out:

- Your first and last name
- Your city
- Your state
- Your gender (boy or girl)
- Your birthday
- Your favorite holiday (or two)

Now, we'll go back to the computer and the Reader Department.

Click on "Update Reader Survey."

The Choose Reader dialog will appear.

[g06 of Choose Reader Dialog]

This dialog box displays all the Readers that have been entered. Your name may be the only one there.

Click on your name in the name list.

Click OK.

The dialog disappears, and is replaced by an onscreen version of the Reader survey.

[g07 of Reader survey screen. Callouts: Scroll Arrows, Scroll Bar]

Your first and last name are already filled out for you. As you enter the rest of your information, you may need to use the scroll bar to scroll the screen down to find all of the information blanks.

Click in the box next to "City:" and type the name of your city.

Click in the box next to "State:" and type the name or abbreviation of your state.

Check the checkbox next to either Boy or Girl.

Click in the box next to "Birthday:" and type in your birthday (mm/dd/yyyy).

Check the checkbox next to your favorite holiday or two.

Click OK.

The Reader Survey screen will close and the Main Menu screen will reappear.

Before we move on to the next department, take a look at the other Reader Department tasks:

- **Print Existing Reader Survey** lets you print out Reader information that you've already entered, in case you want to review it for changes or updates.

- **Delete a Reader** lets you remove a Reader that you've entered, and all newspapers created for that Reader.

- And **Reader Department Help** shows an onscreen explanation of all the Reader Department tasks.

OK, now it's time to visit the Editorial Department.

The Editorial Department

What We'll Do:

1. Create a new newspaper (for you).

2. Update the Newspaper Profile.

New News Is Good News(paper)

Take a look at the Editorial Department.

[g08 of Editorial Department. Callouts: Tasks, Help]

We have a Reader; now we need to create and customize a newspaper for that Reader.

Click on "Create a New Newspaper."

The Create a New Newspaper dialog will open.

[g09 of Create a New Newspaper For: dialog]

Because The Personal Newspaper is, after all, *personal,* each newspaper is created for one and only one Reader. The first thing the program needs to know is who the newspaper is for. The newspaper you create will be linked to the information in that one Reader's Reader survey.

Click on your name.

Click OK.

> By adding "For:" to the dialog name, the potential confusion was (hopefully) eliminated, but the information in this paragraph is still useful, so it was slightly rephrased and left in.

The Create a New Newspaper For: dialog closes and the Newspaper Profile Screen opens. Now that we know who the newspaper is for, it's time to deal with the newspaper itself.

File That Profile

The way to customize a newspaper is by filling out its Newspaper Profile. As with the Reader survey, you have the option of printing it out first and talking it over with the Reader, but we'll skip that step, and go right to filling out the profile.

[g11 of Newspaper Profile screen]

You can name the newspaper anything you want, but it's best to keep the name to 24 characters or less. If you need some help coming up with a name, some possibilities are Tutorial Times, Your Name Gazette, or The Your Family News.

Click in the box next to "Name:" and enter a name for the newspaper.

Each newspaper has to have a start date. This lets the program track stories, birthdays and holidays, and

> Note that there is no longer a graphic #10. It was eliminated in the final rewrite. If you want, you can renumber all the graphics to keep them all in exact order, but if you or someone else has already begin creating the graphics and named them by the original names, it could cause more trouble than it's worth. Just note on the graphics list that #10 has been eliminated.

allow for special editions without losing days on the continuing stories. The default start date is today.

Make sure that "Today" is selected.

The newspapers can be presented in a number of different styles to suit almost any Reader. For this tutorial, pick the tutorial style. This style has been customized to need only the information you entered earlier in this tutorial.

Click on and highlight the Tutorial Style newspaper.

Click OK.

The Update a Newspaper Profile screen closes, and we're back at the Main Menu screen.

Before moving on, take a last look at the Editorial Department. Note that here you can also:

- Create a special edition—we'll do that in a few minutes.
- Delete a newspaper.
- Get help with any of the Editorial Department tasks.

Time to print!

The Print Department

What We'll Do:

1. Preview a newspaper.
2. Print a newspaper.

Hold the Presses

Take a look at the Print Department.

[g12 of Print Department. Callouts: Tasks, Help]

Like the other departments we've visited, it consists of tasks and help.

Now let's take a preview look at our newspaper.

Click on "Preview Newspaper."

The Choose Newspaper dialog appears.

[g13 of Choose Newspaper dialog]

Choose the newspaper we've been working on. Only you know its name.

Click on the newspaper you just profiled.

Click OK.

Now the Choose Dates dialog opens.

[g14 of Choose Dates dialog]

We're only going to print one day's newspaper—today's—so make sure that Today is selected in both the From: and To: columns.

Click on the radio buttons next to "Today" in both the "From:" and "To:" columns.

Notice that you can preview (and print) one, two, or many days at a time—even the whole year at once. If you enter a date that is before your start date or more than a year after it, you'll get an error message.

Click OK.

The Choose Dates dialog will close and the Print Preview screen will appear.

[g15 of Print Preview screen. Callouts: Page Size buttons, Scroll Bars, Previous/Next Day buttons, Print button, Close button]

The newspaper is shown, just as it will print, except that it is shrunk down to fit in the window. You can expand the paper to full size by clicking on the Full Size button. While full size, the whole paper probably won't fit in the window. To see it all, you can either use the scroll bars, or just click and drag the paper itself to move it around the screen.

Click on the Full Size button.

Move the page around on the screen with the scroll bars.

Move the page around on the screen by clicking and dragging the page.

Roll the Presses

We can print the newspaper from here, or go back to the Main Menu screen and print from there. Since we're ready to go, we might as well print here and now.

Make sure the Personal Newspaper CD is in your CD-ROM drive.

This may or may not really be necessary. If you selected "full install" when you installed the program, then you won't need the CD in the drive. If you selected "minimum install," then you'll definitely need the CD. If you're not sure what was installed, put the CD in the drive. It can't hurt.

> This step and the explanation was added to forestall any potential confusion.

Click on the Print button.

A standard Print dialog will open.

Click OK.

The Print dialog will close and the printing process will begin.

While we're waiting for the printer, let's return to the Main Menu screen.

Click the Close button.

As we take a last look at the Print Department, be sure to note Print Department Help is available.

When the paper has been printed, take a look at it. You'll notice that it has a banner, a feature story—about you—with a picture, a joke, a media review, a date countdown, and the first installment of a cliffhanger story.

[g16 of sample newspaper, with callouts: Feature Story, Feature Picture, Joke, Date Countdown, Cliffhanger]

You'll probably notice that the picture isn't very flattering and the joke isn't very funny. We did that on purpose, so we have an excuse to make a special edition of this paper.

Special Edition

What We'll Do:

1. Make today's newspaper into a special edition by changing (and improving) the picture and joke.

2. Print it (if you want to).

You're Special

Look at the Editorial Department on the Main Menu screen again.

[g17 of Editorial Department. Callouts: Tasks, Help]

Let's remake the newspaper we created into a special edition, by replacing the picture and joke.

Click on "Create a Special Edition."

The Choose Newspaper dialog appears.

[g18 of Choose Newspaper dialog]

Choose the same newspaper we just made and printed.

Click on the newspaper you made.

Click OK.

The Choose Newspaper dialog closes and the Choose Dates dialog opens.

[g19 of Choose Dates dialog]

This Choose Dates dialog is just like the Choose Dates dialog we saw when we previewed the newspaper earlier.

We're only going to modify one day's newspaper to make a special edition—today's—so make sure that **Today** is selected in both the **From:** and **To:** columns.

Click on the radio buttons next to "Today" in both the "From:" and "To:" columns.

Click OK.

The Choose Dates dialog appears, and the Special Edition screen opens.

[g19a of Special Edition screen]

It looks very much like the Print Preview screen, with a couple of important differences:

1. It allows you to replace some of the parts of the newspaper, and

2. It has a Cancel button, so you can experiment with changes, and undo them if you don't like them.

> This graphic, which was added between graphics 19 and 20 during the third and last draft (draft 2 isn't shown in this book), can be named 19a to make it easy on the graphic artist and avoid renumbering many graphics.

The parts of the newspaper that you can customize in the Special Edition screen are:

1. The feature story,

2. The feature picture, and

3. The joke.

The banner, the date countdown and the cliffhanger story cannot be changed in this screen—but they can be changed in either the Newspaper Profile screen or the Reader Survey screen.

To change a story or picture, double-click on it.

Double-click on the picture.

The Change a Story or Picture dialog opens.

[g20 of Change a Story or Picture dialog, set to drive C:, and showing the appropriate folders. Callouts: Drive Selector, List box]

You can replace, stories and pictures with text or graphics files on any type of drive that your computer can access, including hard drives, floppies, CDs, removable media and even network drives.

For this tutorial, the files we'll be using are on The Personal Newspaper CD.

Make sure The Personal Newspaper CD is in your CD-ROM drive—even if you performed a full install.

The drive display in the Change a Story or Picture dialog, by default, shows the drive where you installed The Personal Newspaper. Click on the down-arrow next to Drive, and select the drive for your CD. It's usually drive D:, but it could be different.

After you select the drive for your CD, you'll see a number of folders in the list box.

[g21 of Change a Story or Picture dialog, w/ drive D: showing and a couple of folders, including Tutorial in the list box. Tutorial Folder is highlighted and cursor is on it.]

Double-click on the Tutorial folder in the list box.

The list box now displays the contents of the Tutorial folder, which will be two pictures: Editor-female and Editor-male. Since you chose to change a picture in the Special Edition screen, this dialog box will only display pictures—and only those pictures that are in a format that The Personal Newspaper can import.

Note: You may change pictures in newspapers to almost anything as long as they are in one of the right formats. You can even draw your own pictures with any art or paint program. The Personal Newspaper can import pictures as long as they're in .BMP, .WMF, .CLP, .JPG., .TIF (or TIFF) or PICT (Mac) format. Almost any art or paint program can save files in one of these formats. For more information on picture formats and size limitations, see Hints and Tips later in this manual.

Click on either Editor-female or Editor-male—whichever one you personally identify with.

Click OK.

The CD and your hard drive will whir for a moment, then the Change a Story or Picture dialog will disappear.

The new feature picture will be shown in the Special Edition screen. A little better than the other one?

Now let's change the joke.

Double-click on the joke.

The Change a Story or Picture dialog opens again.

Make sure your CD drive is selected, and the list box shows the contents of the Tutorial directory, as it did when we changed the picture. Notice that since you selected a joke, the dialog only shows the files that can be imported into the joke section.

Note: You may change stories in newspapers to almost anything as long as they are in one of the right formats. You can even write your own stories with any text editor or word processor. The Personal Newspaper can import stories from any programs, as long as they're plain text or .RTF format.

Any text editor, like TeachText or SimpleText on the Mac and Notepad on Windows creates plain text. Most word processors, even the fanciest ones, can save files in text or .RTF format. For more information on story formats and size limitations, see Hints and Tips later in this manual.

Click on "Chicken Joke."

Click OK.

The Change a Story or Picture dialog will disappear and the new joke will be shown in the Special Edition screen.

You've just made a special edition. It's that easy.

Now you get to make a decision. You can …

1. Click the Cancel button if you really like the original picture and joke better.

2. Click the Done button to save your changes, in case you want to print later, or

3. Print the special edition now by clicking the Print Page button, clicking OK in the Print dialog, and then clicking Close on the Special Edition screen.

Once you've decided, and performed one of the above three choices, you can congratulate yourself. You've finished the Tutorial.

Tutorial Summary

Congratulations again! You've finished the tutorial.

You now know all the basics you need to know to use The Personal Newspaper. In the last few minutes, you:

Went to the Reader Department and …

1. Added a new Reader,
2. Printed and filled out a Reader survey form, and
3. Entered the data in an onscreen Reader survey form.

Went to the Editorial Department and …

1. Created a new newspaper, and
2. Filled out the newspaper's profile.

Went to the Print Department and …

1. Previewed your newspaper, and
2. Printed it.

Went back to the Editorial Department and …

1. Created a special edition.

Now you can:

1. Quit the program and call it a day, or
2. Start using the program to create newspapers for the early reader in your home.

For more details on any part of this program, see the reference section of this manual.

And, of course, you may repeat this tutorial any time you feel you need a refresher course.

Now, go forth and publish newspapers! (Or take a break and do it tomorrow.)

Reference

Introduction

Welcome to the complete reference to The Personal Newspaper. This part of the manual explains every screen, window, dialog box and control in The Personal Newspaper, First Grade Edition.

If you haven't already installed the program and performed the tutorial, now is the time. Everything in this reference will be easier to absorb after the tutorial.

The Basics

Program Overview

The Personal Newspaper, First Grade Edition, is a program that prints out a beginning Reader newspaper for every day for a full year.

Personal information about the Reader, including name, birthday, pets' names, friends' names, favorite sports, favorite holidays, etc., will be integrated into the feature story, so every day's paper will be about the Reader.

The words used in the stories are all from published lists of words that kindergartners, first graders and second graders learn. The use of the words is graduated—in the early part of the year, only the simplest words will be used, and as time goes on, the vocabulary expands.

There are five parts to each daily newspaper in this edition:

The Banner—the name of the newspaper, the date and the issue number.

The Feature Story—the main story for the day, customized to be about the Reader.

The Daily Joke—a little humor to make the reading more attractive.

The Date Countdown—a listing of how many days until important events, like birthdays, holidays and the last day of school.

The Cliffhanger—a continuing exciting story that lasts the entire year; each day's installment ends with a cliffhanger that is designed to have the child looking forward to the next day's episode.

[g22 of a sample newspaper. Callouts: Banner, Feature Story, Feature Picture, Joke, Date Countdown and Cliffhanger]

In Personal Newspaper versions for older children, the type size is reduced, stories are lengthened, and more stories are added. For instance, in the Second Grade Edition, there is a daily media review, describing a book, movie or piece of educational software.

The Personal Newspaper can print out newspapers in a number of different styles, ranging from traditional to modern to cute and cuddly. The Reader can pick the style they like—and change it during the year. The name of the newspaper is entirely up to the Reader as well.

The Personal Newspaper can generate custom newspapers for more than one Reader, and more than one newspaper for each Reader. But if you keep adding papers or Readers, there will eventually be some recycling of the content.

You and the Reader are not limited to the included content. You can make special editions for any day of the year with your own jokes, feature stories and pictures.

Above all, The Personal Newspaper is simple to use. There are three basic steps:

1. Fill out an onscreen form with information about the Reader (or Readers).

2. Choose the newspaper name and style.

3. Print—for a day, a week or a whole year at once.

Main Menu Screen

The Main Menu screen is your master control panel for controlling The Personal Newspaper.

[g23 of Main Menu screen]

It consists of three departments, dividing the different tasks into logical groups.

At the bottom of the Main Menu screen are three buttons:

About ... opens a message box that gives the date and version of the program. The message can be scrolled to reveal the complete credits for this product.

Overview gives a basic overview of the program.

Quit ends The Personal Newspaper.

Getting Help

The Personal Newspaper has a lot of built-in help. Each department has a help screen, plus there's the Overview button on the Button bar. All you have to do is ask (well, click).

The Departments

The Personal Newspaper is divided into three departments, each of which helps you carry out specific tasks.

Each department has a name, a graphic, a list of tasks and help. To perform a task, simply click on the task's name.

Reader Department

The Reader Department is where you perform all tasks that involve the Readers—the ones for whom the newspapers are printed.

[g24 of Reader Department. Callouts: Name, Tasks, Help]

The tasks that can be performed in this department are:

Add a New Reader—clicking here lets you establish who will read the newspapers. There can be multiple Readers. But eventually, some of the stories will repeat.

Print a Blank Reader Survey—prints out a copy of all the information you can input about each Reader. You don't have to print it out; you can simply enter the information into the computer. But printing it out lets you take your time and talk it over with the Reader, to make sure you have all the names and preferences correct.

Update a Reader Survey—opens the onscreen Reader survey for entering or modifying the information.

Print an Existing Reader Survey—prints out a Reader survey that you've already filled in, completely or partially. This allows you to look at what you have and decide if you want to change anything.

Delete a Reader—removes a Reader from the Reader list. Deleting a Reader deletes any and all of that Reader's newspapers.

And you can also get help with the Reader Department by clicking on **Reader Department Help.**

Editorial Department

The Editorial Department is where you perform all tasks that involve defining and modifying the actual newspapers.

[g25 of Editorial Department. Callouts: Name, Tasks, Help]

The tasks that can be performed in this department are:

Create a New Newspaper—clicking here lets you establish a new newspaper for one of the Readers. There can be multiple newspapers for each Reader. But eventually, some of the stories will repeat.

Print a Blank Newspaper Profile—prints out a copy of all the information you can input about each newspaper. You don't have to print it out; you can simply enter the information into the computer. But printing it out lets you take your time and talk it over with the Reader, to make sure you have the newspaper name and style correct.

Update a Newspaper Profile—opens the onscreen newspaper profile for entering or modifying the information.

Create a Special Edition—lets you customize individual newspapers by replacing the included pictures and stories with your own.

Delete a Newspaper—removes a newspaper from the newspaper list.

And you can also get help with the Editorial Department by clicking on **Editorial Department Help.**

Print Department

The Print Department is where you preview and print the newspapers.

[g26 of Print Department. Callouts: Name, Tasks, Help]

The tasks that can be performed in this department are:

Preview Newspapers—clicking here lets you view and examine one or more days' newspapers prior to printing.

Print Newspapers—prints out newspapers for the date or dates you want.

And you can also get help with the Print Department by clicking on **Print Department Help.**

Screens and Dialogs

There are four main screens in The Personal Newspaper where you will spend some time and energy. They are described in detail here.

Reader Survey Screen

The Reader Survey screen is where you fill in the personal information about a Reader that The Personal Newspaper incorporates into the feature story. The more information you fill in, and the more personal it is, the more the stories will feel tailor-made for the Reader.

You can access the Reader Survey screen through the Reader Department.

You can print out a complete Reader Survey, spend some time with the Reader to answer all the questions, then enter the information into the computer later. Any information you leave out will be filled in with a default in the stories. You can change information at any time to reflect changes in the Reader and the Reader's friends.

[g27 of Reader Survey screen. Callouts: Text Box, Number Selector, Radio Button, Check Boxes, Scroll Bar]

There are four different ways to fill in blank information in the Reader Survey screen:

Text boxes are the most common, and are used for names and addresses. Just click in a text box and type in the information.

Number selectors are used for dates and some other numbers. Click on the down-arrow to open a submenu of possible answers, then click on the answer you want.

Radio buttons are for selecting either/or choices, like boy or girl, or paper, rock or scissors. No matter how many radio buttons there are, one and only one can be selected at a time. Click on the button next to the answer you want. Anything that was selected before will automatically be unselected.

Check boxes are for selecting items from lists. You may select none, one, many or all of the items in a check-box list. Click in an unchecked check box to check it. Click in a checked check box to uncheck it,

When you are done with the Reader Survey screen, click **OK** to save the changes and close the screen. Click **Cancel** to close the screen without saving the changes.

Newspaper Profile Screen

The Newspaper Profile screen is where you name the newspaper and choose its style.

You can access the Newspaper Profile screen by clicking on **Update a Newspaper Profile** in the Editorial Department, and selecting the newspaper whose profile you want to display in the Choose Newspaper dialog (see below).

You can print out a Newspaper Profile, spend some time with the Reader to answer all the questions, then enter the information into the computer later. Any questions you don't answer yourself will be given default values.

[g28 of Newspaper Profile screen. Callouts: Newspaper Name, Start Date, Style Selections]

This screen asks for only three pieces of information:

Newspaper name is what you want to appear in the banner of the newspaper. Some suggestions are The *Your Name* Life and Times, The Personal Picayune, or anything with your name or home town and one of the following: Times, Chronicle, Examiner, Tattler or any other newspapery-sounding word. Then again, you could call your newspaper Harvey. It's up to you.

Newspaper names are best limited to 24 characters. If you go beyond 24, the banner won't look very nice. But it's up to you.

Start Date lets the program know what day the first newspaper will be printed for. The Personal Newspaper prints out a paper for every day of a year. You have to let it know when to start.

Warning: Don't change the start date once you've started printing newspapers, or you'll get repeated stories right away.

Style is the look of the newspaper. Style won't affect the contents (words or feature pictures), just the type, the borders and other incidental graphics that give the paper the feel that the Reader wants. You can change the style on a daily basis if you want. To get an idea of what each style looks like, print out the first week with a different style every day. (You'll have to do this one day at a time.)

When you are done with the Newspaper Profile screen, click **OK** to save the changes and close the screen. Click **Cancel** to close the screen without saving the changes.

Print Preview Screen

The Print Preview screen lets you see what the newspapers will look like before you print them.

You open the Print Preview screen by clicking on **Preview Newspapers** in the Print Department, and selecting a range of dates to display in the Choose Dates dialog (see below).

[g29 of Print Preview screen. Callouts: Scroll Bars, Control Buttons]

The controls for this screen are mostly along the bottom:

Whole Page displays the entire currently previewed newspaper so the whole thing is visible in the Print Preview screen. This is the default setting.

Full Size enlarges the newspaper to approximately full size. Unless you have a very large monitor, the entire full-size newspaper will not be visible. You can move the newspaper on the screen so you can see it all (though not all at once) by using the scroll bars. You can also click and drag the newspaper itself with the mouse to move it around on the screen.

Previous and **Next** change the displayed newspaper to the previous or next day's paper. This is limited to the range of dates you selected in the Choose Dates dialog when you entered the Print Preview screen. The range of selected dates is displayed at the top of the screen.

Print Page sends the currently previewed newspaper to the printer.

Print Range prints the papers for all the days that were selected in the Choose Dates dialog when you entered the Print Preview screen. The range of selected dates is displayed at the top of the screen.

Close closes the Print Preview screen.

Special Edition Screen

The Special Edition screen lets you replace some of the automatic stories and pictures in newspapers with your own stories and pictures.

You get to the Special Edition screen by clicking on **Create a Special Edition** in the Editorial Department, and selecting a range of dates to display in the Choose Dates dialog (see below).

[g30 of Special Edition screen. Callouts: Scroll Bars, Control Buttons, The Newspaper]

The controls for this screen are mostly along the bottom:

Whole Page displays the entire currently previewed newspaper so the whole thing is visible in the Print Preview screen. This is the default setting.

Full Size enlarges the newspaper to approximately full size. Unless you have a very large monitor, the entire full-size newspaper will not be visible. You can move the newspaper on the screen so you can see it all (though not all at once) by using the scroll bars. You can also click and drag the newspaper itself with the mouse to move it around on the screen.

Previous and **Next** change the displayed newspaper to the previous or next day's paper. This is limited to the range of dates you selected in the Choose Dates dialog when you entered the Special Edition screen. The range of selected dates is displayed at the top of the screen.

Print Page sends the currently previewed newspaper to the printer.

Print Range prints the papers for all the days that were selected in the Choose Dates dialog when you entered the Special Edition screen. The range of selected dates is displayed at the top of the screen.

Cancel closes the Print Preview screen without enacting any of the changes you made.

Done enacts the changes you made and closes the Print Preview screen.

The Newspaper itself is what you modify. Double-click on the feature story, the feature picture or the joke to replace them with your own story, picture or joke. The Change a Story or Picture dialog box will open so you can choose the replacement.

The Banner can only be modified in the Editorial Department by selecting **Update a Newspaper Profile.** The Date Count and Cliffhanger can only be modified in the Reader Survey.

Dialog Boxes

There are various dialog boxes in The Personal Newspaper that will appear and ask you for information. They all work in very similar ways. Here is how to enter information into a dialog:

Text boxes let you type in information like names or addresses. Just click in a text box and type in the information.

Radio buttons let you select either/or choices. No matter how many radio buttons there are, one and only one can be selected at a time. Click on the button next to the answer you want. Anything that was selected before will automatically be unselected.

List boxes let you choose one name or item from a list. Click on the name or item you want to select, then click **OK.** You can also double-click on the name or item in the list and the OK will be taken care of automatically.

Drop-down menus contain all the possible choices. Click on the down-arrow to open the menu, then click on the menu item you want.

All dialog boxes have **Cancel** and **OK** buttons. **OK** accepts your choices or entered information and closes the dialog box. **Cancel** closes the dialog box and ignores your choices or entered information.

Here are the dialog boxes:

[g31 of Add a New Reader dialog. Callouts: Text Boxes]

[g32 of Choose a Reader dialog. Callouts: List Box]

[g33 of Create a New Newspaper dialog. Callouts: List Box]

[g34 of Choose a Newspaper dialog. Callouts: List Box]

[g35 of Choose Dates dialog. Callouts: Text Box, Radio Buttons]

[g36 of Choose a Story dialog. Callouts: Drop-Down Menu, List Box]

[g37 of Choose a Picture dialog. Callouts: Drop-Down Menu, List Box]

Hints and Tips

Standard Formats and Parts of the Newspaper

The Personal Newspaper, First Grade Edition creates newspapers that have each of these:

- Banner—The newspaper's name, date and edition.
- Feature story—the main story of the day, which includes some personal information about the Reader.
- Feature picture—the picture of the day.
- Joke—a little humor.
- Date countdowns—vital information like how many days until the Reader's next birthday, the last day of school or favorite holidays.
- Cliffhanger—a continuing story that lasts the whole year, designed to make the child eager to see each day's paper to find out what happened.

Suggested Lengths of Stories for the Different Parts of the Paper

When you import a picture or story into The Personal Newspaper, it will automatically resize the type or graphic to fit the space. If an imported picture is too large, then it will be shrunk so small that it will be hard to see, and a long story might be displayed in type too small to read—especially for a young Reader.

Here are the recommended maximum and absolute maximum sizes for each part of the newspaper:

Part of Paper	Recommended Size	Maximum Size
Banner	24 characters or less	30 (if you really must)
Feature story	100 words or 500 characters	150 words or 750 characters
Feature picture	300w x 400h pixels	600w x 800h pixels
Joke	25 words or 125 characters	40 words or 200 characters

You cannot enter your *own* cliffhangers or date countdowns. You *can* choose which dates to count down and which cliffhanger you want to read in the Reader Survey.

Adding Pictures

The Personal Newspaper allows you to put your own pictures into the newspapers.

These pictures can come from many sources, including:

- Clip art that comes with many programs you may already own,
- Clip art that is free over the Internet,
- Low-cost clip art—CDs full of pictures that can be bought for very little at your local software store,

- Pictures and drawings that you or your child make with a paint or draw program, and

- Your own family photos.

Scanners—computer peripherals that take a digital picture of your photographs (or almost anything that fits into the scanner) so they can be displayed on a computer and inserted into various programs, including The Personal Newspaper—are priced very low these days. If you don't have or want to buy one, you may know someone, possibly at work, who will lend you theirs, or scan some photos for you. If all else fails, there are services that will scan your photos and put them onto a CD for a nominal charge.

The Personal Newspaper will import and print any computer graphics files as long as they are in one of the following formats:

- .JPG—a standard format for graphics on the Internet,

- .BMP and .WMF—standard formats for Windows-based paint and draw programs,

- .CLP—a standard clip art format,

- PICT—a standard format for Mac-based paint and draw programs, or

- .TIF (or TIFF)—a standard format for both Windows- and Mac-based paint and draw programs.

Adding Stories

The Personal Newspaper allows you to put your own feature stories and jokes into the newspapers.

These stories can come from many sources, including:

- Kids' joke sites on the Internet,

- Other interesting sites on the Internet, including news sites, or

- Any word processor—stories and jokes written by you or your child.

The Personal Newspaper will import and print any text as long as it is in one of the following formats:

.TXT—the basic, plain text that is created from programs like NotePad in Windows or TeachText or SimpleText on the Mac. Most word processors—even the big, fancy ones—can save files in .TXT format.

.RTF (rich text format)—this is a standard format that almost all word processors can read and write. It is often used as an intermediary format for getting text from one program to another.

If you get stories or jokes from the Internet, they may be in another format, usually HTML or .HTM. You may have to paste these files into a program like NotePad or SimpleText, edit out some of the symbols and garbage (formatting information that you don't need for The Personal Newspaper) and save them as texts file before importing them into your newspapers.

Important Warning: Material on the Internet may be copyrighted material. Check carefully before you copy. In most cases, if you are allowed to copy, it is still illegal to use jokes or stories you get from the Internet for other than personal use. No selling newspapers.

Your Hints and Tips

If you find that you've come up with a good idea that saves time or energy with The Personal Newspaper, share it with others on The Personal Newspaper Discussion Group at:

www.untechnicalpress/personalnewspaper/discussion.

Appendices

Appendix 1—Troubleshooting

The Personal Newspaper has been carefully designed and thoroughly tested, so it should present very few, if any, problems or complications.

Just in case, here are some troubleshooting tips:

For problems installing The Personal Newspaper:

- Be sure your computer meets the System Requirements, as stated on the box and at the beginning of this manual.

- Read the installation instructions carefully. You may be skipping a step.

- If AutoPlay doesn't work (nothing happens after you've put in the CD and waited a minute or two), then **open (click on) the Start menu** in the lower-left corner of your screen, and **select Run.** When the Run dialog box opens, **type "D:\setup"** in the little box in the middle, then **click OK.** (D is the usual designation for the CD-ROM drive. If your CD-ROM drive has a different letter, type that one instead of D.)

- Be sure you know the letter designation for your CD-ROM drive.

For problems starting The Personal Newspaper:

- There may or may not be an icon for The Personal Newspaper on your desktop screen. If not, then you must start the program through the Start menu: **open the Start menu (click on it),** then **select Program Files,** then **select Personal Newspaper,** then **select Personal Newspaper again.** It should work.

- If you still can't start The Personal Newspaper, or it is missing from the Start menu, then chances are the program wasn't installed or the installation was somehow interrupted. In this case, go back and install the program again.

For problems using The Personal Newspaper:

- Be sure to click on the Help option for each department for quick reminders of what each task in each department does.

- Many things must be done in a certain order. Read through the tutorial for a good example of how to create a newspaper from step one through printing.

- Beyond the tutorial, there is a lot of useful, helpful information in the reference section of this manual. Take a look through it. Chances are you'll find answers to your questions.

If these tips don't help:

- Look at the Readme file on the Personal Newspaper CD. It is called Readme.txt, and will contain any last-minute information about the program, including troubleshooting tips. The Readme file will be automatically displayed at the end of the installation. You can also see it by **double-clicking on My Computer** (in the upper-left corner of your screen), then **double-clicking on the Personal Newspaper CD,** then **double-clicking on Readme.txt.**

- Look at the UnTechnical Software website Help page. It has all the latest tips and solutions for problems that we found after this manual was printed. The URL for this website is:

  www.untechnicalpress/personalnewspaper/tips

- Look at The Personal Newspaper Discussion Group website. It is where people like you who have discovered useful hints, tips and solutions to problems share their knowledge with others. The URL for this website is:

  www.untechnicalpress/personalnewspaper/discussion

- Contact the UnTechnical Software Tech Support group. You'll find many ways to contact them in Appendix 2.

Appendix 2—Support and Contact Information

[This will be the standard contact page from previous manuals. Insert at layout.]

Appendix 3—For Parents and Teachers

The Personal Newspaper, First Grade Edition was designed and created to encourage reading and to make reading fun. It can be used as a home educational aid, and can also be adapted for classroom use.

You can customize the newspapers to the visual style and types of stories that the Reader wants to see and read. And you can change the styles and stories as the child's interest changes.

The vocabulary in the stories is carefully selected and graduated, to begin with very few words and slowly use more and more throughout the year. By the time the child has read a year's worth of personalized newspapers, they will have been exposed to the majority of recommended words that first graders should know, plus a number of words from the second grade list.

When using The Personal Newspaper with your child or student, get them involved in the process. Let *them* fill out the Reader Survey, even if they need a little help. Let *them* choose the paper's name and visual style. Give the child as much control over the process as possible. Make sure they know it's *their* newspaper.

After only a few weeks of reading the papers generated by the program, encourage the child to create their own stories for their newspapers. For the younger ones, let them dictate to you and you can type them (or write them by hand and type them in later) and enter them into special editions. As the children get a little older, they can write—or type—their own stories, and even take over the control of The Personal Newspaper to make their own special editions.

Their stories can be about anything at all: summer vacations, movies they saw, their favorite games, even fights with siblings. The subject doesn't matter nearly as much as the fact that they're creating a story about their own lives.

Check out our website's education page:

www.untechnicalpress/education

for more ways to get educational value out of The Personal Newspaper, and for availability of teacher's guides for this product.

Above all, educational activities that involve The Personal Newspaper should be fun. Please.

Index

[Note: The Index will be created after the first round of layout.]

Problems and Solutions

Problems that you might run into during this stage—and their solutions—are:

• Things keep changing!

You have to go through the rewrite over and over, changing things, then changing them back, then changing them again.

Welcome to the wonderful world of software. A certain amount of change, even chaos, is an essential part of the creative process. Besides, if all projects ran perfectly smoothly—no bumps, no problems, no last second re-re-rewrites—then you wouldn't have any good war stories to trade with other writers.

Complications and Opportunities

Here are some likely complications for this stage, and opportunities to help, learn or have fun:

• Understanding chaos and the development process.

Depending on the project and the people, chaos can be very bad, or quite OK. The more creative a product is and the more it has to do with entertainment rather than business, the more the development process need a little freedom, even a little chaos. And some people just can't be creative, or *as* creative, in a tightly regimented working environment.

• Learning to live with—but limit—chaos.

The more times you have to go through drafts and testing, and rewrite and re-rewrite, the less organized, managed or planned the project is. The less organized, managed or planned a project is, the more chaotic it is. While, as stated above, some chaos can be good for a project, too much chaos leads to "projects from hell." We all need to experience a horrible project, maybe two, to appreciate a well-run project. But once you've had the experience, you may be able to help limit chaos to manageable levels.

You're in the middle of the process, talking to everyone on the project and analyzing the product and the process in detail. You may not be intentionally or even consciously analyzing the process, but in the course of running from person to person to dig up information you need, you'll be learning almost as much about how and where work is done and who makes decisions (or doesn't make them) as you learn about the product itself.

If you keep your eyes and ears open, you'll likely be able to suggest ways that will simplify the process, especially those that relate to information gathering, communication, writing, testing and editing.

Be sure not to suggest too much regimentation. While it will make your job easier, it won't necessarily work for all projects. Many people in software, especially entertainment software, are in that industry because they don't want or can't handle regimentation.

As a writer—yes, even a technical writer—you are constantly being called upon to use your creativity. Especially as a technical writer, you are required to be creative and meet deadlines, sometimes in a strictly regimented environment. Not everyone can do what you do. Be understanding.

- **Start taking notes for the postmortem.**

It's never too early to start making lists of problems and roadblocks to bring up in the postmortem meeting.

- **Start taking notes for features to add to the next version of the program.**

If a product is successful, chances are that the company will want a version 2. Now is a good time for someone to put together a list of all the features that were dropped because of time or budget, and all the new features that people want to add, but can't.

Make a quick round of the team for suggestions. Use this time to remind them that feature freeze has been enacted (if it has) and while they can't add their wonderful ideas now, they will have the opportunity to get them into the next version.

- **Continue making backups.**

All it takes is one flaky computer.

Stage 7: Detailed Editing—The Line Edit

This chapter covers the line edit. You've fought the good fight, grabbed information from your teammates like a dentist pulling teeth, written and rewritten the manual, possibly many times. You feel pretty good. Fulfilled. You've really accomplished something.

It's time for another humbling experience. No matter how careful you are, if you have a good editor, you'll soon find many red marks all over your pretty manuscript.

The sections are:

- Preparing for the Line Edit
- Selected Sample Edits
- Problems and Solutions
- Complications and Opportunities

Preparing for the Line Edit

Chances are, you'll only have one or two people give your final draft a line edit. Chances are also that others will want to see the final draft, if not to edit, review or comment, but just to see how the manual is progressing.

Ask your editor or writing manager who will be giving the "official" line edit(s), and ask around to find out who else wants a copy. While you'll pay the most attention to the designated line editor(s), don't ignore comments or edits from any other source. The more eyes that see the draft, the more mistakes will be caught.

Preparation of the draft itself was covered in the previous chapter, but double-check with the line editor(s), and double-space their printout if that's their preference. Editors have to examine each and every word, each and every letter and each and every punctuation mark. Be kind to them and give them the final draft in the format they prefer.

You probably won't need a cover letter for the copies that go to the line editors, but you will want one for everyone else. In the cover letter, give the same information as before, but point out that this is a final draft, and reviewers should be mainly concerned with clarity, style and typos. Any major changes in the structure or areas of coverage will cause the project to run late. Of course, if anyone notices errors in the program descriptions, ask them to point them out.

Your draft may include graphics—either in the document itself or printed separately—or it may be totally without graphics. For this example, we'll assume that the editor(s) will have access to the program and won't need your graphics yet. If you do need to supply the graphics for this editing stage on your project, see the next section for a description of preparing graphics.

At this point, depending on the company's work process, you may just hand over the draft to the editor and you're done (except for graphics). At other companies, you'll enter the line editor's edits into your draft and carry on through the layout process.

Selected Sample Edits

Here are two pages that typify the types of edits that a good line editor will make.

A key to proofreaders' marks can be found in the Exhibits section.

Reference

Introduction

Welcome to the complete reference to The Personal Newspaper. This part of the manual explains every screen, window dialog box and control in The Personal Newspaper, First Grade Edition.

If you haven't already installed the program and experienced the tutorial, now is the time. Everything in this reference will be easier to absorb after the tutorial.

#

The Basics

Program Overview

The Personal Newspaper, First Grade Edition, is a program that prints out a beginning Reader newspaper for every day for a full year.

Personal information about the Reader, including name, birthday, pets names, friends' names, favorite sports, favorite holidays, etc., will be integrated into the feature story, so every day's paper will be about the Reader.

tr

The words used in the stories are all from published lists of words that kindergartners, first graders and second graders learn. The use of the words is graduated—in the early part of the year, only the simplest words will be used, and as time goes on, the vocabulary expands.

⊙

There are five parts to each daily newspaper in this edition:

bf   The Banner—the name of the newspaper, the date and the issue number.

The Feature Story—the main story for the day, customized to be about the Reader.

The Daily Joke—a little humor to make the reading more attractive.

The Date Countdown—a listing of how many days until important events, like birthdays, holidays and the last day of school.

ℓ / ¹⁄ₘ   **The Cliffhanger**—a continuing exciting story that lasts the entire year; each day's installment ends with a cliffhanger that is designed to have the child looking forward to the next day's episode.

[g22 of a sample newspaper. Callouts: Banner, Feature Story, Feature Picture, Joke, Date Countdown and Cliffhanger]

In Personal Newspaper versions for older children, the size of the type is reduced, stories are lengthened, and more stories are added. For instance, in the Second Grade

uc   edition, there is a daily media review, describing a book, movie or piece of educational software.

The Personal Newspaper can print out newspapers in a number of different styles, ranging from traditional to modern to cute and cuddly. The Reader can pick the style they like—and change it during the year. The name of the newspaper is entirely up to the Reader as well.

The Personal Newspaper can generate custom newspapers for more than one Reader, and more than one newspaper for each Reader. But if you keep adding papers or   more stet
Readers, there will eventually be some recycling of the content.

You and the Reader are not limited to the included content. You can make special editions for any day of the year with your own jokes, feature stories and pictures.

Above all, The Personal Newspaper is simple to use. There are three basic steps:

1. Fill out an onscreen form with information about the Reader (or Readers).
2. Choose the newspaper name and style.
3. Print—for a day, a week or a whole year at once.

Main Menu Screen

lc   The Main Menu screen is your master control panel for controlling The Personal Newspaper.

[g23 of Main Menu screen]

It consists of three departments, dividing the different tasks into logical groups.

At the bottom of the Main Menu screen are three buttons:

About … opens a message box that gives the date and version of the program. The message can be scrolled to reveal the complete credits for this product.

bf   Overview gives a basic overview of the program.

Quit ends The Personal Newspaper.

Getting Help

The Personal Newspaper has a lot of built in help. Each department has a help screen, plus there's the Overview button on the Button bar. All you have to do is ask (well … click).

Problems and Solutions

Problems that you might run into during this stage—and their solutions—are:

- **There's still no editor.**

Find one. Even if you skipped using a real editor in previous stages, *you need one now.* There are many freelance editors all over the country that will do a good job for an hourly fee. Depending on experience and the part of the country they live in, rates range from $15.00 to $50.00 per hour. A manual the size of this sample would take an experienced editor three or four hours at the most to edit. They won't be fact-checking or comparing it against the program, just editing the words, phrases, punctuation and consistency.

There's no excuse for a company that won't supply the funds for a freelance editor if there isn't someone on staff.

If you can't find one or the company won't pay for it, then find someone on your own. A friend, perhaps another writer you know. Someone.

Of course, it's better to have a staff editor or combination writer/editor so they'll be more familiar with the company's style.

- **There are too many editors.**

Sometimes you'll get comments and corrections from more people than you expect. Look them all over. If anything conflicts with your "main" editor, defer to the professional.

Complications and Opportunities

Here are some likely complications for this stage, and opportunities to help, learn or have fun:

- **Your turn as editor.**

If you have good editing skills, you may be called upon to edit another writer's project. The trick here is to think like an editor, not a writer. It's not your job to rewrite the document or change the writer's style, just correct typos and errors (basic proofreading), identify inconsistencies and point out awkward or unclear passages. It never hurts to take a class or three in editing.

- **People want major changes.**

Usually, by the time you've got your final draft, you've got to rush it through editing and layout and get it into production as quickly as you can.

Even though you've said in the cover letter that this edit is only for grammar, typos, and errors about the actual product, someone is bound to demand major structural changes. And it's usually someone in management that has finally gotten around to looking at the manual, even though you've supplied that person with every draft.

This is a time for diplomacy. No matter how tempted you are to find new uses for the paper shredder, it behooves your career to calmly explain to this person—with witnesses, if possible—that their suggestions are great, and you only wish they had spoken up sooner (like when you gave them the first 17 drafts).

You continue by explaining that the problem is the timing. You'd like to rewrite and incorporate the new suggestions, but that would delay the manual getting to layout by a week, and that could cause the product to miss its shipping date. You then make the offer that if that person will arrange for the company to change its shipping date, you'll make the changes.

Unless your manual really is bad, and would hurt the company's reputation, you'll be leaving that meeting and getting ready for layout.

Stage 8: Preparing the Manual for Layout

This chapter explains and shows how to prepare and organize all your files so they'll be ready to hand over to the graphic artist.

The sections are:

- What You'll Deliver
- Preparing the Final Draft and Style Sheet
- Preparing Graphics
- Problems and Solutions
- Complications and Opportunities

What You'll Deliver

This is what you'll give the graphic artist:

1. The draft in electronic form—cleaned up and in the proper format.

2. The draft, printed—so the graphic artist can see what tables or bullets or numbers may have been lost during the import to the page layout program.

3. Style sheet—a list of all the styles you've included and assigned in the draft.

4. Screenshots in electronic format—in the format that the artist wants.

5. Printouts of the screenshots, with their names or numbers, and callouts for graphic artist reference.

6. Graphics list—a printed list of all the graphics, their names, descriptions, callouts and status.

7. Cover letter and notes.

Preparing the Final Draft and Style Sheet

Technically, your job is the writing, and the graphic artist's job is the formatting. But you can make the artist's life a little easier if you format your document cleanly.

Ideally, you will organize and format your document and styles from the beginning of the project, so little or no cleanup is needed. But in the rush at the end of a project, we often fall back on old habits, and format in the quickest way, even though we or the graphic artist will eventually have to fix it to make the layout go smoothly.

You may just give the draft as is to the graphic artist, but you might want to clean it up a little first.

Warning: if you make *any* changes to your finished draft, be extra careful, work slowly and triple-check everything you do. And save backup copies.

Before you start messing with your draft to prepare it for the graphic artist (if you *do* mess with it), first print it out. You may want to keep a copy for yourself, so print two.

Depending on how much busywork you want to pass on to the graphic artist, you may want to clean up all of the things covered in the following bullet points. If you can't or don't, then list these things in your cover letter or notes.

- Remove extra returns—space between paragraphs and sections helps make a draft readable. But extra returns are a pain for graphic artists. Spacing between paragraphs and sections is (should be) done through spacing assigned to paragraph styles. You won't need to add the spacing into the styles before you hand over the draft. The graphic artist will have to change them anyway for the new layout. The printed copy of the draft—with all the spacing—will give the artist a reference for what space is needed where.

- Remove the table of contents. While necessary for the editing stages, the table of contents most likely won't import into the page layout program, and if it does, it probably won't be able to update to the new pages. Remove it, and let the graphic artist create a fresh one.

- Make sure *everything* is a style. Your notes and warnings that are formatted differently from the body or normal text should be defined as styles, and assigned. Instructions in the tutorial should be a formatted style. Even your bullet points and numbered lists should be defined and assigned as styles. That way the graphic artist can easily redesign the style and change all the bullets or numbers in seconds instead of searching through every line and modifying them one by one.

- Remove all graphics. You may have placed some screenshots into the document for the reviewers and editors. Take them out. The graphic artist will want to batch process all the graphics before placing them into the document.

- There may even be a problem with tables. If your graphic artist's page layout program can't import tables from your word processor, then turn the tables into columns of tab-delimited text. Don't do this unless you know for a fact that the tables won't import. Recreating tables is a lot of work.

If you really want to get on your graphic artist's good side, don't use your word processor's built-in bulleting or numbering. The automatic bullets and numbers are often lost during import. Instead, create a style for bullets and a style for numbers. Assign these styles as needed. If you use these styles often, create a custom toolbar button to make them easier to assign.

It is helpful for the graphic artist if you list and describe the styles you've created. You don't have to actually define the font, the paragraph aspects, etc., just describe what function the style performs.

Here's a sample style sheet for the sample project:

Style Sheet for The Personal Newspaper User Manual

Heading 1—	for chapter names. Include in table of contents.
Heading 2—	for major divisions within the chapters. Include in table of contents.
Heading 3—	for subdivisions within the chapters. Include in table of contents.
Heading 4—	used only in tutorial. Do not include in table of contents.
Instructions—	instructions for readers to follow during tutorial. Need to be big, bold, clear, and easy to read with good spacing above and below.
Normal or Body—	the standard body text.
Normal with Bullet—	body text, indented with bulleted hanging indent.
Normal with Number—	body text, indented with number in hanging indent.
Indent—	indents paragraphs that follow and relate directly to bullet points to match the bullet-point text indent.
Normal Question—	used to emphasize questions that act sort of like low-level headings.
Quote—	body text, italic. Only used once.
Normal Bold—	standard body text set to bold. Used for list headings and a few lines in the installation and troubleshooting sections, and for questions.
Note—	body text, bold and italic, must stand out. Used for important notes and warnings.

One last thing: a cover letter. It doesn't have to be long or fancy. All you need to include in it are delivery and contact information and anything else special that the artist needs to know.

List what you're delivering now, and what else you'll be delivering and when you'll be delivering it. Give your name, phone number and email address so you can be contacted with questions. Mention things like how you use brackets for notes to the artist and calls for graphics.

You can now deliver the electronic draft, printed draft, style sheet and cover letter. This will keep the graphic artist busy for a couple of days while you prepare the graphics. Deliver the printed part in person if you can, and either email the electronic files or deposit them in the designated location on the company net.

Preparing Graphics

Simple software manuals like the sample project only require screenshots for graphics. Some may require graphs and flowcharts that you can do yourself. In some cases, a project may need custom technical drawings. If you do need technical drawings, define them and find someone to create them as soon as you can. You may not have to actually find the artist, but you will have to give the list of drawings and clear descriptions to somebody.

If you wait until you're about to start layout to put together the list, you're in trouble. Luckily for us, this project needs only screenshots.

The first step in preparing graphics is to make your graphics list. Go through the entire final draft and copy all the graphics calls into a new file. It should look something like this:

[g01 of run dialog w/D:\setup typed in]

[g02 of Icon]

[g03 of Main Menu screen, large, with callouts for Departments, Help, button bar]

[g04 of Reader Department. Callouts: Tasks, Help]

[g05 of Add a New Reader dialog]

[g06 of Choose Reader dialog]

[g07 of Reader Survey screen. Callouts: Scroll Arrows, Scroll Bar]

[g08 of Editorial Department. Callouts: Tasks, Help]

[g09 of Create a New Newspaper For: dialog]

[g11 of Newspaper Profile screen]

[g12 of Print Department. Callouts: Tasks, Help]

[g13 of Choose Newspaper dialog]

[g14 of Choose Dates dialog]

[g15 of Print Preview screen. Callouts: Page Size buttons, Scroll Bars, Previous/Next Day buttons, Print button, Close button]

[g16 of Sample Newspaper, with callouts: Feature Story, Feature Picture, Joke, Date Countdown, Cliffhanger]

[g17 of Editorial Department. Callouts: Tasks, Help]

[g18 of Choose Newspaper dialog]

[g19 of Choose Dates dialog]

[g19a of Special Edition screen]

[g20 of Change a Story or Picture dialog, set to drive C:, and showing a couple of folders. Callouts: Drive Selector, List box]

[g21 of Change a Story or Picture dialog, w/ drive D: showing and a couple of folders, including Tutorial in the list box. Tutorial Folder is highlighted and cursor is on it.]

[g22 of a Sample Newspaper. Callouts: Banner, Feature Story, Feature Picture, Joke, Date Countdown and Cliffhanger]

[g23 of Main Menu screen]

[g24 of Reader Department. Callouts: Name, Tasks, Help]

[g25 of Editorial Department. Callouts: Name, Tasks, Help]

[g26 of Print Department. Callouts: Name, Tasks, Help]

[g27 of Reader Survey screen. Callouts: Text Box, Number Selector, Radio Button, Check Boxes, Scroll Bar]

[g28 of Newspaper Profile screen. Callouts: Newspaper Name, Start Date, Style Selections]

[g29 of Print Preview screen. Callouts: Scroll Bars, Control Buttons]

[g30 of Special Edition screen. Callouts: Scroll Bars, Control Buttons, The Newspaper]

[g31 of Add a New Reader dialog. Callouts: Text Boxes]

[g32 of Choose a Reader dialog. Callouts: List Box]

[g33 of Create a New Newspaper dialog. Callouts: List Box]

[g34 of Choose a Newspaper dialog. Callouts: List Box]

[g35 of Choose Dates dialog. Callouts: Text Box, Radio Buttons]

[g36 of Choose a Story dialog. Callouts: Drop-Down Menu, List Box]

[g37 of Choose a Picture dialog. Callouts: Drop-Down Menu, List Box]

Next, unbold the list, then go through it get rid of the opening brackets and the "g"s. Replace the word "of" with a tab, and replace the close brackets with four tabs. On short lists, you can do this by brute force, but on longer lists you'll want to use "find and replace" or a fancy macro.

Next, highlight the whole list and turn it into a table. Add a row on the top with these column titles: Name, Description/Captions/Callouts, Status, Notes, I18N, and GA Use.

Now you've got your list.

Name	Description/Captions/Callouts	Status	Notes	I18N	GA Use
01	Run dialog w/D:\setup typed in				
02	Icon				
03	Main Menu screen, large, with callouts for Departments, Help, button bar				
04	Reader Department. Callouts: Tasks, Help.				
05	Add a New Reader dialog				
06	Choose Reader dialog				
07	Reader Survey screen. Callouts: scroll arrows, scroll bar				
08	Editorial Department. Callouts: Tasks, Help				
09	Create a New Newspaper For: dialog				
10	Graphic Deleted				
11	Newspaper Profile screen				
12	Print Department. Callouts: Tasks, Help				
13	Choose Newspaper dialog				
14	Choose Dates dialog				
15	Print Preview screen. Callouts: Page Size buttons, Scroll Bars, Previous/Next Day buttons, Print button, Close button				
16	Sample Newspaper, with callouts: Feature Story, Feature Picture, Joke, Date Countdown, Cliffhanger				
17	Editorial Department. Callouts: Tasks, Help				
18	Choose Newspaper dialog				
19	Choose Dates dialog				
19a	Special Edition screen				
20	Change a Story or Picture dialog, set to drive C:, and showing a couple of folders. Callouts: Drive Selector, List box				
21	Change a Story or Picture dialog, w/ drive D: showing and a couple of folders, including Tutorial in the list box. Tutorial Folder is highlighted and cursor is on it.				

Name	Description/Captions/Callouts	Status	Notes	I18N	GA Use
22	Sample Newspaper. Callouts: Banner, Feature Story, Feature Picture, Joke, Date Countdown and Cliffhanger				
23	Main Menu screen				
24	Reader Department. Callouts: Name, Tasks, Help				
25	Editorial Department. Callouts: Name, Tasks, Help				
26	Print Department. Callouts: Name, Tasks, Help				
27	Reader Survey screen. Callouts: Text Box, Number Selector, Radio Button, Check Boxes, Scroll Bar				
28	Newspaper Profile screen. Callouts: Newspaper Name, Start Date, Style Selections				
29	Print Preview screen. Callouts: Scroll Bars, Control Buttons				
30	Special Edition screen. Callouts: Scroll Bars, Control Buttons, The Newspaper				
31	Add a New Reader dialog. Callouts: Text Boxes				
32	Choose a Reader dialog. Callouts: List Box				
33	Create a New Newspaper dialog. Callouts: List Box				
34	Choose a Newspaper dialog. Callouts: List Box				
35	Choose Dates dialog. Callouts: Text Box, Radio Buttons				
36	Choose a Story dialog. Callouts: Drop-Down Menu, List Box				
37	Choose a Picture dialog. Callouts: Drop-Down Menu, List Box				

The Name column is self-explanatory.

The Description/Captions/Callouts holds all the information you need to take the shot.

Status is where you mark each graphic either done, FPO (temporary For Position Only) or put a date when it will be ready.

Notes is a place for comments like, "Keep this graphic large, the reader needs to see the detail," or "Try to keep this on the same page as the previous three paragraphs."

I18N is for marking those graphics that have no text and can be used without modification in foreign language versions of the manual.

GA Use is a courtesy—a place for the graphic artist to mark their progress or status.

Print out the list and start taking the screenshots.

Whatever computer you have, it will have a built-in keyboard command to either save the screen to a file or copy it to the clipboard in memory. Either way, you can then paste or load the screen into a paint program for cropping, converting and saving.

There are a number of commercial and shareware products that make taking screenshots, cropping and converting quick and easy. Check a few of them out and pick one you like.

When all your graphics are ready, place them into a document (a word processor document will do), along with their name (number). Add captions and callouts to each graphic that has them. They don't have to be perfect or pretty—that's the graphic artist's job. They just have to be there with lines pointing to the right places so the graphic artist knows what to do.

Once that's all done, deliver the electronic graphics files via network or email, and deliver the graphics list and printouts to the graphic artist, preferably in person. Adding a cover letter listing what you're handing over and where you put the electronic files couldn't hurt.

One last important thing: keep a copy of all of the electronic graphics files. The first thing the graphic artist is likely to do is batch convert all the files to grayscale for printing in the manual. You may need the original color versions for the onscreen help. If you don't keep a copy, you'll be recreating all the graphics from scratch.

Problems and Solutions

Problems that you might run into during this stage—and their solutions—are:

- **You messed up the draft while trying to clean it up.**

Don't mess with your original. Once you have that master all edited, make a backup copy or three and work on cleaning up a copy to hand over to graphic arts. If anything goes wrong, start over with a fresh copy.

Complications and Opportunities

Here are some likely complications for this stage, and opportunities to help, learn or have fun:

- **This may be an opportunity to learn about layout, design and page layout programs.**

If the graphic artist is willing, and it won't prevent you from meeting your next deadline, you may be able to spend a little time sitting with the artist during the design and layout process. Other than doing it yourself, the best way to learn is to watch an expert and ask questions.

- **This may also be an opportunity to play with graphics programs.**

You may be able to get fancy with the graphics. Making flowcharts or other graphics is a nice break from a word processor—if you have the time.

Stage 9: Making It Look Good—Layout and Final Edits

This chapter covers the layout process. You've written the manual. You've prepared the graphics. You've handed everything over to the graphic artist. Your work isn't done.

The sections are:

- The Graphic Artist
- Writers' Contributions to Layout: Editing, Index, Table of Contents
- Final Edits
- Problems and Solutions
- Complications and Opportunities

The Graphic Artist

The design and layout of the manual is the graphic artist's responsibility. Unless the company or product line is new, the artist will most likely be working from an established look-and-feel template, possibly making a few changes here and there to suit the particular product.

If at all possible, the writer should be involved in the whole process. Graphic artists concentrate on the look and feel of the book and the pages. They rarely read any of the text. Since they don't read it, they don't have the context to know if a graphic is the right one for a particular page or if a paragraph is missing.

Also, graphic artists are notoriously bad typists. If you make changes or corrections to a layout draft that consist of more than one or two words, supply the words electronically (pre-spell-checked), so the artist can copy and paste them in. Even if the changes are only one or two words, recheck every correction you ask the graphic artist to make.

You and your manual need graphic artists to finish your job. If you're on good terms with the artists, you'll get better work, and it'll happen faster. If you're on bad terms with the artists, then when you need a rush job to meet your deadline, they'll be taking a long lunch. The best way to get on bad terms with a graphic artist is to call one "the layout person." That word/title "artist" is important to them. Calling a graphic artist a "layout person" is like calling a writer a "typist."

You generally won't be sitting next to the graphic artist the whole time (unless you have the time, want to learn about page layout and the graphic artist is a willing teacher). While the graphic artist makes the first pass through the manual, you'll generally be working on the addendum, Quick-Start guide or onscreen help. But you will want to be available for questions and checking details, and drop in every so often to see how the manual is progressing.

Writers' Contributions to Layout: Editing, Index, Table of Contents

During the layout process, long before a draft has been prepared and sent out for editing, writers should check the following things:

- That the import process didn't lose anything, including tables, bullets and numbers from lists.
- That all the artist's styles make sense for their purpose. (Don't redesign the styles, but make sure the artist knows what function the text serves. It makes more sense for instructions that the customer follows be large, clear, simple and bold than thin and fancy script.)

Once the artist has made a first pass, you'll want to check the following:

- That all lines and paragraphs have been assigned their proper style: heading levels, quote, instruction, etc.
- That all headings are at the right level and in the right place.
- That all the graphics are in the right places and are as clear as possible for a test print.
- That all the captions and callouts are in the right places, and the lines that go from the callout text to a spot on the graphic point to the correct spot on the correct graphic.
- That the table of contents contains all the heading levels that you specified in your style sheet. When the page layout program generates the table of contents, it will include every heading with the selected styles. From there,

you may want to pare it down. Partly because of size constraints, and partly for reader convenience. A chapter may have a lot of heading 3s that really don't need to be in the contents, and another may have some heading 4s that do. It's a matter of what the reader is likely to need or want to find.

At this point, you'll also define the index.

The easiest way to create an index is for the writer to mark up the first rough layout, indicating the words and phrases that you want in the index. A highlighting pen works well for this, and distinguishes the index selection from those red pen corrections. From this draft, the graphic artist creates a first draft of the index, with the tools built into the layout program. The writer then edits this index draft, changing the names of things when it's helpful, grouping similar subjects under new headings, and making capitalization, fonts and font properties consistent.

If the manual is very small—like the sample project—then you may be able to get away with a simple, single-level index. If it's a bit larger, then you can start with a single-level index, then regroup the index points and give them group headings to make a still fairly simple two-level index. If the manual is very large and complex, then you may want to bring in a professional indexer.

Generally, the writer and graphic artist will make a few rounds of corrections before the draft gets sent out for in-house review and editing. As with the drafts, only a few people will actually want to carefully edit it. Most will just want to see it and know that progress is being made.

Before the laid-out manual is distributed for edit and review, check:

- That all notes, questions, calls for graphics, brackets, etc., have been removed from the document.

- That page numbers are continuous, and that any headers and footers give the correct title and chapter names.

- That the table of contents contains everything you want, and only what you want, and that the page references are correct.

- That the index is neat, and all the page references are correct.

- That the text flows properly from page to page, with no paragraphs or parts of paragraphs accidentally hidden.

- That there is a consistent look from page-to-page and chapter-to-chapter.

Here's a hint: when editing laid-out pages, also look at them upside down. Your eyes look for the way things align and lay on the page without getting distracted by the words.

Final Edit(s)

After you've been over the manual a few times, and it seems very wonderful to you, it's time for distribution for review and edit.

Arranging this may be your job or it may be up to the graphic artist. If you're involved, make sure each reviewer's name is on the draft itself, and include the usual cover letter.

Most of the best edits and corrections will come from the "official" editor(s), but check every page of every draft that is returned to you. There's usually a typo or two that get past the editor(s), but is noticed by others.

After the graphic artist inputs all the corrections, check them carefully against the marked up manuscripts.

- Make sure all typed-in words are spelled correctly.
- And make sure that the changes haven't caused any text-flow problems. It's very easy for one additional word to change the flow, misaligning many pages.

Problems and Solutions

Problems that you might run into during this stage—and their solutions—are:

• The product is still changing (arrrrrgggggh).

Ah, yes. The nightmare of software documentation. Somebody has added a new feature or decided to leave one out, and just got around to telling you.

The manual has to accurately describe the product. Talk it over with the producer to decide what to do. You have three choices:

1. Change the manual, if you can do it without missing your deadline.
2. Talk to the producer and see if that change is really necessary. At this point it may be faster and cheaper to change the product instead of the manual.
3. Cover the change in the addendum or Readme (the last resort).

• The layout is moving too slowly.

Sometimes, if there are lots of changes and corrections, the graphic artist can get bogged down. When things take too long, you may be able to sit with the graphic artist and do anything you can to help. This includes organizing the pages with edits, getting the printed corrections from the printer and checking them against the edits, putting together a master copy of all the final corrected pages, and even getting coffee.

Don't smother, and don't become another boss. Be an able assistant. When things bog down, the artist is likely to feel pressure and get into a bad mood. Artists in bad moods work slower and make more mistakes. Try to relieve the pressure any way you can.

Complications and Opportunities

Here are some likely complications for this stage, and opportunities to help, learn or have fun:

- **Great opportunity to learn about page layout.**

If you're sitting with the graphic artist and doing the page-by-page print/edit cycle, you'll pick up some basics of page design. Pay a little attention, and you'll also learn about the page layout program.

- **You may be expected to do the layout, or to input the edits.**

In some instances, especially with outside contractors, the writer may be responsible for the layout. If you know what you're doing, contracting for a finished product can be lucrative. If you don't know what you're doing, you should subcontract someone who does.

Even as an employee, you may be able to—or be expected to—help input the edits into the draft using the page layout program. This speeds up the process, dividing the work between the graphic artist and you. Of course, you have to know how to operate the program. And be sure to install all the fonts used in the manual in your computer, or the pages will all be wrong.

Stage 10: Printing and Final Production

This chapter covers the last stage of producing a manual.

The sections are:

- Final Preparation
- Blueline—The Last Line of Defense
- The Payoff
- Problems and Solutions
- Complications and Opportunities

Final Preparation

At this point, the graphic artist gathers up all the electronic files from the page layout program, plus all the processed graphics, and fills out a form that lists the program used, all the fonts needed, and any other special information that the printer needs, and hands it off to the manufacturing person on the project (if there is one), or gives it directly to the printer.

Blueline—The Last Line of Defense

These days there is no Linotronic printout stage—printers go directly from electronic files to film. This takes a few days. Ideally, although many people skip this stage, the printer will make a blueline print from the film, and submit it back to you to check.

The blueline should be checked very carefully for:

- Overall look,
- Missing parts of letters,
- Spots on parts of pages where there shouldn't be any,
- Pagination,
- Clear graphics, and
- Correct text flow from page-to-page.

If you find any other problems with the manual at this point, you're in trouble. If you did your job well, and edited carefully, there shouldn't be anything more than a few spots for the printer to clean up on the film negative.

The Payoff

The next time you see the manual, two to six weeks later, it will be printed and bound with your name on it somewhere (hopefully). See the finished sample manual in the Exhibits section.

Take a moment and admire your work. If you're into collecting mementos, grab a copy and ask everyone who worked on it with you to sign the title page.

Now get back to work.

Problems and Solutions

Problems that you might run into during this stage—and their solutions—are:

• **Somebody requests a major change at the blueline stage.**

It happens. Your best tactic at this point is to laugh loud and long, pretending and hoping that it's a joke. If you laugh loud enough, you might even convince the person you're laughing with (or at) that they meant it as a joke all along. Even if they didn't.

If that doesn't work, remind yourself that violence is probably against company policy, and that maiming a manager is a good way to forfeit a large percentage of your year-end bonus.

Seriously though, if there really is a problem, if the manual really can't ship in its current state, then it's back to rewriting and re-laying out. If this happens, the company has lost a lot of time and money. Printers don't make negatives for free. You might also have lost your time slot for printing and lose more time. Somebody's head will—and should—roll.

• **You want or need to update the manual, but they printed a year's supply to get a good price.**

Make the changes to the manual and the addendum if there is one, and have it ready for the next printing. It's up to the producer to decide when to incorporate the new material into the shipping product.

Complications and Opportunities

Here are some likely complications for this stage, and opportunities to help, learn or have fun:

• **Your main opportunity here is to relax.**

If you took care of the addendum or Quick-Start guide and the onscreen help while the manual was printing, you may be just about done with the project. You'll be coming off of a major multi-week crunch, and slowing down a little will help you prepare for the postmortem—and maybe a well-earned break.

Stage 11: Producing the Addendum or Quick-Start Guide

This chapter covers the production of an addendum or Quick-Start guide. The Personal Newspaper doesn't have an addendum, but since many projects do, it will be covered briefly here.

The sections are:

- A Project in Miniature
- Problems and Solutions
- Complications and Opportunities

A Project in Miniature

An addendum or Quick-Start guide is handled much the same as a manual, except each stage is much smaller and finished much more quickly. The stages you will go through are:

1. Research
2. Outline
3. Structural Edit
4. Writing
5. Content Edit and Test
6. Rewrite
7. Line Edit
8. Prepare for Layout
9. Layout and Final Edits
10. Production (w/blueline)

If you can get fast turnaround from editors and reviewers, the whole process from beginning up to layout can be a week or less. Layout can take from two days to a week or more, depending on the graphic artist, the editing turnaround and how much design is involved. (If it's not a new line of products, a template will be available and will speed things up considerably.)

Typical contents of the addendum or Quick-Start guide are discussed in detail earlier in this book, plus a checklist can be found in the Exhibits section.

Problems and Solutions

Problems that you might run into during this stage—and their solutions—are:

- **The addendum or Quick-Start guide is really long.**

If the addendum or Quick-Start guide gets to be more than 24 pages or so, you might as well put that information into the manual. It saves money in printing and in assembly.

Long Quick-Start guides or addenda are not very useful for readers. They're no different from having the information split between two manuals. Beyond that, they are very inelegant, and are a sign that the company (or the writer) isn't really in control of the product.

Ideally, if you have to make a long addendum for the initial shipping, you'll be able to move most of the corrections into the manual for the second shipping.

Complications and Opportunities

Here are some likely complications for this stage, and opportunities to help, learn or have fun:

- **The addendum has to cover multiple computer platforms.**

This is typical, as it allows multiple versions of a program to be manufactured, distributed and sold in a single package. It saves time, money, shipping and storage costs.

Just keep it well-organized, with a good table of contents that directs the reader to the right computer platform. Keep is as simple and small as you can.

- **Someone wants to get fancy.**

One way companies handle two-platform addenda (or even manuals) is to have two separate documents bound back-to-back and upside down. If you open one side, it's the document for one platform. If you turn it over, it's the document for the other platform.

This relieves the reader of the necessity of paging through information on a platform they don't have, but can be expensive. Much of the information in the documents will be the same for both platforms, and you'll have to print (and pay for) a lot of duplication.

Stage 12: Producing Onscreen Help

This chapter covers the writer's job in preparing onscreen help. These days, onscreen or online help is almost a required part of any software product. Even if people never use it.

The sections are:

- A Little Background
- Timing
- Extra Reading
- Writing for the Screen
- Onscreen Help for The Personal Newspaper
- Problems and Solutions
- Complications and Opportunities

A Little Background

More and more, software companies depend on onscreen and online help to enhance or replace printed documentation.

In many ways it's a wonderful thing.

- It's always there; you don't have to search through (or store) shelves full of manuals.
- You can use the computer to search the whole text for words or phrases, so you don't have to depend on the author to include everything you want to look up in the index.
- It can be updated for accuracy on a daily basis without throwing out old versions of the manual and printing new ones.

But, in other ways, it isn't so wonderful.

- It is very hard for many people to read a lot of text on their computer screens.
- Many onscreen help systems are badly written, badly organized, and useless.
- It ties the reader to their computer and the reader's hand to the mouse or keyboard. (You can't take the manual with you to the beach for some fun summer reading.)

- Printed docs, especially tutorials, can be set next to the screen and readers can quickly move their eyes between book and screen. But when the instructions are on the screen, they will often obscure the part of the program they are describing.

- Many customers don't like, don't understand, and even fear onscreen help systems.

If only for financial reasons—the cost of paper has been rising in cost almost as much as computer hardware has been falling—onscreen documentation, manuals and help systems are the future. To make them truly useful, help systems must be written, organized and presented well, and computer displays have to continue to improve in resolution and readability.

Timing

If the help system is a supplement to the manual, you'll want to begin work on it while the manual is in the earliest stages of layout. If the help system covers more ground than the manual—or replaces it—then you've got to start a lot sooner.

This timing works well because it's easiest to wait until all the manual writing is done. You'll finish in the weeks after layout, while the printer is producing the manuals.

Extra Reading

Both Windows and Macintosh have extensive, flexible, powerful ways to create and present help, and integrate it into programs. And there are many tools, commercial and shareware, to let non-programmers create and debug systems.

Designing, creating and testing onscreen documentation is the subject for another book An explanation of all the tools is another half-dozen books.

Writing for the Screen

Writing text for onscreen reading is slightly different from writing for print. Because it's harder for many people to read from a screen, you should keep onscreen text short, to the point, and heavy on step-by-step procedures, as opposed to background explanations. Because screens are lower resolution than printing presses, text on a screen has to be larger than text in print to be equally readable.

Since scrolling is a hassle for many readers, and if you scroll to see the bottom of the text, you may lose the graphic on top, try to write in screen-size chunks. Work with whoever is laying out the pages for onscreen reading so each screen page mostly or completely fits on an average screen without much scrolling.

Onscreen Help for The Personal Newspaper

The help system for The Personal Newspaper doesn't use (or need) the standard Windows or Macintosh help systems. It consists of a series of single-screen bitmap graphics, text included.

The screens needed are:

- Product Overview,
- The About Screen with Credits,
- Reader Department Help,
- Editorial Department Help, and
- Print Department Help.

To make them, it is basically a matter of slightly (if at all) editing down the manual sections on these subjects so they'll fit on a screen along with a graphic, calling out the graphic, and handing it over to a computer artist on the development team.

Problems and Solutions

Problems that you might run into during this stage—and their solutions—are:

- **Difficulty cutting the text down to one screen.**

Add a second screen for that topic. Put a "More" button on the first screen to reach it.

- **Last-minute decisions to add more help screens.**

For this program, within this system, it's not really a problem. You can turn around a screen's worth of wisdom on any subject within this program in 15 minutes. For other projects, adding more help screens at the last minute may or may not be a problem. Generally, with a custom help system (as opposed to the standard Windows or Mac systems) it's more of a problem for the programmers than for the writers.

• **Last-minute decision to change the system to the standard Windows help system.**

This can be a problem, depending on the time allowed, your ability to create a Windows help system, and the availability of someone to help.

For this simple program, it doesn't make sense to bother with a fancy help system. But these last-minute changes do happen. The more you know, the easier these surprises are to handle.

Complications and Opportunities

Here are some likely complications for this stage, and opportunities to help, learn or have fun:

• **Thinking ahead.**

If you think the company may eventually turn this program into a budget-line product, or might want to bundle it with educational computer systems, then it'll need an onscreen manual. If you have the time, this is a good opportunity to learn how to create a help system (or other onscreen manual system) with a real project. Turn the full manual into an electronic, onscreen manual.

Stage 13: Writing the Readme

This chapter covers the Readme file. The Readme (a.k.a. README, a.k.a. read.me, a.k.a. readme.txt) is a long-standing tradition in software development.

The sections are:

- The Last Word
- Writing the Readme
- The Personal Newspaper Readme
- Problems and Solutions
- Complications and Opportunities

The Last Word

In the olden days, the Readme file served as the complete documentation, and on some shareware, still does. Today, it's generally used as a cheap way to include last-minute information—the inevitable information that becomes known after the manuals and addenda are printed.

There may be errors in the manual and/or changes in the program that should be pointed out. With many programs, there will be troubleshooting tips, or hardware or software incompatibilities that you won't know about until the program has been released and tried on thousands of machines with different combinations of motherboards, graphics cards and other hardware and software variables.

The Readme file is useful—the information needs to be somewhere. The problem with it is that computer novices don't know to look for it. Make sure the customer knows it exists and how to find it. Refer to it in the manual and/or Quick-Start guide.

Readme files are easy—simple text, no formatting, no testing. They go on the disk uncompressed. They are readable by almost any computer.

They are also cheaper to update than a manual or addendum. Since disks can be pressed in high volume in a short time, they aren't usually manufactured in huge quantities ahead of time and stored. They're generally made when they're needed. You won't have to throw out obsolete versions when you update.

It's sometimes better to add a one-page piece of paper to the box than put information into a Readme. It's easier for the customer to find and use, but more expensive to manufacture.

Writing the Readme

Traditionally, programmers or producers put the Readme file together, incorporating notes from testers. But, if you can, at least give it a once-over (rewrite and edit) to make sure that your customers will understand everything. It wouldn't hurt for you to take charge of it, and gather, compile and edit all the information, then write it. Be sure to send it around for a quick content check.

Keep these files short. Don't use one for an addendum. Only for an addendum to the addendum.

Having the words "Read" and "me" in the name of the file is traditional, but not absolutely necessary. Now that you can use longer file names, feel free to use names that will make more sense to the customer, such as "Last-Minute Info.txt."

Always start a Readme by identifying the program and stating the function of the file. It also never hurts to have a date in the file, so both you and the customer know how up-to-date it is.

Below is a sample Readme file for The Personal Newspaper. It was intentionally kept as short as possible, but you may want to add more to yours. Possible additional sections include Technical Tips and Contact Information.

The Sample Project's Readme

THE PERSONAL NEWSPAPER

LAST-MINUTE INFO 1-1-2001

This file contains helpful information about installing and using The Personal Newspaper, First Grade Edition, that became available after the manual was printed.

CONTENTS

I.   Installation Tips

II.   Printing Tips

III.   New Program Features

I. INSTALLATION TIPS

Tip 1: We have found that some people have trouble installing The Personal Newspaper while other programs are running. This is because The Personal Newspaper's installer needs a lot of memory. Close or Quit all other programs before installing, and you shouldn't have any problems.

Tip 2: While installing, think carefully about whether you want the minimum installation or the full installation. Minimum installation takes up much less disk space, but runs a little slower and requires you to have The Personal Newspaper CD in the CD-ROM drive whenever you run the program. Full installation doesn't require the CD and runs faster, but takes up a lot more room on your hard disk. See The Personal Newspaper Editor-In-Chief's Guide for more details.

II. PRINTING TIPS

If you have problems printing, first make sure that your printer is plugged into the wall, connected to your computer, filled with paper and turned on. If it still won't print, chances are you installed The Personal Newspaper with the minimum installation—it won't print unless The Personal Newspaper CD is in your CD-ROM drive. Put the CD in, and your printing problems should be solved.

III. NEW PROGRAM FEATURES

The Personal Newspaper now imports an additional graphics format. You can now use Encapsulated PostScript (.EPS) graphics in your special editions.

Problems and Solutions

Problems that you might run into during this stage—and their solutions—are:

• **You want to add some nice formatting to the Readme file.**

Traditionally, Readme files are simple text. If they're short enough, they won't need any formatting, other than using caps for headings. You can't go wrong with plain text, since every computer can read it and display it with a utility that comes with every operating system, like Notepad or TeachText. If you want or need to do a little extra formatting to bring out headings, you can use Write or WordPad for Windows and SimpleText for Mac, but be sure to stay with fonts that come with the computer. Don't count on customers having a particular word processor, or even Acrobat.

• **You've been given enough information for the Readme to fill a manual.**

Leave out things that are covered in the manual or in the help system. If there's still a lot, you may not have been complete enough in your writing—or the program was still in poor shape when you finished. Move sections to the help system, if you can. If a lot of the information is general technical information that isn't program-specific, then put it into a separate technical Readme file that can be included with other programs as well. Be sure to refer to all Readme files in the manual and/or addendum.

Complications and Opportunities

Here are some likely complications for this stage, and opportunities to help, learn or have fun:

• **You can put much of the Readme info into the help file.**

It is actually better to add as much last-second information as you can to the help file. Make it easy on yourself, or whoever will be adding the information in subsequent updates, and put in a heading with links to the various areas traditionally covered in the Readme (hints, corrections, new features, troubleshooting), even if you have nothing to say at the time. When it needs to be added, all anyone has to do is paste in the text and recompile. With no new links, there should be very little testing needed for the new version.

Of course, if the customer can't install the program, they'll have trouble accessing the help file, so a Readme may still be necessary.

Stage 14: Cleaning Up— The Project Backup

This chapter covers the cleanup process. The manual, and possibly an addendum are done and printed. The help system is finished and tested, the Readme file is done. But your job isn't. What follows is one of the most boring parts of the project, but it doesn't last very long.

The sections are:

- Backup
- Problems and Solutions
- Complications and Opportunities

Backup

You should make a backup copy of everything you generated or were involved with. You may be called upon to update the docs in the future. The better you've prepared your material, the easier it will be.

Some people like to keep copies of everything both electronically and in print, filling a notebook with paper and disks for each project. Others just keep electronic copies.

You want to keep a copy of everything that will help you—or someone else— come in and update or modify everything with the least amount of time and trouble.

You should include:

- Final text before layout for manual and addendum or Quick-Start guide
- All the graphics from the docs, screenshots you took and other graphics you had others generate
- Graphics list
- Help system text
- Interim help system files (formatted text that is ready to be compiled into a help system)
- Finished help system

- List of tools used for generating the help (so the next person will be able to recreate your environment)
- Readme file text

• **Any other documents, requests, forms, etc., that you created or used during the project.**

If the graphic artist doesn't keep a good copy of the page layout files, ask for and include those with your backup. Don't forget to get copies of all the modified graphics and a list of the fonts, programs and tools the graphic artist used.

Once you have everything gathered, make a couple or three copies. One for you to hang onto, one for either the writing manager or producer, and one to go into offsite storage. (Many companies keep backup copies of all vital data offsite in a fireproof vault, in cast there's a fire or flood at the office.)

Small projects, like The Personal Newspaper will fit onto a single 100MB Zip disk. Most projects will fit onto a CD, which hold six times as much and costs about a tenth as much as a Zip disk. Any software company will either have a CD writer that you can use, or someone to write CDs for you.

Problems and Solutions

Problems that you might run into during this stage—and their solutions—are:

• **Time**

Either you're an employee with pressure to move on to the next project, or you're a contractor with pressure to get out and stop charging. Either way, you may have to explain the advantages—in terms of money savings—of preparing this project backup.

Complications and Opportunities

Here are some likely complications for this stage, and opportunities to help, learn or have fun:

• **Opportunity to establish a project backup tradition.**

If your company doesn't normally keep backups of the docs, it's time to start.

Stage 15: Looking Back— The Postmortem: Lessons Learned

This chapter covers the postmortem process. It's time to look back—hopefully fondly—on the project with 20-20 hindsight.

The sections are:

- The Postmortem
- Problems and Solutions
- Complications and Opportunities

The Postmortem

A postmortem is a look back at a project to identify what went right—things to do again on the next project—and what went wrong—things to avoid on the next project.

Postmortems can be as informal as a short meeting—or an evening at the local bar. They can also be very formal, with multi-hundred-page reports generated and distributed to management and other project teams.

Whether you're required to or not, it's worth your while to think over your part of the project you just finished.

- How long did it take?
- How long should it have taken?
- What were the barriers that stopped you or slowed you down?
- What were the events or tools that really helped you get your job done?
- Who on the team was helpful?
- Who off the team helped?
- How much time did you spend just waiting for information?
- What can you change to make the next project better or faster?

- How was communication, in general, on the team?
- How might you use your writing skills to improve the communication?
- Any other comments, events or incidents you want people to know or think about?

Problems and Solutions

Problems that you might run into during this stage—and their solutions—are:

- **The company doesn't have a tradition of postmortems.**

Start it. You may not be able to convince the company to change its ways instantly, but you probably could convince the producer to have a short team meeting to talk it all over. At worst you could bring up the subject at the traditional post-project blow-out party, and get a few people talking about what went right and wrong and what to do about it next time.

Complications and Opportunities

Here are some likely complications for this stage, and opportunities to help, learn or have fun:

- **Track yourself.**

Keep your own records on each project you work on. Track how long it took you, what problems you had, what skills you lacked, what tools you needed. After a few projects, you'll be in a better position to make time estimates on new projects, and be able to ask for the time and tools you'll need up front.

The End

Congratulations. You've waded through the grueling process of creating a software manual. The finished product can be found in the Exhibits section below.

There is a lot information in this book, with many variations and complications to cover as many types of projects and working situations as possible. If you feel overwhelmed by data overload, don't worry. After you work on a project or three, and have a framework of personal experience to build on, all the information in this book will fall into place.

I've covered a lot in this book—too much according to some—but if you feel I missed something, let me know. If you face other situations, complications and opportunities during your writing experiences, and would like to share them with others in future updates of this book, please pass them on. Contact information can be found in the Appendices.

A few last words on writing in the technical world:

Writing something you can be proud of is one of the great joys of life, yet writing a good manual is one of the most under-appreciated tasks you can take on. But don't despair. Whether they realize it or not, your readers' lives are made a little better, a little easier, a little less complicated because of your work. And sometimes they do realize it. And the feeling you get from someone telling you your manual was helpful or useful or wonderful is just as good as being told your novel was riveting or your screenplay was really scary.

Today's fast-paced, ever-more-technical world needs more and better human-to-human communication. It needs writers who can simplify and humanize technology. I salute you, and wish you well.

Part 3

Exhibits

The sections are:

- New Employee/Onsite Contractor Checklist

- Parts of the Manual Checklist

- Quick-Start Guide (or Addendum) Checklist

- Key to Proofreaders' Marks

- Preparing a Draft for Layout Information Sheet

- About the Sample Project Documentation

- Sample Project Proposal

- Sample Project Initial Design Document

- The Finished Sample Project Manual

This section contains sample documents, forms and checklists that are useful for almost any project, along with the sample project documentation.

New Employee/Onsite Contractor Checklist

When you start a new job or move to a new project, you'll need a bit of information and a pile of supplies before you can get started. This checklist will help you get organized.

Basics

❏ Desk

❏ Chair

❏ Paper, pens, pencils

❏ Stapler

❏ Paper clips

❏ Whiteboard, w/markers and eraser

Computer and Software

❏ Computer

Type: _____

Other specs: _____

_____

❏ Printer access (and location)

Software

❏ Word Processor

❏ Spreadsheet

❏ Other:

❏ Other:

❏ Email account

❏ Network organization

People

❏ To whom do you report?

❏ Name and number and email

❏ Peer support (someone with a similar job that's been there a while who can answer questions)

Job-specific Items for a Writer

❏ Dictionary

❏ Other reference books

❏ Company style guide

❏ Screen capture and graphic-editing software

Project-specific Items

❏ Team member contact list

❏ Project-specific network locations

❏ Customer analysis from marketing

❏ Project documentation (or location)

Parts of the Manual Checklists

Here are reminder checklists to make sure you include or knowingly exclude each part of the manual.

Front Matter

- ❏ Title Page
  - ❏ Manual and program title
  - ❏ Manual author's name
  - ❏ Software designers' or producers' names
  - ❏ Publisher name
- ❏ License
  - ❏ Software license agreement
  - ❏ Copyright for manual and software
  - ❏ Publisher contact information

- ❏ Trademark declarations
- ❏ ISBN number
- ❏ Credits (may appear as appendix)
  - ❏ Software credits
  - ❏ Manual credits
  - ❏ Thanks and special thanks
- ❏ Table of Contents
- ❏ Acknowledgements, dedications

Introduction

- ❏ Welcome
- ❏ Product description
  - ❏ What it does
  - ❏ Package contents
  - ❏ Prerequisites, hardware, software and knowledge
  - ❏ How product fits into product line, customer's working style, etc.

- ❏ Description of manual and its organization
- ❏ Installation and startup directions
  - ❏ Full installation and startup
  - ❏ Reference to separate installation card or booklet
- ❏ Plea to fill out registration card

Tutorial

- ❏ Tutorial introduction
  - ❏ Welcome
  - ❏ Explain contents and structure
  - ❏ Point out instruction text
  - ❏ Notify graphic artist re: instruction text
  - ❏ Tone
  - ❏ Short (avg. reading time:_____)
- ❏ Lesson introduction (if tutorial is broken up into more than one lesson)
  - ❏ Explain lesson contents
  - ❏ Make sure computer is ready
- ❏ Main body of tutorial (or lesson if tutorial is broken up into more than one lesson)
  - ❏ Make sure computer and files are ready
  - ❏ Instructions marked for different typestyle

- ❏ Instruction steps numbered
- ❏ Triple-tell format
- ❏ Enough graphics
- ❏ Enough series graphics
- ❏ File saved at end of each lesson
- ❏ Tutorial (or lesson) can be completed in 20 minutes or less
- ❏ Lesson summary (if tutorial is broken up into more than one lesson)
  - ❏ Summarize lesson content
  - ❏ Invite to next lesson, allow quitting
- ❏ Tutorial summary
  - ❏ Congratulate
  - ❏ Summarize whole tutorial
  - ❏ Invite to use program
  - ❏ Tell where and how to get help
  - ❏ Tell that they can repeat the tutorial later
- ❏ Other

Reference

- ❏ Introduction
- ❏ Functional overview
- ❏ Detailed mode description
- ❏ Detailed menu description
- ❏ Detailed toolbar description

- ❏ Detailed window and dialog description
- ❏ Detailed control description

Additional Information

- ❑ Technical background
- ❑ Technical inner-workings explanation
- ❑ Hints and tips for use

- ❑ Strategies
- ❑ Educational background material
- ❑ Historical material

Back Matter

- ❑ Appendices
- ❑ Lists and resources
- ❑ Bibliographies
- ❑ Troubleshooting tips
- ❑ Help with operating system and operating system extensions
- ❑ Company and support contact information
- ❑ Detailed technical specs, or technical theory of operation (for hardcore audience only)

- ❑ Data file formats
- ❑ Frequently Asked Questions
- ❑ Command summaries, keyboard shortcuts
- ❑ Charts of related information
- ❑ Credits
- ❑ Glossary
- ❑ Index

Quick-Start Guide (or Addendum) Checklist

- ❑ Welcome
- ❑ System requirements
- ❑ Program installation instructions
- ❑ Program starting instructions
- ❑ Where to get more information

- ❑ Where to get help
- ❑ Machine-specific file loading and saving
- ❑ Reference charts
- ❑ Corrections or additions to the manual

Key to Proofreaders' Marks

Delete and Insert

Mark	Example
ℓ	Delete, take out
	Delete and close up
l/s	LETTER SP A CE
#	Insert space(more space)
□	Em quad space or indention
stet	Let it stand (all ~~matter~~ above dots)

Punctuation Marks

Mark	Meaning
⊙	Period
^,	Comma
⊙;	Semicolon
\\“/	Open quotes
\\”/	Close quotes
?/	Question mark
!/	Exclamation point
=	Hyphen
(/)	Parenthesis
:/	Colon
\\’/	Apostrophe

Style of Type

Mark	Example
wf	Wrong **style of type**
lc	Set in LOWERCASE or ~~LOWERCASE~~
lc + caps	Lower case with Initial Caps
sc	SET IN small capitals
rom	Set in roman type
ital	*Set in* italic *type*
lf	Set in lightface type
bf	Set in boldface type
uc or caps	SET IN capital letters

Spacing

Example	Mark
Close up en tirely; take out space	⊂
Less space between words	◡
Insertspace	#

Paragraphing and Positions

Example	Mark
Center	] [
] Move to right	]
[Move to left	[
Lower (letter or words)	⊔
Raise (letter or words)	⊓
Align horizontally	=
Align vertically	||
Begin a paragraph	¶
No paragraph	no ¶
Run in	run in
flush ¶ |← No paragraphs indentation	
Transpose lettesr in a word	tr
Transpose enclosed in circle matter	tr

Miscellaneous

Example	Mark
Broken type	X
Invert (upside-down type)	⌒/
Push down|space	↓
Spell out Pres. Bremer	ⓢⓟ
OK “with corrections”	ok w/c
or “as corrected”	ok a/c
Insert (caret)	∧
Em (long dash)	1/m
En (short) dash	1/n

Preparing a Draft for Layout Information Sheet

This combination worksheet and checklist is for your own use, to help you gather the information you'll need to prepare your draft for hand-off to graphic arts.

Info for You

Document Name: _____ Draft#: _____ Due Date: _____

Deliver electronic versions to: _____

Email: _____ Phone/Ext.: _____

Location on Net: _____

Deliver printed versions to: _____

Location: _____

Electronic Format for text:

       ❏ Mac   ❏ PC

       ❏ Word Processor (_____)   ❏ .RTF   ❏ SimpleText   ❏ Other _____

       ❏ Styles/headings assigned   ❏ Styles/heading marked in text [H1]

Electronic Graphics Format(s)

❏ TIF   ❏ PICT   ❏ PCX   ❏ JPG   ❏ BMP   ❏ WMF   ❏ Other _____

Info for Graphic Artist

Draft Contains:

       ❏ Number of Tables_____   ❏ Number of Graphics_____

       ❏ Other _____

               Printed Draft Number of Pages _____

               Printed Graphics Number of Pages _____

Info from Graphic Artist

Estimated date/time for pre-edit edit _____

Checklist

Printed Draft

       ❏   Page numbers

Printed Graphics

       ❏   Page numbers

       ❏   Graphics named, marked up for callouts and captions

Other Printed Material

       ❏   Cover letter/notes

       ❏   Style definitions

       ❏   Graphics list

Electronic Graphics

       ❏   Backed up

           Location _____

About the Sample Project Documentation

Here are the two source documents for the sample project, plus the finished manual.

Notice the differences in the product from the beginning (the proposal) to the Initial Design Document. And the differences between the design doc and the final manual.

Part of the change is a result of thinking about the concept and fleshing out the ideas.

Part of it is because of the writing process. (When you write a manual for a product, and define every button and every step and every process, you're bound to find areas that need simplification and improvement.)

Part of it is from having typical customers actually use the product, following the instructions in the manual, and letting you know what they think.

Part of it is just because a fresh set of eyes (or two or seven) are taking a look at it, and noticing awkward things that the original team members don't notice any more.

Proposal Notes

The proposal is a typical five-page or less software product proposal. Some companies prefer them to be no more than two pages. Other companies don't want them at all.

The headings and topics covered are standard. The people reading and evaluating the proposal need to know what the product is, who it's for, how hard it's going to be to develop, how long it will take, what the market is, what the competition is, etc. If you can encapsulate all that in very few pages—a writing feat—and it makes business sense for the company, you've got a good chance of having your concept considered.

Design Document Notes

This document—what there is of it—is approximately at the level of detail of an Initial Design Document. Sometimes called a script, it serves the same purpose as a script in a movie. It describes what the audience will see, hear and experience. It is usually written by the program's designer, producer or project manager.

This is only a partial design doc. It only includes the parts of an actual document that directly apply to the purposes of this book, and those are admittedly sparse.

An actual Initial Design Doc might also contain any or all of the following:

- Far better artwork,
- Sample output,
- Market analysis,
- Cost-of-goods analysis,
- Break-even calculations,
- Sales projections,
- Company-specific information on how the product fits the product line and complements other products, and
- Almost anything that the management team wants to see and hear.

It might be presented through a full-blown presentation at a management meeting. After all, the goal of this document is as much to get the project approved and funded as it is to actually design the product—maybe more so.

While a few of the technical details are mentioned here, if only to bring them up as warnings, the majority of the technical methods and details used to implement the script are written by the lead engineer in the technical design document.

In theory, extensive prototypes would be made based on this document—and its corresponding initial Technical Design Document—then extensively tested. This testing leads to a rethinking, refining and redesign. After that, another more detailed design document would be created, and the final product would be built based on it. Of course there should be more testing and refinement, but hopefully the second round of the document would be 70–90% accurate.

In practice, many development teams skip the Detailed Design Document. Sometimes this causes problems, sometimes it doesn't. In the case of The Personal Newspaper, a very simple program that doesn't break new conceptual or technical ground, another round of design docs probably would have helped, but might not have sped up the process. The manual itself served the purpose of testing and refining the design.

Note the differences in the product between the design doc and the first manual draft, as well as the differences between the first and final manual drafts. It's all part of the development process.

Manual Notes

This is the final sample manual, all laid out and looking pretty. It took around three rounds of edits between the author and the graphic artist, then another two rounds with a fresh editor.

It would theoretically be printed at around 8.5 x 5.5 inches, but has been reduced in size here to save a few trees.

No manual is ever perfect, and this one is no exception. Looking at it, you will no doubt find areas that need work, additional explanations that should be added, and possibly even a typo or two.

Part of the reason for this is that this is only a sample project—there is no program of *The Personal Newspaper* to test the manual against with typical users. Another part of the reason for this is purely practical and time-based.

As tempting as it is to rewrite and polish this manual again and again, it serves its purpose. And just as software projects have time and budget limits, so do book projects. If *The Personal Newspaper* is ever actually developed, it will be modified and expanded to the point where the manual will need extensive changes. That's when you'll see a (nearly) perfect version of this manual.

Product Proposal

The Personal Newspaper

A line of products, plus add-ons.

Proposal by Michael Bremer
UnTechnical Software

Uncle Michael's Theorem of Reading and Education

A good education is important.

Good reading skills are the basis of a good education.

Good reading skills are gained by reading—a lot of reading.

We are most likely to read if we find the material interesting.

We all find nothing in this world more interesting than ourselves.

Therefore: If we give kids a daily newspaper that talks about *them*—what they like and don't like, what they do, what they want to do—they'll read it. Every day. And that's a good first step toward a good education.

Working Title

The Personal Newspaper

Product Category and Target Audience

The Personal Newspaper can be fit into any line of educational software for the home. It can also be sold to and used in classrooms. It will be targeted for ages 5 or 6 (or whenever a child starts showing an interest in reading) on up. Different add-ons and version/edition variations can make it a viable product/engine all the way through elementary school, if not middle school. It can also be used in remedial reading courses.

Note: We also have the option of making The Classroom Newspaper, a modified version that is specifically designed for classroom use.

Brief Description of the Product

Personal Newspaper is a versatile, expandable engine that creates daily personalized newspapers with personalized stories. Readers (children from 5 up) will enjoy reading because *their* names and *their* friends and *their* birthdays and *their* pets and *their* likes and *their* dislikes will appear in fun, easy-to-read stories.

The single Personal Newspaper engine can be tailored, by altering the included stories, pictures, fonts and newspaper layouts, into 6 or more age-specific products (for first through sixth grades), with little or no programming beyond the initial shipping version.

In addition, Personal Newspaper will be designed from day one to accept additional stories and graphics, so we can create an unlimited number of general and subject-specific add-on packs without any programmer time, and very little testing time.

Classroom Newspaper could be based on the same engine, but with an altered database to handle the students, stories and features of an entire classroom. It will also have a few special features to help teachers track student progress with the product.

Similar Products Currently on the Market

There is nothing else exactly like it. There are "publishing" programs that let you make newspapers, and "make your own storybook" products, but nothing that generates actual stories about the reader on a daily basis.

Special Technical Requirements

A small amount of disk space (or a lot, depending on installation options), a CD-ROM drive and printer will be required. A sound card is optional. Additional hard disk space will be needed for story add-on packs.

Expanded Description of the Product

The Personal Newspaper will be designed around the metaphor of a newspaper office. It will consist of six departments.

1. **Reader Department**—This is where the parent or teacher (Editor-in-Chief) fills out a small database about the child (the Reader), consisting of name, age, gender, birthday, friends' names and birthdays, family members' names, nicknames and birthdays, pets and their names, favorite sports, etc., etc., etc., etc.

   In addition, reading preferences can be set for each reader: if someone won't read anything but sports stories, they'll get all sports stories; if all the child will read are fuzzy animal stories, then they'll get fuzzy animal stories. The point here is to give the readers what they want—so they'll read.

2. **Editorial Department**—This is where the Editor-in-Chief chooses the name and look of the newspaper, and customizes papers with their own stories and pictures.

3. **Print Department**—Where the papers can be previewed and printed, from a day to a year at a time.

4. **Story Department**—Where teachers, parents or kids can write their own stories for the newspaper.

5. **Print Department**—Where teachers, parents or kids can draw their own pictures for the newspaper.

6. **Help Department**—An onscreen guide to all the features and functions.

The Stories

The stories that come with the product and are used to create (at least) a year's worth of newspapers will be a mixed spattering of:

- Cute animal stories
- Future/space stories
- Scary stories
- Kids' movie reviews
- Historical characters
- Birthday countdown
- Grimm's Fairy Tales
- Sports stories
- Science stories
- Silly stories
- Famous Americans
- Advice column
- Holiday countdowns
- Aesop's Fables
- Jokes and cartoons
- Silly advertisements
- Kids' book reviews
- Famous people in the news
- Trivia facts
- Long serial stories
- Parodies of Grimm and Aesop

Stories will be written in appropriate lengths and using the appropriate vocabulary and font size for the age of the reader. The vocabulary will be graduated, so new words are introduced throughout the year's newspapers.

Stealth Learning

One of the ways we will encourage reading is to include serialized daily cliffhanger stories that will make the reader want to find out what happens next. If the child has the desire to read more, and reads the whole year's worth of papers in one sitting, that's just fine. They've gained the learning and love of reading that we're trying to teach. After finishing the papers early, it'll be time for the reader to start writing their own stories or for the parent to buy the next year's Personal Newspaper.

Add-ons

To extend the usefulness of the product beyond a year, many add-on Personal Newspaper Story Packs that can be grouped by subject matter (to keep the Reader interested) and by reading level (to keep the Reader on a reading-improvement track) will be available. One or more add-on Story Packs can be made for each of the story subjects above, plus there are limitless possibilities, including:

- Pictures to write stories about
- Story starters (fill-in-the-blank stories)

There are also many possible custom educational add-ons and versions:

- Daily newspaper stories that recount the time of cavemen, the Civil War, WWI, WWII, dinosaurs, the American Revolution, or any other time that can be studied in history or social studies.

Technical Issues and Logistics

Personal Newspaper is technically simple for production for both Windows and Macintosh. It is primarily a database (nothing new here) that generates small reports and prints them out (not rocket science).

The main issues in creating a successful Personal Newspaper are:

- Careful up-front design
- Great content

Resources

A lot of the writing can be done by our staff writers, but we can also make good use of local freelancers. In addition, we should be able to license a lot of the material (jokes, cartoons, book and movie reviews, clip art and graphics) from existing sources at a very low cost.

We will of course bring in educators to write or help write the special educational/historical versions and add-ons.

There are reference books with word lists for various grade levels that we can use as a vocabulary guide.

Why The Personal Newspaper Is a Good Product for the Company

- **First and foremost: leverage.** Personal Newspaper is an engine that can be designed and programmed once, and used to make a number of different products and add-on products. The First Grade edition through the Sixth Grade editions will all be created out of the same engine, but with different stories, fonts and newspaper layouts. That's 6 (or more if we decide to extend the line above 6th or below 1st grades) products for the price of 2. And when it comes to the add-ons, that's 10 or 20 products for the price of 1.

- **Low risk, low cost, high return.** There are no programming risks, nothing technically new or untried. The content is completely within the capabilities of our current writing and art staff, plus licensing additional material is cheap and unlimited. Even selling at a relatively low wholesale price, our break-even point will be low.

- **It's both educational and creative.** Yes, the content is all there for the Reader—at first. But when the time comes when the Readers will want to talk or write back with letters to the editor and stories of their own, Personal Newspaper can handle it. They'll be able to create *their* newspaper from scratch, something they can be proud of.

- **It can be used in the home and in school.** It will be easy to write useful teacher's guides for this product.

- **It's fast.** If given full staffing, the first complete product can be designed, programmed, tested and completed in 6 to 9 months. Additional full versions can be ready in an additional 3 to 6 months. Add-on products can be generated in 2 to 4 months.

- **It's flexible.** We can create many of these products simultaneously, and sit on them until a slow quarter, then release 1, or 3 or 5 products as needed to take up the slack.

Marketing Hooks

- We can include coupons for kids' books that are reviewed. We can include excerpts from the books in serials.

- The contest possibilities are limitless.

Suggested Platform(s)

Windows and Macintosh.

THE READER'S NAME TRIBUNE

A Personal Newspaper for Your Name!

Date	© 2000 UnTechnical Press, unless otherwise noted.	Volume I Issue 1

HEADLINE FOR MAIN STORY

Byline for Main or Feature Story— This is the body for the Main Story. The length of this body will depend on the grade level. This is the story that will be personalized for the Reader, and will be customized to be personal and special, like a birthday or holiday, whenever possible.

For first graders, this story will appear in at least 14 pt. type and be no more than six or seven sentences in two paragraphs. Volume I in the banner indicates that this is the first-grade edition.

Inserted into this story is the Feature Story picture or photograph. It will generally be line art, but may also be gray-scale.

JOKE OF THE DAY HEAD (+ Logo)

Joke Body, up to a couple sentences in case it's a riddle.

Joke Answer Body, perhaps upside-down, perhaps in italics.

COUNTDOWNS HEAD (+ Logo)

xx days until Reader's birthday.

xxx days until Christmas.

xx weeks until something else.

xx days until summer vacation.

CLIFFHANGER (+ Logo)

This is the body copy for the second story—the cliffhanger. It will only be slightly personalized for the Reader, mostly the names, and will be fairly short.

Cliffhangers are stories told in 365 segments, each ending with, of course, a cliffhanger, so the child will be eager to get the next day's paper. The point sizes of all stories need to self-adjust to fill out the space available.

If the child actually reads all the stories ahead of time on their own, we consider it a success.

(continued tomorrow …)

The Personal Newspaper

Initial Design Document

Presented to UnTechnical Press

Concept Summary

*It's breakfast time. Your parents are drinking their coffee and reading the newspaper. They occasionally comment to each other on a story. You're eating your cereal and reading **your own newspaper.** You occasionally comment to them about a story—and remind them that it's only 259 days until your next birthday.*

The Personal Newspaper is a program for Windows (and possibly also Macintosh) that creates a daily newspaper for and about individual children.

Classroom Newspaper is an expanded version of Personal Newspaper, with modified and extended database capabilities, special features that relate to classrooms and class scheduling, and a teacher's guide. It will be covered in detail in another document.

Educational Attributes

The Personal Newspaper is a program to build language arts for kids in grades K through 6. It encourages kids to read a little every day.

The stories will be written with a graduated vocabulary, so that over the course of a year, the child will be exposed to the standard vocabulary of their grade level.

The point size of the type also changes with the vocabulary and age level, allowing more and/or longer stories to fit onto the page as kids get older and become better readers.

One possible option to include in the program is to display words that appear for the first time in bold print so parents and teachers can easily pick them out ahead of time. Adults can then either have the kids look them up in the dictionary, or use them in conversation, to make sure the kids know what they mean then when they see them in writing.

After a while, just reading the paper won't be challenging enough—the kids will want to write their own stories about themselves and their friends, and draw pictures to go with them. And the program will fit all of it to the page and add other stories to fill the space.

Features and Use

Installation

The Personal Newspaper must be installed to a hard disk before use. The setup must be done by an adult or an older child with reading and typing ability.

In the Windows version, AutoPlay will be supported. Manual installation instructions will be given to cover those machines where AutoPlay doesn't work.

The main decision for the user during installation is how much disk space to use. It will have at least two options, one using as little disk space as possible, and the other putting the entire program on the hard drive.

Basic Use

Basic use consists of:

1. Filling in a database about the reader (the child for whom the newspapers will be personalized and printed),

2. Naming the newspaper and selecting its style (design, fonts, etc.),

3. Choosing the range of date(s) to print a paper for, and

4. Printing.

The database will include personal information ranging from birthdate and gender (to get the pronouns right) to friends' names, pets' names, and likes and dislikes. Everything in the database will be inserted into various stories in various days' newspapers to personalize the paper to the reader.

If any fields are left out of the database, whether by mistake or intent, a default value will be used, so all stories will still make sense.

Advanced Use

If and when parents—and children—want to take more control of the paper, they can include their own stories or pictures in any day's paper. Stories and pictures can be created in other applications and imported, or may be created within The Personal Newspaper.

Basic Design

Overview

The Personal Newspaper is an easy-to-use front end for a database—actually for a number of databases.

All functions will be listed on and accessed through the Main Menu screen.

Main Menu Screen

The Main Menu screen is the center of activity and "home base" of The Personal Newspaper.

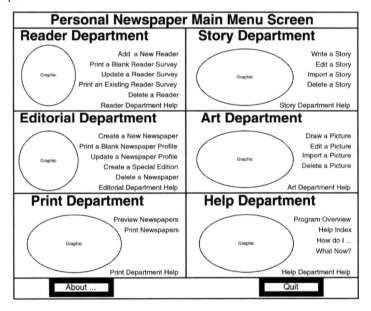

The Main Menu screen will consist of a title bar, six departments and a button bar.

Each task that the user can perform through the program will be clearly named in text. The user clicks on the name of the task to activate it.

The example above is, of course, only a functional schematic. The actual screen may be drawn to resemble a newspaper office, divided into functional departments.

The Departments

The departments divide the program's possible tasks into logical and functional groups.

Reader Department

The Reader Department contains all the functions that relate to the readers—in this case, the children for whom the newspapers will be customized and printed. Its options are:

- Add a New Reader—Open a new database file for a child.

- Print a Blank Reader Survey—Print out a copy of all the database questions and blanks that the program can use in personalized newspapers. Printing out allows parents and children to talk over the answers away from the computer, at their leisure.

- Update a Reader Survey—Enter data into a reader's database.

- Print an Existing Reader Survey—Print out a reader's database that has already been updated. For checking or modifying.

- Delete a Reader—Removes a reader database.

- Reader Department Help—Opens the context-sensitive help system to a section on the Reader Department.

Editorial Department

The Editorial Department contains all the functions that relate to the newspaper itself. Its options are:

- Create a New Newspaper—Establish a new newspaper database.

- Print a Blank Newspaper Profile—Print out a copy of all the options for customizing the look and feel of a newspaper.

- Update a Newspaper Profile—Edit the look and feel of a newspaper.

- Create a Special Edition—Modify or change the stories or pictures of a day's newspaper.

- Delete a Newspaper—Remove the newspaper database.

- Editorial Department Help—Opens the context-sensitive help system to a section on the Editorial Department.

Print Department

The Print Department contains all the functions that let the user preview or print newspapers. Its options are:

- Preview Newspapers—Display a print-preview screen for selected dates' newspapers.

- Print Newspapers—Print out the finished product for any number of days, from one to 365.

- Print Department Help—Opens the context-sensitive help system to a section on the Print Department.

Story Department

The Story Department contains all the functions that relate to creating, editing or importing text for use in a newspaper. Its options are:

- Write a Story—Open a built-in text-editor.

- Edit a Story—Open an existing story in the built-in text-editor.

- Import a Story—Find and import (change format and copy) a text file created with another application.

- Delete a Story—Remove a text file that has been imported.

- Story Department Help—Opens the context-sensitive help system to a section on the Story Department.

Art Department

The Art Department contains all the functions that relate to creating, editing or importing pictures for use in a newspaper. Its options are:

- Draw a Picture—Open a built-in drawing program.

- Edit a Picture—Open an existing drawing in the built-in drawing program.

- Import a Picture—Find and import (change format and copy) a picture created with another application.

- Delete a Picture—Remove a picture that has been imported.

- Art Department Help—Opens the context-sensitive help system to a section on the Art Department.

Help Department

The Help Department supplies access to all the available onscreen help. Its options are:

- Program Overview—Displays a help screen that gives a basic overview of the program.

- Help Index—Displays a listing of all the topics covered in the onscreen help system.

- How Do I …—Lists and gives simple instructions for common tasks performed within the program.

- What Now?—Displays a screen that analyzes what the user has done with the program and lists the possible things that the user can do now. (May be optional.)

- Help Department Help—Opens the context-sensitive help system to a section on the Help Department.

The Work Flow

Here is an explanation of the functional path that each department option follows.

Reader Department

Function   Screens and dialogs

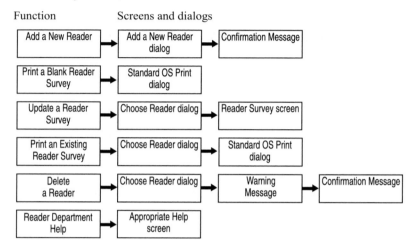

Editorial Department

Function   Screens and dialogs

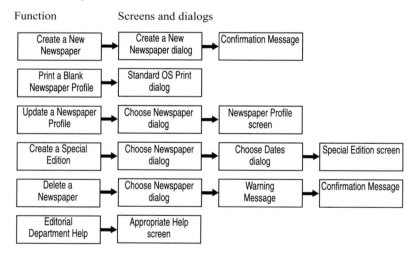

Print Department

Function   Screens and dialogs

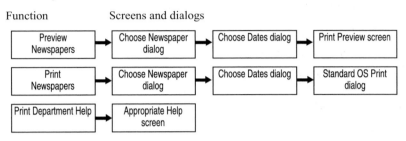

Story Department

Function   Screens and dialogs

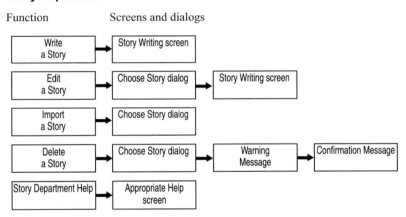

Art Department

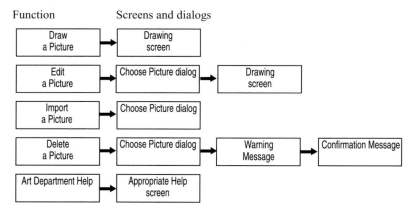

Function | Screens and dialogs

Draw a Picture → Drawing screen

Edit a Picture → Choose Picture dialog → Drawing screen

Import a Picture → Choose Picture dialog

Delete a Picture → Choose Picture dialog → Warning Message → Confirmation Message

Art Department Help → Appropriate Help screen

Help Department

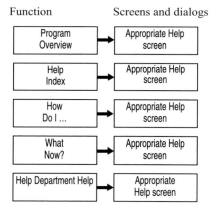

Function | Screens and dialogs

Program Overview → Appropriate Help screen

Help Index → Appropriate Help screen

How Do I ... → Appropriate Help screen

What Now? → Appropriate Help screen

Help Department Help → Appropriate Help screen

Sample Dialogs and Screens

Here is a sampling of schematic drawings of the various dialogs and screens mentioned in the previous section.

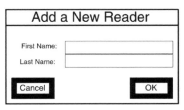

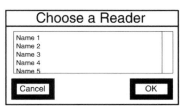

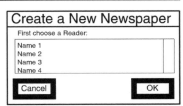

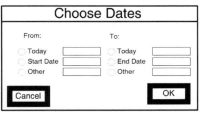

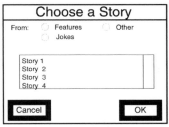

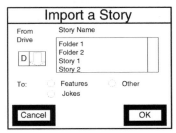

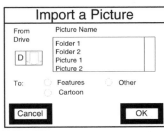

Reader Survey Screen

Fill out this information about the reader. Include as much or as little as you want, but the more information you include, the more personal the newspapers will be

First Name: [Your]   Last Name: [Name]
Address: [ ]
City: [ ]   State: [ ]   Zip: [ ]

Check one: ❑ Boy ❑ Girl   Birthday (mm/dd/yyyy): [ ]

Mother	First Name: [ ]	Last Name: [ ]	Nick Name: [ ]
Father	First Name: [ ]	Last Name: [ ]	Nick Name: [ ]

Pet 1	Name: [ ]	Nick Name: [ ]	
Pet 2	Name: [ ]	Nick Name: [ ]	
Pet 3	Name: [ ]	Nick Name: [ ]	

Friend 1	First Name: [ ]	Last Name: [ ]	Nick Name: [ ]
Friend 2	First Name: [ ]	Last Name: [ ]	Nick Name: [ ]
Friend 3	First Name: [ ]	Last Name: [ ]	Nick Name: [ ]

Favorite Holidays (check all that apply):
❑ Christmas   ❑ Chanukah   ❑ Kwanza   ❑ New Year's Eve
❑ Ground Hog Day   ❑ Independence Day   ❑ Halloween

Scroll-bar

Newspaper Profile Screen

Newspaper Name: [ ]

Start Date: ◯ [Today's Date]   ◯ [Other Date]

Style:

Style 1	Style 2	Style 3	Style 4	Style 5
Style 6	Style 7	Style 8	Style 9	Style 10

[Cancel]   [OK]

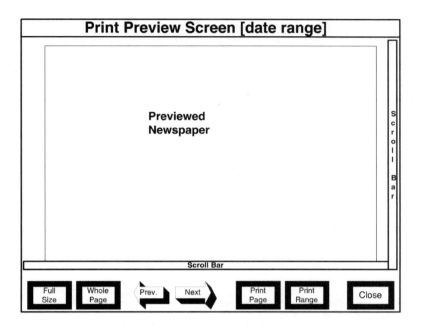

Print Preview Screen [date range]

Previewed
Newspaper

Scroll Bar

Scroll Bar

| Full Size | Whole Page | Prev. | Next | Print Page | Print Range | Close |

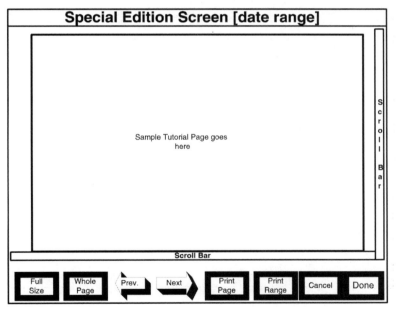

Special Edition Screen [date range]

Sample Tutorial Page goes
here

Scroll Bar

Scroll Bar

| Full Size | Whole Page | Prev. | Next | Print Page | Print Range | Cancel | Done |

Story Writing Screen

Headline:
Story:

S
c
r
o
l
l

B
a
r

| New Story | Save | Save As... | Print | Copy | Paste | Help | Close |

The Documentation

The documentation will consist of a standard printed manual, onscreen help, and possible Quick-Start Guide.

Printed Manual

The manual will be 40 to 60 pages at approx. 8.5 x 5.5 inches (company standard). At this low page count, it can be saddle-stitched (stapled), which costs less than perfect binding.

The cover will be 4-color, the inside pages will be one-color.

Onscreen Help

Onscreen help will be standard Windows Help for the Windows versions. If a Macintosh version is created, we'll weigh the options at that time.

Quick-Start Guide

At the very least, this will consist of a single page in the CD jewelcase (the back of the color front cover), and at most will be 24 pages (the maximum that will fit in a standard jewelcase).

If it's a single page, it will contain installation and starting instructions only. Beyond that, it may contain machine-specific information (for multiple platforms), reference charts, and possibly some troubleshooting and tech-support information.

The Databases

Reader Database

Here is a preliminary list of fields for the Reader Database. More possibilities will no doubt occur as the first round of stories are being written.

- Child's name: first, last and middle
- Child's nickname(s)
- Address, City, State
- Gender (to get the pronouns correct)
- Date of birth
- Place of birth
- Hobbies
- Favorite sports, position played
- Favorite subjects in school
- What they want to be when they grow up (a number of choices)
- Favorite color
- Favorite food(s)
- Foods they hate
- Where they might want to live when they grow up
- How many children they want to have
- Pets: their names, genders, ages, type of pet, favorite pet tricks, etc.
- Friends names, genders, ages, birthdays, nicknames
- Friends' family pets, type of pet, favorite tricks, age, etc.
- Parents' and siblings' names, ages, genders, birthdates, nicknames
- Favorite holidays (to track in the date countdowns)
- Blanks for other days to track (last day of school, etc.)
- Choice of cliffhanger stories
- Choice of "theme" for the main story (sports, cute animals, science, history, biographies, silly stuff, etc.)
- School name, classroom, grade, teacher's name, gender
- Favorite non-pet animals

- Names of heroes, role models, etc., with genders

The Internal Databases

The Stories

The stories themselves will be stored in a database, and accessed as needed for printing.

General Knowledge

In addition to the variables in the reader database, stories can be written with other variables that refer to a general knowledge database. This will allow more variation in the stories, and allow stories to cover timely issues.

This will include:

- A list of many sports, what their highest awards are, and special tournament years (i.e., the World Cup is only every four years).

- Olympic events and years

- Pet species and breeds, anecdotes and fun facts

- Wild animals, anecdotes and fun facts about different species

- List of books common to the age group, along with short synopsis

- List of songs and musical artists popular with the age group

As the stories are written, more and more of these subjects will be added.

TPN

THE PERSONAL NEWSPAPER

EDITOR-IN-CHIEF'S HANDBOOK

Designed and Produced
by Chris Orny

Handbook Written by
Michael Bremer

UnTechnical Press

TPN

UnTechnical Press

P.O. Box 272896
Concord, CA 94527

925 825-1655

www.untechnicalpress.com

This manual describes The Personal Newspaper, a program that has been designed, but not yet built. This manual and its contents contain a copy-righted design for this program. This manual is being distributed as part of a book or as an electronic book for the purpose of serving as a learning aid to writers who want to write manuals. Purchase of this manual in any form does not convey any ownership of the design of The Personal Newspaper, or any rights to use the design of the program or the contents of the manual as the basis of any work or product.

A free demo version of this program is made available to people who have purchased a book or electronic book that contains this manual. Its purpose is to aid writers in practicing taking screenshots and writing manuals. Pos-session of this demo program does not convey any rights to or ownership of the program or its design. The program may not be distributed beyond the initial book-owner without the express permission of UnTechnical Press.

Anyone with an interest in pursuing the design or publishing of this product should contact UnTechnical Press at the address above.

All names that appear in this book, other than Michael Bremer, Tom Bentley, Richard Bagel and Kevin Kraus are, as far as we know, fictional. Anyone who by chance is known by those names owns no rights to this program and deserves no credit. So there.

Windows, Windows 95, NotePad, TeachText, SimpleText, Mac and Macintosh are trademarks or registered trademarks of their respective owners.

TPN

CREDITS

THE PROGRAM

Designed and Produced by: Chris Orny
Lead Engineer: Brian Ranier
Engineer: Joe Okenso
Lead Artist: Sue Topper
Artist: Kevin Kraus
Lead Tester: Dan Amity
Testers: Crash N. Berns
Sound: The Noise Boys
Product Manager: Horace Ecksley
Contributing Story Writers: Bob Smith, Debbie Jones, Laura White, Steve Black

THE MANUAL

Written by: Michael Bremer
Design and Layout: Richard Bagel
Editor: Tom Bentley
Writing Manager: William Ordyss

THE PACKAGE

Package Design: Package Design, Inc.
Package Illustration: Illustrators Anonymous (We put the "ill" in illustration.)

SPECIAL THANKS TO:

Company President: C. P. Resident
VP Product Development: Barry Eeren
VP Marketing: Della Fenster
Manufacturing: Fred Osilin
Graphic Arts Manager: Linda Earnest
And Bob's cat

THE DEMO PROGRAM

Design, Production, Programming: Michael Bremer
Art: Kevin Kraus, Richard Bagel

CONTENTS

INTRODUCTION 5
  WELCOME 5
  WHAT CAN YOU DO WITH THE PERSONAL NEWSPAPER? ... 5
  WHY THE PERSONAL NEWSPAPER? 5
  THE PERSONAL NEWSPAPER PRODUCT LINE 6
  REGISTERING THE PERSONAL NEWSPAPER 6
  ABOUT THIS MANUAL 6
  GETTING STARTED 7
    SYSTEM REQUIREMENTS 7
    INSTALLING THE PERSONAL NEWSPAPER 7
    STARTING THE PERSONAL NEWSPAPER 9

TUTORIAL 10
  INTRODUCTION TO THE TUTORIAL 10
  BEFORE YOU BEGIN 10
  A TOUR OF YOUR PERSONAL NEWSPAPER OFFICE 10
  THE READER DEPARTMENT 12
  THE EDITORIAL DEPARTMENT 15
  THE PRINT DEPARTMENT 17
  SPECIAL EDITION 20
  TUTORIAL SUMMARY 25

REFERENCE 26
  INTRODUCTION 26
  THE BASICS 26
  THE DEPARTMENTS 29
    READER DEPARTMENT 29
    EDITORIAL DEPARTMENT 30
    PRINT DEPARTMENT 31
  SCREENS AND DIALOGS 31
    READER SURVEY SCREEN 31
    NEWSPAPER PROFILE SCREEN 32
    PRINT PREVIEW SCREEN 34
    SPECIAL EDITION SCREEN 35
    DIALOG BOXES 36
  HINTS AND TIPS 39

APPENDICES 42
  APPENDIX 1—TROUBLESHOOTING 42
  APPENDIX 2—SUPPORT AND CONTACT INFORMATION 44
  APPENDIX 3—FOR PARENTS & TEACHERS 45

INDEX 46

THE PERSONAL NEWSPAPER

4

INTRODUCTION

WELCOME ...

... to The Personal Newspaper, First Grade Edition, the program that prints out customized, personalized newspapers for early readers.

We trust—in fact, we guarantee—that you will find this product both useful and fun.

WHAT CAN YOU DO WITH THE PERSONAL NEWSPAPER?

As owner and Editor-in-Chief of this program, you can create and print daily personalized newspapers for the early readers in your family—for every day for a whole year.

These newspapers feature stories about the Readers, their families, friends, pets and hobbies. They also feature jokes, important date countdowns and exciting cliffhanger stories that will have kids wanting to read tomorrow's paper today.

Newspapers can be customized to the individual Readers' tastes—if the Readers love sports, they'll get a lot of sports stories; if they don't like sports, but love cute animals, they'll get cute animal stories.

And beyond that, you can replace any day's automatic stories, jokes and pictures with your own stories, jokes and pictures, allowing you to make special editions to announce or commemorate special family outings and events.

WHY THE PERSONAL NEWSPAPER?

We'll let our company president field this question:

"We believe that good reading skills are the foundation of a good education. We also believe that people who enjoy reading read more and gain more skills faster.

We created The Personal Newspaper to provide every child with daily reading material that they will enjoy."

— C. P. Resident, Company President

THE PERSONAL NEWSPAPER

5

GETTING STARTED

Installing and starting The Personal Newspaper for Windows 95 or later is easy. Just follow the instructions below.

Note: If you have The Personal Newspaper for another operating system, then refer to the Quick-Start guide for installation and starting instructions for your computer.

SYSTEM REQUIREMENTS

This program will run on any PC-compatible computer running Windows 95 or later, with:

- 16 MB RAM
- Hard disk with at least 10 MB free (120 MB for full installation so you can run it without the CD)
- CD-ROM drive
- Any printer supported by Windows

A color monitor and a sound card with speakers are nice, but not absolutely necessary.

INSTALLING THE PERSONAL NEWSPAPER

The Personal Newspaper must be installed before it can be used. To install:

1. Make sure your computer meets the system requirements above.
2. Start your computer and put the Personal Newspaper CD into your CD-ROM drive.
3. If AutoPlay works on your computer, **click on "Install The Personal Newspaper"** when the AutoPlay screen opens, then skip to step 6.

If AutoPlay doesn't work (nothing happens after you've put in the CD and waited a minute or two), then **open (click on) the Start menu** in the lower-left corner of your screen, and **select Run.**

Let's face it: when it comes to interesting subjects to read about, nothing beats ourselves. We make your child the star of a daily newspaper, so even reluctant Readers will want to read—every day.

THE PERSONAL NEWSPAPER PRODUCT LINE

The Personal Newspaper comes in editions for first through sixth grades. Plus, there are separately available Personal Newspaper Add-on Packs of specially stories that let you customize the paper even more perfectly to your child's reading interests.

REGISTERING THE PERSONAL NEWSPAPER

Now would be a good time to fill out the registration card. Registering provides you with extended technical support. And we keep registered owners notified of new products and add-ons, updates, upgrades and special events like story contests.

ABOUT THIS MANUAL

This manual is short and simple—and very useful.

It has a tutorial that will guide you through every step of creating and printing newspapers.

It also has a reference section that explains all the menus, screens, windows and dialog boxes.

At the end of the manual, you'll find:

- some troubleshooting tips—just in case,
- contact information if you have questions or need support, and
- useful information for parents and teachers on getting the most educational value from The Personal Newspaper.

4. When the Run dialog box opens, **type "D:\setup"** in the little box in the middle, then **click OK.** (D is the usual designation for the CD-ROM drive. If your CD-ROM drive has a different letter, type that one instead of D.)

5. Installation will now begin. Just answer the questions, and the computer will take care of all the work.

You'll only have two questions to answer:

Where would you like The Personal Newspaper to be installed?

Unless you have a preference, just **click OK** to accept the default location:

C:\Program Files\Personal Newspaper.

Would you like the minimum installation or the full installation?

The minimum installation only takes up 10 MB of your hard drive, but requires that you always have the Personal Newspaper CD in your CD-ROM drive whenever you print from the program.

The full installation takes up 120 MB of your hard drive, but can perform almost any task without the CD in the drive.

The choice is between space and convenience. If you're not sure, just **click OK** to accept the default minimum installation.

6. Once the installation is complete, it's time to start The Personal Newspaper.

THE PERSONAL NEWSPAPER

8

STARTING THE PERSONAL NEWSPAPER

For your convenience a Personal Newspaper icon has been added to your desktop.

Note: if you don't want the icon on your desktop, just drag it to the Recycle Bin. You can start the program by opening the Start menu, then selecting Program Files, then Personal Newspaper then Personal Newspaper again.

Turn the page to begin a quick tutorial that will teach you everything you need to know to use The Personal Newspaper.

THE PERSONAL NEWSPAPER

9

TUTORIAL

INTRODUCTION TO THE TUTORIAL

Welcome to The Personal Newspaper tutorial.

In this tutorial, you will learn how to create, view, customize and print a sample newspaper.

One point first:

While reading this tutorial, when you see text that looks like this, it is an instruction for you to follow.

Relax and enjoy yourself. You've just been put in charge of a newspaper.

BEFORE YOU BEGIN

Make sure your computer is on and your printer is hooked up, loaded with paper and turned on.

Start The Personal Newspaper.

If you haven't already installed the program, please refer to Getting Started in the Introduction chapter (or Quick-Start guide, if your version of The Personal Newspaper is for a computer other than Windows) for installation and starting instructions.

A TOUR OF YOUR PERSONAL NEWSPAPER OFFICE

WHAT WE'LL DO:

1. Take a quick look at the opening screens.
2. Get acquainted with the Main Menu screen.

MAKE A SPLASH

As the program starts, you will be entertained by the appearance and disappearance of a couple of "splash screens." These are screens that let you know what company made this product (UnTechnical Press), and announce the product itself (The Personal Newspaper).

THE PERSONAL NEWSPAPER

10

Once those screens have passed, we begin the actual program at the Main Menu screen.

WHAT'S ON THE MENU?

The Main Menu screen is the heart of The Personal Newspaper.

Reader Department	Editorial Department	Print Department
Add a New Reader	Create a New Newspaper	Preview Newspapers
Print a Blank Reader Survey	Print a Blank Newspaper Profile	Print Newspapers
Update a Reader Survey	Update a Newspaper Profile	Print Dept. Help
Print an Existing Reader Survey	Create a Special Edition	
Delete a Reader	Delete a Newspaper	
Reader Dept. Help	Editorial Dept. Help	

About...	Overview	Quit

Think of yourself as the Editor-in-Chief of a local newspaper. You are in a big office, overlooking the entire company. This screen represents your newspaper office, filled with your eager-to-please employees. Anytime you want anything done, just click. (Of course, as Editor-in-Chief you have every right to yell orders in a gruff voice while you click.)

The Main Menu screen is divided into three departments and a Button bar.

Everything you can do—and could ever want to do—with this program is done through one of the three departments.

Each department has a picture showing what goes on there, plus a list of all the different tasks that that department handles. When you want to carry out a task, you just click on it—*but don't click yet.* We want to finish looking around first.

THE PERSONAL NEWSPAPER

11

At the bottom of the screen is the Button bar. It lets you quit (not now, of course), find out who made this program (About ...), and get an overview description of this program whenever you want.

One last thing before we move on—notice that at the bottom of each department is a way to access help for that department. Click on each department's help for a complete explanation of all of that department's tasks.

Now let's take a look at the Reader Department.

THE READER DEPARTMENT

WHAT WE'LL DO:

1. Look over the Reader Department tasks.
2. Add a new Reader.
3. Input information about the new Reader.

WHAT GOES ON HERE?

Take a look at the Reader Department.

Notice that there are five different tasks that can be performed in this department—plus a way to get help.

Let's start at the beginning, and add a new Reader.

INCREASING CIRCULATION

Click on "Add a New Reader."

The Add a New Reader dialog opens.

For this tutorial, go ahead and use your own name.

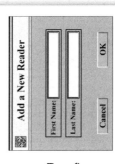

Click in the box next to "First Name:" and type in your first name.

Click in the box next to "Last Name:" and type in your last name.

Click OK.

The Add a New Reader dialog disappears and you are back at the Main Menu screen.

DRAWING A BLANK

We could go ahead and start filling in the information about the new Reader right now by clicking on Update Reader Survey. But we won't.

First, we'll print out a blank Reader survey to look over.

When gathering information about a Reader other than yourself, you may want to sit with that person and the blank survey and talk it over away from the computer. You can fill out the survey by hand, then come back to the computer later and enter the information.

Click on "Print Blank Reader Survey."

Depending on your computer and printer this may take a few minutes. You may want to take this time to practice yelling, "And don't call me chief!" in your gruffest voice.

Once the Reader survey is printed, look it over. All the information on the survey will be used in various newspaper stories about the Reader.

For the purposes of this tutorial, you won't need to fill in all the information. The special tutorial newspaper that we'll be printing later only uses a few bits of information.

On the blank Reader survey form, fill out:

- Your first and last name
- Your city
- Your state
- Your gender (boy or girl)
- Your birthday
- Your favorite holiday (or two)

Now, we'll go back to the computer and the Reader Department.

Click on "Update Reader Survey."

The Choose a Reader dialog will appear.

This dialog box displays all the Readers that have been entered. Your name may be the only one there.

Click on your name in the name list.

Click OK.

The dialog disappears, and is replaced by an onscreen version of the Reader survey.

Choose a Reader
Whose Reader Survey would you like to update?
Your Name
Cancel   OK

The Personal Newspaper® — Reader Survey

Fill out this information about the reader. Include as much or as little as you want, but the more information you include, the more personal the newspapers will be.

First Name: Your   Last Name: Name
Address:
City: State: Zip:
Check one: ☐Boy ☐Girl   Birthday (mm/dd/yyyy):
Relationship: First Name: Last Name: Nick Name: Birthday
Mother
Father
☐Brother ☐Sister
☐Brother ☐Sister
☐Brother ☐Sister
☐Brother ☐Sister
Cancel   OK

Scroll Arrow
Scroll Bar
Scroll Arrow

Your first and last name are already filled out for you. As you enter the rest of your information, you may need to use the scroll bar to scroll the screen down to find all of the information blanks.

Click in the box next to "City:" and type the name of your city.

Click in the box next to "State:" and type the name or abbreviation of your state.

Check the checkbox next to either Boy or Girl.

THE PERSONAL NEWSPAPER

14

Click in the box next to "Birthday:" and type in your birthday (mm/dd/yyyy).

Check the checkbox next to your favorite holiday or two.

Click OK.

The Reader Survey screen will close and the Main Menu screen will reappear.

Before we move on to the next department, take a look at the other Reader Department tasks:

- **Print Existing Reader Survey** lets you print out Reader information that you've already entered, in case you want to review it for changes or updates.

- **Delete a Reader** lets you remove a Reader that you've entered, and all newspapers created for that Reader.

- And **Reader Department Help** shows an onscreen explanation of all the Reader Department tasks.

OK, now it's time to visit the Editorial Department.

THE EDITORIAL DEPARTMENT

WHAT WE'LL DO:

1. Create a new newspaper (for you).
2. Update the Newspaper Profile.

NEW NEWS IS GOOD NEWS(PAPER)

Take a look at the Editorial Department.

We have a Reader; now we need to create and customize a newspaper for that Reader.

Click on "Create a New Newspaper."

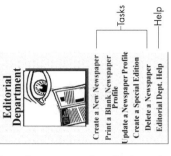

Editorial Department

Create a New Newspaper
Print a Blank Newspaper Profile
Update a Newspaper Profile
Create a Special Edition
Delete a Newspaper
Editorial Dept. Help

— Tasks
— Help

THE PERSONAL NEWSPAPER

15

Left page (16)

TPN

The Create a New Newspaper For: dialog will open.

Because The Personal Newspaper is, after all, *personal*, each newspaper is created for one and only one Reader. The first thing the program needs to know is who the newspaper is for. The newspaper you create will be linked to the information in that one Reader's Reader survey.

Click on your name.

Click OK.

The Create a New Newspaper For: dialog closes and the Newspaper Profile Screen opens. Now that we know who the newspaper is for, it's time to deal with the newspaper itself.

FILE THAT PROFILE

The way to customize a newspaper is by filling out its Newspaper Profile. As with the Reader survey, you have the option of printing it out first and talking it over with the Reader, but we'll skip that step, and go right to filling out the profile.

You can name the newspaper anything you want, but it's best to keep the name to 24 characters or less. If you need some help coming up with a name, some possibilities are Tutorial Times, The Your Name Gazette, or The Your Family News.

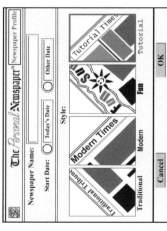

Right page (17)

TPN — *TPN*

Click in the box next to "Name:" and enter a name for the newspaper.

Each newspaper has to have a start date. This lets the program track stories, birthdays and holidays, and allow for special editions without losing days on the continuing stories. The default start date is today.

Make sure that "Today" is selected.

The newspapers can be presented in a number of different styles to suit almost any Reader. For this tutorial, pick the tutorial style. This style has been customized to need only the information you entered earlier in this tutorial.

Click on and highlight the Tutorial Style newspaper.

Click OK.

The Update a Newspaper Profile screen closes, and we're back at the Main Menu screen.

Before moving on, take a last look at the Editorial Department. Note that here you can also:

• Create a special edition—we'll do that in a few minutes.
• Delete a newspaper.
• Get help with any of the Editorial Department tasks.

Time to print!

THE PRINT DEPARTMENT

WHAT WE'LL DO:

1. Preview a newspaper.
2. Print a newspaper.

HOLD THE PRESSES

Take a look at the Print Department. Like the other departments we've visited, it consists of tasks and help.

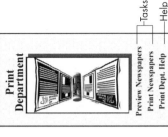

Tasks
Help

Now let's take a preview look at our newspaper.

Click on "Preview a Newspaper."

The Choose a Newspaper dialog appears.

Choose the newspaper we've been working on. Only you know its name.

Click on the newspaper you just profiled.

Click OK.

Now the Choose Dates dialog opens.

We're only going to print one day's newspaper—today's—so make sure that Today is selected in both the From: and To: columns.

Click on the radio buttons next to "Today" in both the "From:" and "To:" columns.

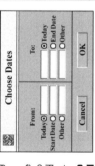

Notice that you can preview (and print) one, two, or many days at a time—even the whole year at once. If you enter a date that is before your start date or more than a year after it, you'll get an error message.

Click OK.

The Choose Dates dialog will close and the Print Preview screen will appear.

The newspaper is shown, just as it will print, except that it is shrunk down to fit in the window. You can expand the paper to full size by clicking on the Full Size button. While full size, the whole paper probably won't fit in the window. To see it all, you can either use the scroll bars, or just click and drag the paper itself to move it around the screen.

Click on the Full Size button.

Move the page around on the screen with the scroll bars.

THE PERSONAL NEWSPAPER

18

Move the page around on the screen by clicking and dragging the page.

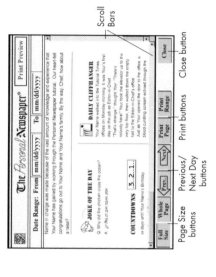

Scroll Bars

Close button

Page Size buttons   Previous/Next Day buttons   Print buttons

ROLL THE PRESSES

We can print the newspaper from here, or go back to the Main Menu screen and print from there. Since we're ready to go, we might as well print here and now.

Make sure the Personal Newspaper CD is in your CD-ROM drive.

This may or may not really be necessary. If you selected "full install" when you installed the program, then you won't need the CD in the drive. If you selected "minimum install," then you'll definitely need the CD. If you're not sure what was installed, put the CD in the drive. It can't hurt.

Click on the Print button.

A standard Print dialog will open.

Click OK.

The Print dialog will close and the printing process will begin.

While we're waiting for the printer, let's return to the Main Menu screen.

THE PERSONAL NEWSPAPER

19

Click the Close button.

As we take a last look at the Print Department, be sure to note Print Department Help is available.

When the paper has been printed, take a look at it. You'll notice that it has a banner, a feature story—about you—with a picture, a joke, a date countdown, and the first installment of a cliffhanger story.

You'll probably notice that the picture isn't very flattering and the joke isn't very funny. We did that on purpose, so we have an excuse to make a special edition of this paper.

Banner · Feature · Feature Story · Cliffhanger · Joke · Date Countdown

SPECIAL EDITION

WHAT WE'LL DO:

1. Make today's newspaper into a special edition by changing (and improving) the picture and joke.

2. Print it (if you want to).

YOU'RE SPECIAL

Look at the Editorial Department on the Main Menu screen again.

Let's remake the newspaper we created into a special edition, by replacing the picture and joke.

Editorial Department

Create a New Newspaper
Print a Blank Newspaper Profile
Update a Newspaper Profile
Create a Special Edition
Delete a Newspaper
Editorial Dept. Help

Click on "Create a Special Edition."

The Choose a Newspaper dialog appears.

Choose a Newspaper

Newspaper Name · Reader Name

Newspaper 1 · Your Name

Cancel · OK

Choose the same newspaper we just made and printed.

Click OK.

The Choose Newspaper dialog closes and the Choose Dates dialog opens.

Choose Dates

From:
Today
Start Date
Other

To:
Today
End Date
Other

Cancel · OK

This Choose Dates dialog is just like the Choose Dates dialog we saw when we previewed the newspaper earlier.

We're only going to modify one day's newspaper to make a special edition—today's—so make sure that **Today** is selected in both the **From:** and **To:** columns.

Click on the radio buttons next to "Today" in both the "From:" and "To:" columns.

Click OK.

The Choose Dates dialog disappears, and the Special Edition screen opens.

It looks very much like the Print Preview screen, with a couple of important differences:

1. It allows you to replace some of the parts of the newspaper, and

2. It has a Cancel button, so you can experiment with changes, and undo them if you don't like them.

The parts of the newspaper that you can customize in the Special Edition screen are:

1. The feature story,

2. The feature picture, and

3. The joke.

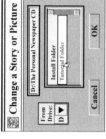

Drive Selector   List Box

The banner, the date countdown and the cliffhanger story cannot be changed in this screen—but they can be changed in either the Newspaper Profile screen or the Reader Survey screen.

To change a story or picture, double-click on it.

Double-click on the picture.

The Change a Story or Picture dialog opens.

You can replace, stories and pictures with text or graphics files on any type of drive that your computer can access, including hard drives, floppies, CDs, removable media and even network drives.

For this tutorial, the files we'll be using are on The Personal Newspaper CD.

Make sure The Personal Newspaper CD is in your CD-ROM drive—even if you performed a full install.

The drive display in the Change a Story or Picture dialog, by default, shows the drive where you installed The Personal Newspaper.

Click on the down-arrow next to "From Drive", and select the drive for your CD.

It's usually drive D:, but it could be different.

THE PERSONAL NEWSPAPER

 22

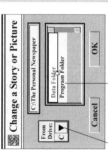

After you select the drive for your CD, you'll see a number of folders in the list box.

Double-click on the Tutorial folder in the list box.

The list box now displays the contents of the Tutorial folder, which will be two pictures: Editor-female and Editor-male. Since you chose to change a picture in the Special Edition screen, this dialog box will only display pictures—and only those pictures that are in a format that The Personal Newspaper can import.

Note: You may change pictures in newspapers to almost anything as long as they are in one of the right formats. You can even draw your own pictures with any art or paint program. The Personal Newspaper can import pictures as long as they're in .BMP, .WMF, .CLP, .JPG, .TIF (or TIFF) or PICT (Mac) format. Almost any art or paint program can save files in one of these formats. For more information on picture formats and size limitations, see Hints and Tips later in this manual.

Click on either Editor-female or Editor-male—whichever one you personally identify with.

Click OK.

The CD and your hard drive will whir for a moment, then the Change a Story or Picture dialog will disappear.

The new feature picture will be shown in the Special Edition screen. A little better than the other one?

Now let's change the joke.

Double-click on the joke.

The Change a Story or Picture dialog opens again.

Make sure your CD drive is selected, and the list box shows the contents of the Tutorial directory, as it did when we changed the picture. Notice that since you selected a joke, the dialog only shows the files that can be imported into the joke section.

THE PERSONAL NEWSPAPER

23

Note: You may change stories in newspapers to almost anything as long as they are in one of the right formats. You can even write your own stories with any text editor or word processor. The Personal Newspaper can import stories from any programs, as long as they're plain text or .RTF format.

Any text editor, like TeachText or SimpleText on the Mac and Notepad on Windows creates plain text. Most word processors, even the fanciest ones, can save files in text or .RTF format. For more information on story formats and size limitations, see Hints and Tips later in this manual.

Click on "Chicken Joke."

Click OK.

The Change a Story or Picture dialog will disappear and the new joke will be shown in the Special Edition screen.

You've just made a special edition. It's that easy.

Now you get to make a decision. You can ...

1. Click the Cancel button if you really like the original picture and joke better.

2. Click the Done button to save your changes, in case you want to print later, or

3. Print the special edition now by clicking the Print Page button, clicking OK in the Print dialog, and then clicking Close on the Special Edition screen.

Once you've decided, and performed one of the above three choices, you can congratulate yourself. You've finished the Tutorial.

TUTORIAL SUMMARY

Congratulations again! You've finished the tutorial.

You now know all the basics you need to know to use The Personal Newspaper. In the last few minutes, you:

Went to the Reader Department and ...

1. Added a new Reader,
2. Printed and filled out a Reader survey form, and
3. Entered the data in an onscreen Reader survey form.

Went to the Editorial Department and ...

1. Created a new newspaper, and
2. Filled out the newspaper's profile.

Went to the Print Department and ...

1. Previewed your newspaper, and
2. Printed it.

Went back to the Editorial Department and ...

1. Created a special edition.

Now you can:

1. Quit the program and call it a day, or
2. Start using the program to create newspapers for the early reader in your home.

For more details on any part of this program, see the reference section of this manual.

And, of course, you may repeat this tutorial any time you feel you need a refresher course.

Now, go forth and publish newspapers! (Or take a break and do it tomorrow.)

REFERENCE

INTRODUCTION

Welcome to the complete reference to The Personal Newspaper. This part of the manual explains every screen, window, dialog box and control in The Personal Newspaper, First Grade Edition.

If you haven't already installed the program and performed the tutorial, now is the time. Everything in this reference will be easier to absorb after the tutorial.

THE BASICS

PROGRAM OVERVIEW

The Personal Newspaper, First Grade Edition, is a program that prints out a beginning Reader newspaper for every day for a full year.

Personal information about the Reader, including name, birthday, pets' names, friends' names, favorite sports, favorite holidays, etc., will be integrated into the feature story, so every day's paper will be about the Reader.

The words used in the stories are all from published lists of words that kindergartners, first graders and second graders learn. The use of the words is graduated—in the early part of the year, only the simplest words will be used, and as time goes on, the vocabulary expands.

There are five parts to each daily newspaper in this edition:

The Banner—the name of the newspaper, the date and the issue number.

The Feature Story—the main story for the day, customized to be about the Reader.

The Daily Joke—a little humor to make the reading more attractive.

The Date Countdown—a listing of how many days until important events, like birthdays, holidays and the last day of school.

The Cliffhanger—a continuing exciting story that lasts the entire year; each day's installment ends with a cliffhanger that is designed to have the child looking forward to the next day's episode.

In Personal Newspaper versions for older children, the type size is reduced, stories are lengthened, and more stories are added. For instance, in the Second Grade Edition, there is a daily media review, describing a book, movie or piece of educational software.

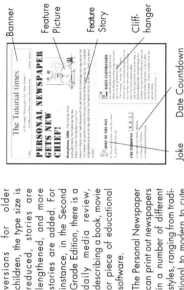

Banner

Feature Picture

Feature Story

Cliff-hanger

Joke   Date Countdown

The Personal Newspaper can print out newspapers in a number of different styles, ranging from traditional to modern to cute and cuddly. The Reader can pick the style they like—and change it during the year. The name of the newspaper is entirely up to the Reader as well.

The Personal Newspaper can generate custom newspapers for more than one Reader, and more than one newspaper for each Reader. But if you keep adding papers or Readers, there will eventually be some recycling of the content.

You and the Reader are not limited to the included content. You can make special editions for any day of the year with your own jokes, feature stories and pictures.

Above all, The Personal Newspaper is simple to use. There are three basic steps:

1. Fill out an onscreen form with information about the Reader (or Readers).

2. Choose the newspaper name and style.

3. Print—for a day, a week or a whole year at once.

MAIN MENU SCREEN

The Main Menu screen is your master control panel for controlling The Personal Newspaper.

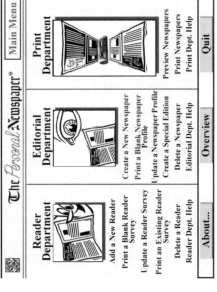

It consists of three departments, dividing the different tasks into logical groups.

At the bottom of the Main Menu screen are three buttons:

About ... opens a message box that gives the date and version of the program. The message can be scrolled to reveal the complete credits for this product.

Overview gives a basic overview of the program.

Quit ends The Personal Newspaper.

GETTING HELP

The Personal Newspaper has a lot of built-in help. Each department has a help screen, plus there's the Overview button on the Button bar. All you have to do is ask (well, click).

THE DEPARTMENTS

The Personal Newspaper is divided into three departments, each of which helps you carry out specific tasks.

Each department has a name, a graphic, a list of tasks and help. To perform a task, simply click on the task's name.

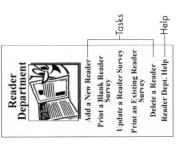

READER DEPARTMENT

The Reader Department is where you perform all tasks that involve the Readers—the ones for whom the newspapers are printed.

The tasks that can be performed in this department are:

Add a New Reader—clicking here lets you establish who will read the newspapers. There can be multiple Readers. But eventually, some of the stories will repeat.

Print a Blank Reader Survey—prints out a copy of all the information you can input about each Reader. You don't have to print it out; you can simply enter the information into the computer. But printing it out lets you take your time and talk it over with the Reader, to make sure you have all the names and preferences correct.

Update a Reader Survey—opens the onscreen Reader survey for entering or modifying the information.

Print an Existing Reader Survey—prints out a Reader survey that you've already filled in, completely or partially. This allows you to look at what you have and decide if you want to change anything.

Delete a Reader—removes a Reader from the Reader list. Deleting a Reader deletes any and all of that Reader's newspapers.

And you can also get help with the Reader Department by clicking on **Reader Department Help.**

EDITORIAL DEPARTMENT

Editorial Department

Create a New Newspaper
Print a Blank Newspaper Profile
Update a Newspaper Profile
Create a Special Edition
Delete a Newspaper — Tasks
Editorial Dept. Help — Help

The Editorial Department is where you perform all tasks that involve defining and modifying the actual newspapers.

The tasks that can be performed in this department are:

Create a New Newspaper—clicking here lets you establish a new newspaper for one of the Readers. There can be multiple newspapers for each Reader. But eventually, some of the stories will repeat.

Print a Blank Newspaper Profile—prints out a copy of all the information you can input about each newspaper. You don't have to print it out; you can simply enter the information into the computer. But printing it out lets you take your time and talk it over with the Reader, to make sure you have the newspaper name and style correct.

Update a Newspaper Profile—opens the onscreen newspaper profile for entering or modifying the information.

Create a Special Edition—lets you customize individual newspapers by replacing the included pictures and stories with your own.

Delete a Newspaper—removes a newspaper from the newspaper list.

And you can also get help with the Editorial Department by clicking on **Editorial Department Help.**

PRINT DEPARTMENT

Print Department

Preview Newspapers
Print Newspapers — Tasks
Print Dept. Help — Help

The Print Department is where you preview and print the newspapers.

The tasks that can be performed in this department are:

Preview Newspapers—clicking here lets you view and examine one or more days' newspapers prior to printing.

Print Newspapers—prints out newspapers for the date or dates you want.

And you can also get help with the Print Department by clicking on **Print Department Help.**

SCREENS AND DIALOGS

There are four main screens in The Personal Newspaper where you will spend some time and energy. They are described in detail here.

READER SURVEY SCREEN

The Reader Survey screen is where you fill in the personal information about a Reader that The Personal Newspaper incorporates into the feature story. The more information you fill in, and the more personal it is, the more the stories will feel tailor-made for the Reader.

You can access the Reader Survey screen through the Reader Department.

You can print out a complete Reader Survey, spend some time with the Reader to answer all the questions, then enter the information into the computer later. Any information you leave out will be filled in with a default in the stories. You can change information at any time to reflect changes in the Reader and the Reader's friends.

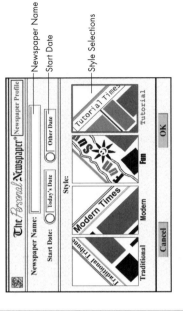

Newspaper Name
Start Date
Style Selections

You can print out a Newspaper Profile, spend some time with the Reader to answer all the questions, then enter the information into the computer later. Any questions you don't answer yourself will be given default values.

This screen asks for only three pieces of information:

Newspaper name is what you want to appear in the banner of the newspaper. Some suggestions are The Your Name Life and Times, The Personal Picayune, or anything with your name or home town and one of the following: Times, Chronicle, Examiner, Tattler or any other newspapery-sounding word. Then again, you could call your newspaper Harvey. It's up to you.

Newspaper names are best limited to 24 characters. If you go beyond 24, the banner won't look very nice. But it's up to you.

Start Date lets the program know what day the first newspaper will be printed for. The Personal Newspaper prints out a paper for every day of a year. You have to let it know when to start.

*Warning: **Don't change** the start date once you've started printing newspapers, or you'll get repeated stories right away.*

Style is the look of the newspaper. Style won't affect the contents (words or feature pictures), just the type, the borders and other incidental graphics that give the paper the feel that the Reader wants. You can change

THE PERSONAL NEWSPAPER 33

There are four different ways to fill in blank information in the Reader Survey screen:

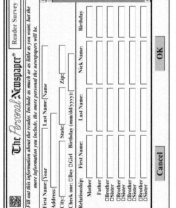

Text boxes are the most common, and are used for names and addresses. Just click in a text box and type in the information.

Radio buttons are for selecting either/or choices, like boy or girl, or paper, rock or scissors. No matter how many radio buttons there are, one and only one can be selected at a time. Click on the button next to the answer you want. Anything that was selected before will automatically be unselected.

Drop-down menus are used for dates and some other numbers. Click on the down-arrow to open a submenu of possible answers, then click on the answer you want.

Check boxes are for selecting items from lists. You may select none, one, many or all of the items in a check-box list. Click in an unchecked check box to check it. Click in a checked check box to uncheck it,

When you are done with the Reader Survey screen, click **OK** to save the changes and close the screen. Click **Cancel** to close the screen without saving the changes.

NEWSPAPER PROFILE SCREEN

The Newspaper Profile screen is where you name the newspaper and choose its style.

You can access the Newspaper Profile screen by clicking on **Update a Newspaper Profile** in the Editorial Department, and selecting the newspaper whose profile you want to display in the Choose Newspaper dialog (see below).

THE PERSONAL NEWSPAPER 32

Full Size enlarges the newspaper to approximately full size. Unless you have a very large monitor, the entire full-size newspaper will not be visible. You can move the newspaper on the screen so you can see it all (though not all at once) by using the scroll bars. You can also click and drag the newspaper itself with the mouse to move it around on the screen.

Previous and **Next** change the displayed newspaper to the previous or next day's paper. This is limited to the range of dates you selected in the Choose Dates dialog when you entered the Print Preview screen. The range of selected dates is displayed at the top of the screen.

Print Page sends the currently previewed newspaper to the printer.

Print Range prints the papers for all the days that were selected in the Choose Dates dialog when you entered the Print Preview screen. The range of selected dates is displayed at the top of the screen.

Close closes the Print Preview screen.

SPECIAL EDITION SCREEN

The Special Edition screen lets you replace some of the automatic stories and pictures in newspapers with your own stories and pictures.

Page Size buttons — Previous/Next Day buttons — Print Page — Print Range — Cancel button — Done button — Print buttons — Scroll Bars — Done button

THE PERSONAL NEWSPAPER

35

---

the style on a daily basis if you want. To get an idea of what each style looks like, print out the first week with a different style every day. (You'll have to do this one day at a time.)

When you are done with the Newspaper Profile screen, click **OK** to save the changes and close the screen. Click **Cancel** to close the screen without saving the changes.

PRINT PREVIEW SCREEN

The Print Preview screen lets you see what the newspapers will look like before you print them.

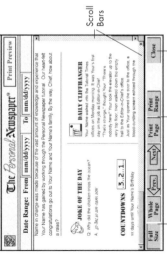

Full Size — Page Size buttons — Whole Page — Previous/Next Day buttons — Print Page — Print Range — Print buttons — Close button — Scroll Bars

You open the Print Preview screen by clicking on **Preview Newspapers** in the Print Department, and selecting a range of dates to display in the Choose Dates dialog (see below).

The controls for this screen are mostly along the bottom:

Whole Page displays the entire currently previewed newspaper so the whole thing is visible in the Print Preview screen. This is the default setting.

THE PERSONAL NEWSPAPER

34

You get to the Special Edition screen by clicking on **Create a Special Edition** in the Editorial Department, and selecting a range of dates to display in the Choose Dates dialog (see below).

The controls for this screen are mostly along the bottom:

Whole Page displays the entire currently previewed newspaper so the whole thing is visible in the Print Preview screen. This is the default setting.

Full Size enlarges the newspaper to approximately full size. Unless you have a very large monitor, the entire full-size newspaper will not be visible. You can move the newspaper on the screen so you can see it all (though not all at once) by using the scroll bars. You can also click and drag the newspaper itself with the mouse to move it around on the screen.

Previous and **Next** change the displayed newspaper to the previous or next day's paper. This is limited to the range of dates you selected in the Choose Dates dialog when you entered the Special Edition screen. The range of selected dates is displayed at the top of the screen.

Print Page sends the currently previewed newspaper to the printer.

Print Range prints the papers for all the days that were selected in the Choose Dates dialog when you entered the Special Edition screen. The range of selected dates is displayed at the top of the screen.

Cancel closes the Print Preview screen without enacting any of the changes you made.

Done enacts the changes you made and closes the Print Preview screen.

The Newspaper itself is what you modify. Double-click on the feature story, the feature picture or the joke to replace them with your own story, picture or joke. The Change a Story or Picture dialog box will open so you can choose the replacement.

The Banner can only be modified in the Editorial Department by selecting **Update a Newspaper Profile.** The Date Count and Cliffhanger can only be modified in the Reader Survey.

DIALOG BOXES

There are various dialog boxes in The Personal Newspaper that will appear and ask you for information. They all work in very similar ways.

Here is how to enter information into a dialog:

Text boxes let you type in information like names or addresses. Just click in a text box and type in the information.

Radio buttons let you select either/or choices. No matter how many radio buttons there are, one and only one can be selected at a time. Click on the button next to the answer you want. Anything that was selected before will automatically be unselected.

List boxes let you choose one name or item from a list. Click on the name or item you want to select, then click **OK.** You can also double-click on the name or item in the list and the OK will be taken care of automatically.

Drop-down menus contain all the possible choices. Click on the down-arrow to open the menu, then click on the menu item you want.

All dialog boxes have **Cancel** and **OK** buttons. **OK** accepts your choices or entered information and closes the dialog box. **Cancel** closes the dialog box and ignores your choices or entered information.

Here are the dialog boxes:

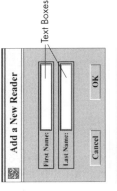
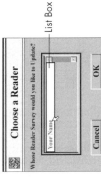

Hints and Tips

Standard Formats and Parts of the Newspaper

The Personal Newspaper, First Grade Edition creates newspapers that have each of these:

- Banner—The newspaper's name, date and edition.
- Feature story—the main story of the day, which includes some personal information about the Reader.
- Feature picture—the picture of the day.
- Joke—a little humor.
- Date countdowns—vital information like how many days until the Reader's next birthday, the last day of school or favorite holidays.
- Cliffhanger—a continuing story that lasts the whole year, designed to make the child eager to see each day's paper to find out what happened.

Suggested Lengths of Stories for the Different Parts of the Paper

When you import a picture or story into The Personal Newspaper, it will automatically resize the type or graphic to fit the space. If an imported picture is too large, then it will be shrunk so small that it will be hard to see, and a long story might be displayed in type too small to read—especially for a young Reader.

Here are the recommended maximum and absolute maximum sizes for each part of the newspaper:

Part of Paper	Recommended Size	Maximum Size
Banner	24 characters or less	30 (if you really must)
Feature story	100 words or 500 characters	150 words or 750 characters
Feature picture	300w x 400h pixels	600w x 800h pixels
Joke	25 words or 125 characters	40 words or 200 characters

You cannot enter your own cliffhangers or date countdowns. You can choose which dates to count down and which cliffhanger you want to read in the Reader Survey.

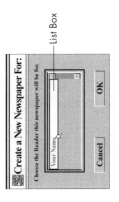
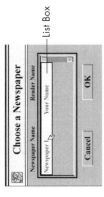
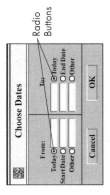
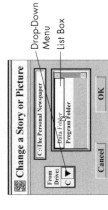

ADDING PICTURES

The Personal Newspaper allows you to put your own pictures into the newspapers.

These pictures can come from many sources, including:

- Clip art that comes with many programs you may already own,
- Clip art that is free over the Internet,
- Low-cost clip art—CDs full of pictures that can be bought for very little at your local software store,
- Pictures and drawings that you or your child make with a paint or draw program, and
- Your own family photos.

Scanners—computer peripherals that take a digital picture of your photographs (or almost anything that fits into the scanner) so they can be displayed on a computer and inserted into various programs, including The Personal Newspaper—are priced very low these days. If you don't have or want to buy one, you may know someone, possibly at work, who will lend you theirs, or scan some photos for you. If all else fails, there are services that will scan your photos and put them onto a CD for a nominal charge.

The Personal Newspaper will import and print any computer graphics files as long as they are in one of the following formats:

- .JPG—a standard format for graphics on the Internet,
- .BMP and .WMF—standard formats for Windows-based paint and draw programs,
- .CLP—a standard clip art format,
- .PICT—a standard format for Mac-based paint and draw programs, or
- .TIF (or TIFF)—a standard format for both Windows- and Mac-based paint and draw programs.

ADDING STORIES

The Personal Newspaper allows you to put your own feature stories and jokes into the newspapers.

These stories can come from many sources, including:

- Kids' joke sites on the Internet,
- Other interesting sites on the Internet, including news sites, or
- Any word processor—stories and jokes written by you or your child.

The Personal Newspaper will import and print any text as long as it is in one of the following formats:

.TXT—the basic, plain text that is created from programs like NotePad in Windows or TeachText or SimpleText on the Mac. Most word processors—even the big, fancy ones—can save files in .TXT format.

.RTF (rich text format)—this is a standard format that almost all word processors can read and write. It is often used as an intermediary format for getting text from one program to another.

If you get stories or jokes from the Internet, they may be in another format, usually HTML or .HTM. You may have to paste these files into a program like NotePad or SimpleText, edit out some of the symbols and garbage (formatting information that you don't need for The Personal Newspaper) and save them as text files before importing them into your newspapers.

Important Warning: Material on the Internet may be copyrighted material. Check carefully before you copy. In most cases, if you are allowed to copy, it is still illegal to use jokes or stories you get from the Internet for other than personal use. No selling newspapers.

YOUR HINTS AND TIPS

If you find that you've come up with a good idea that saves time or energy with The Personal Newspaper, share it with others on The Personal Newspaper Discussion Group at:

www.untechnicalpress.com/personalnewspaper/discussion

APPENDICES

APPENDIX 1—TROUBLESHOOTING

The Personal Newspaper has been carefully designed and thoroughly tested, so it should present very few, if any, problems or complications.

Just in case, here are some troubleshooting tips:

For problems installing The Personal Newspaper:

- Be sure your computer meets the System Requirements, as stated on the box and at the beginning of this manual.

- Read the installation instructions carefully. You may be skipping a step.

- If AutoPlay doesn't work (nothing happens after you've put in the CD and waited a minute or two), then **open (click on) the Start menu** in the lower-left corner of your screen, and **select Run.** When the Run dialog box opens, **type "D:\setup"** in the little box in the middle, then **click OK.** (D is the usual designation for the CD-ROM drive. If your CD-ROM drive has a different letter, type that one instead of D.)

- Be sure you know the letter designation for your CD-ROM drive.

For problems starting The Personal Newspaper:

- There may or may not be an icon for The Personal Newspaper on your desktop screen. If not, then you must start the program through the Start menu: **open the Start menu (click on it)**, then **select Program Files,** then **select Personal Newspaper,** then **select Personal Newspaper again.** It should work.

- If you still can't start The Personal Newspaper, or it is missing from the Start menu, then chances are the program wasn't installed or the installation was somehow interrupted. In this case, go back and install the program again.

For problems using The Personal Newspaper:

- Be sure to click on the Help option for each department for quick reminders of what each task in each department does.

- Many things must be done in a certain order. Read through the

tutorial for a good example of how to create a newspaper from step one through printing.

- Beyond the tutorial, there is a lot of useful, helpful information in the reference section of this manual. Take a look through it. Chances are you'll find answers to your questions.

If these tips don't help:

- Look at the Readme file on the Personal Newspaper CD. It is called Readme.txt, and will contain any last-minute information about the program, including troubleshooting tips. The Readme file will be automatically displayed at the end of the installation. You can also see it by **double-clicking on My Computer** (in the upper-left corner of your screen), then **double-clicking on the Personal Newspaper CD,** then **double-clicking on Readme.txt.**

- Look at the UnTechnical Press website Help page. It has all the latest tips and solutions for problems that we found after this manual was printed. The URL for this website is:

  www.untechnicalpress.com/personalnewspaper/tips

- Look at The Personal Newspaper Discussion Group website. It is where people like you who have discovered useful hints, tips and solutions to problems share their knowledge with others. The URL for this website is:

  www.untechnicalpress.com/personalnewspaper/discussion

- Contact the UnTechnical Press Tech Support group. You'll find many ways to contact them in Appendix 2.

APPENDIX 2—SUPPORT AND CONTACT INFORMATION

All UnTechical Press products are carefully designed and extensively tested to provide problem-free use. But if you do have a problem, we're here to help.

Before calling for technical support, please first make sure that:

1. The program is installed properly according to the installation instructions in this manual.

2. That the Personal Newspaper CD is in the CD-ROM Drive.

If you've done that, and are still having problems with The Personal Newspaper, then contact our Technical Support Department.

- Tel: 555 555-0000,
- Fax: 555 555-0001
- Email: PNhelp@untechnicalpress.com.

If you call, be at your computer, with the disk and manual handy, ready to solve the problem.

If you fax or email, be sure to include as much information about your problem as possible, plus whatever basic information about your computer you can supply (type of computer, amount of memory, etc.). Also be sure to supply a way to contact you by phone, fax or email.

Other sources of help:

If you have an Internet connection, you can get technical support as well as hints and tips to get more out of the product at the following website: www.untechnicalpress.com/personalnewspaper.

More contact information:

Customer Service
Tel: 800 555-0002
Fax: 555 555-0003

Email: UPCS@untechnicalpress.com

US Mail: UnTechnical Press Customer Service,
P.O. Box 272896, Concord, CA 94527

APPENDIX 3—FOR PARENTS & TEACHERS

The Personal Newspaper, First Grade Edition was designed and created to encourage reading and to make reading fun. It can be used as a home educational aid, and can also be adapted for classroom use.

You can customize the newspapers to the visual style and types of stories that the Reader wants to see and read. And you can change the styles and stories as the child's interest changes.

The vocabulary in the stories is carefully selected and graduated, to begin with very few words and slowly use more and more throughout the year. By the time the child has read a year's worth of personalized newspapers, they will have been exposed to the majority of recommended words that first graders should know, plus a number of words from the second grade list.

When using The Personal Newspaper with your child or student, get them involved in the process. Let them fill out the Reader Survey, even if they need a little help. Let them choose the paper's name and visual style. Give the child as much control over the process as possible. Make sure they know it's their newspaper.

After only a few weeks of reading the papers generated by the program, encourage the child to create their own stories for their newspapers. For the younger ones, let them dictate to you and you can type them (or write them by hand and type them in later) and enter them into special editions. As the children get a little older, they can write—or type—their own stories, and even take over the control of The Personal Newspaper to make their own special editions.

Their stories can be about anything at all: summer vacations, movies they saw, their favorite games, even fights with siblings. The subject doesn't matter nearly as much as the fact that they're creating a story about their own lives.

Check out our website's education page:

www.untechnicalpress.com/education

for more ways to get educational value out of The Personal Newspaper, and for availability of teacher's guides for this product.

Above all, educational activities that involve The Personal Newspaper should be fun. Please.

INDEX

.BMP 23, 40
.CLP 23, 40
.HTM 41
.JPG 23, 40
.PICT 40
.RTF 24, 41
.TIF 23
.TIF (or TIFF) 40
.TXT 41
.WMF 23, 40

A
About 28
Add a New Reader 12, 29
Adding pictures 40

B
Banner 20, 26, 39
Blank Reader Survey 13

C
C. P. Resident 5
Cancel 36
CD-ROM 7
CD-ROM drive 19, 22
Change a Story or Picture dialog 22
Check boxes 32
Chicken joke 24
Choose a Newspaper 18, 21
Choose Dates 18, 21
Cliffhanger 26, 39
Clip art 40
Close 35
Copyrighted material 41
Create a New Newspaper 15, 30
Create a New Newspaper For: 16
Create a Special Edition 30, 36

D
Daily Joke 26
Date countdowns 26, 39
Delete a Newspaper 30
Delete a Reader 29
Dialog boxes 36
Done 36
Drop-down menus 32, 37

E
Editor-in-Chief 5, 11
Editorial Department 15, 30
Editorial Department Help 30

F
Family photos 40
Feature picture 39
Feature Story 20, 26, 39
Full installation 8
Full Size 35, 36
Full Size button 18

G
Getting Help 28
Getting Started 7

H
Hints and Tips 39
HTML 41

I
Installing 7

J
Joke 39

L
List boxes 37

M
Main Menu screen 11, 28
Minimum installation 8

N
Newspaper name 33
Newspaper Profile 16
Newspaper Profile Screen 32
Next 35, 36
Notepad 24

O
Opening screens 10
Overview 28

P
Parents 45
Parts of the Newspaper 39
Personal Newspaper Discussion Group 41
Personal Newspaper product Line 6
PICT 23
Preview Newspapers 17, 31, 34
Previous 35, 36
Print a Blank Newspaper Profile 30
Print a Blank Reader Survey 13, 29
Print an existing Reader Survey 29
Print Department 17, 31
Print Department Help 31
Print dialog 19
Print Newspapers 17, 31
Print Page 35, 36
Print Preview screen 18, 34
Print Range 35, 36
Problems installing 42
Problems starting 42
Problems using 42
Program overview 26

Q
Quit 28

R
Radio buttons 32, 37
Reader Department 12, 29
Reader Department Help 29
Reader Survey screen 31
Reference 26
Registering 6
Registration card 6

S
Scanners 40
SimpleText 24
Special Edition screen 21, 35
Splash screens 10
Standard Formats 39
Start Date 17, 33
Starting The Personal Newspaper 9
Style 33
System Requirements 7

T
Teachers 45
TeachText 24
Text boxes 32, 37
TIFF 23
Troubleshooting 42
Tutorial 10
Tutorial Summary 25

U
Update a Newspaper Profile 30, 32, 36
Update a Reader Survey 14, 29

W
Welcome 5
Whole page 34, 36

Part 4

Appendices and Index

The sections are:

- Recommended Reading

- Contact Information

- Author Bio

- About UnTechnical Press

- Index

These appendices offer an assortment of information on other good books, the publisher and the author.

Recommended Reading

Writing and Editing

The Elements of Style, by Strunk and White

The Writer's Journey, by Christopher Vogler

On Writing Well, by William Zinsser

The Elements of Editing, by Arthur Plotnik

Pinkert's Practical Grammar, by Robert Pinckert

Technical Editing, by Judith A. Tarutz

Zen and the Art of Writing: Essays on Creativity, by Ray Bradbury

Comedy Writing Step by Step, by Gene Perret

Comedy Writing Secrets, by Melvin Helitzer

The Copywriter's Handbook, by Robert W. Bly

Writing for Children & Teenagers, by Lee Wyndham

The Craft of the Screenwriter, by John Brady

The Complete Book of Scriptwriting, by J. Michael Straczynski

Necessary Reference Books

Dictionary, Webster's 10th or later

Children's Dictionary

Thesaurus

Books of Quotes

Rhyming Dictionaries

Dictionaries of Slang and Euphemisms

Collections of Cliches

Almanacs

Joke Books

Comic Collections

Fowler's Modern English Usage

Wired Style, edited by Constance Hale

The Chicago Manual of Style

The New Well-Tempered Sentence, by Karen Elizabeth Gordon

The Transitive Vampire, by Karen Elizabeth Gordon

Children's Writer's Word Book, by Alijandra Mogilner

Interface Design (and design in general)

Macintosh Human Interface Guidelines, by Apple Computer, Inc.

The Windows Interface, Microsoft Press

TOG on Interface, by Bruce Tognazzini

The Elements of Friendly Software Design, by Paul Heckel

The Art of Human-Computer Interface Design, edited by Brenda Laurel

Computers as Theatre, by Brenda Laurel

Understanding Comics, by Scott McCloud

The Design (or Psychology) of Everyday Things, by Donald A. Norman

Turn Signals Are the Facial Expressions of Automobiles, by Donald A. Norman

Things That Make Us Smart, by Donald A. Norman

The Visual Display of Quantitative Information, by Edward R. Tufte

Envisioning Information, by Edward R. Tufte

Anything by R. Buckminster Fuller (not easy reading)

The World, Technology and Our Times

The Popcorn Report, by Faith Popcorn

Future Shock, by Alvin Toffler

The Third Wave, by Alvin and Heidi Toffler

Mirror Worlds, by David Gelernter

Out of Control, by Kevin Kelly

The Dictionary of Cultural Literacy, by Hirsch, Kett, Trefil

Creativity

A Whack on the Side of the Head, by Roger von Oech

A Kick in the Seat of the Pants, by Roger von Oech

The Care and Feeding of Ideas, by Bill Backer

Drawing on the Right Side of the Brain, by Betty Edwards

Anything by Philip K. Dick or Philip Jose Farmer

The Oz books by L. Frank Baum are also marvels of creativity

Children's Books and Magazines

Anything by James Howe, L. Frank Baum, Bruce Coville and Roald Dahl. R. L. Stein, too

Cricket (Magazine)

Nickelodeon Magazine

Popular Science

Chaos, by James Gleick

Three Scientists and Their Gods, by Robert Wright

The Blind Watchmaker, and other books by Richard Dawkins

The Cartoon Guide to Genetics, by Larry Gonick and Mark Wheelis

Calculus Gems: Brief Lives and Memorable Mathematics, by George F. Simmons

The Case for Mars, by Robert Zubrin

Godel, Escher, Bach: An Eternal Golden Braid, by Douglas Hofstadter

The Mind's I, by Douglas Hofstadter

A Brief History of Time, by Stephen Hawking

Genius, by James Gleick

Longitude, by Dava Sobel

Complexity, by Roger Lenin

Life of the Cosmos, by Rick Smolin

On Human Nature, by Edward O. Wilson

Broca's Brain, by Carl Sagan

How Things Work, and other books by by David MacAulay

The Naked Ape, by Desmond Morris

Powers of Ten, by Charles and Ray Eames

'Surely You're Joking, Mr. Feynman!': Adventures of a Curious Character, by Edward Hutchings (Editor), Ralph Leighton, Richard Phillips Feynman, Albert Hibbs

Coming of Age in the Milky Way, by Timothy Ferris

The Man Who Mistook His Wife for a Hat: And Other Clinical Tales, by Oliver W. Sacks

Connections, and other books by James Burke

Product Development

Debugging the Development Process, by Steve Maguire

Managing Software Maniacs, by Ken Whitaker

Rapid Development, by Steve McConnell

Dynamics of Software Development, by Jim McCarthy

Manuals

Maxis: *SimAnt, SimLife, El-Fish, Widget Workshop* and *SimCity 2000* are my favorites.

Apple: Most of the Macintosh manuals are pretty well done.

Adobe: for wonderful examples of manuals that explain very complex subjects in a clear, well-organized way, read the manuals for *Photoshop* or *After Effects.*

Other Recommended Reading

You Just Don't Understand, by Deborah Tannen (about male/female language differences)

The Shockwave Rider, by John Brunner

Ender's Game, by Orson Scott Card

Something by William Gibson (short stories: *Burning Chrome,* 1st novel: *Neuromancer*)

Educational frameworks from various states, at least California and Texas

Read screenplays (not novelizations) of movies you've seen. (A lot of these are now available in stores. And check out www.script-o-rama.com.)

Contact Information

If you have suggestions for improvements to this book, let us know.

If you find a typo or other mistake, let us know. But please be nice.

If you send a message, please state the book title, edition and page number, if applicable.

You can contact us about this book in the following ways:

Email:	Michael@untechnicalpress.com
US mail:	Michael Bremer
	c/o UnTechnical Press
	P.O. Box 272896
	Concord, CA 94527
FAX:	925 825-4601

And check out the website: www.untechnicalpress.com.

Author Bio

Michael Bremer has written or edited the manuals, screen text, interactive help, teacher's guides, packaging and marketing materials for dozens of computer games, beginning with SimCity in 1989. For many years, he was Director of Creative Services at Maxis, Inc., heading up the Writing, Audio/Music/Video and Internationalization groups. After a stint as a Senior Game Designer at Electronic Arts, he is now an independent writer, publisher and consultant, and a founding member of the Remedial Film School.

About UnTechnical Press

UnTechnical Press publishes books and provides information to help people use, understand and explain today's technology.

UnTechnical Press Books for Writers provide writers—current, aspiring and student—with the tools, knowledge and skills they need to communicate complex technical information to any audience.

UnTechnical Press Books for Business help managers and business owners understand and use the latest technologies and management methods in today's workplace.

Advice from the Neighborhood Nerd is a series of books for the consumer audience, especially the newcomer to computers and technology.

Index

.RTF, 56

A

A4, 89
Abbreviations, 22
About manuals, 14
About software products, 15
About this book, 12
Acknowledgments, 33
Acorn, 85
Addenda, 52
Additions, 51
Adobe Acrobat, 57, 243
After-market books, 48
All about manuals, 27
Amiga, 85
Appendices, 45, 305–309
Apple Guide, 57
Arrrrrgggggh, 229
Assumptions and methods, 13
Atari ST, 85
Author bio, 309
Avoiders, 29

B

Back matter parts, 45
Back up your files, 165
Bagel, Richard, 98
Basic questions, 96
Big projects, 83
Bite-sized chunks, 24
Blueline, 231
Bottom-up approach, 107
Box copy, 53
Budget line, 101

C

Choosing your role, 19
Close-ended products, 16
Code and fix, 74
Colby, Frank Moore, 25
Companies and their systems, 59–82
Company attitude, 60
Company structure, 96
Consistency, 22
Console machines, 86

Contact information, 309
Contracting, 94
Contractor, 106
Corporate culture, 97
Corrections, 51
Cost of changes, 82
Cover letter, 220
Credits, 46
Credits and special thanks, 32
Cue cards, 56
Cultural conversion, 88
Cultural references, 88
Customer Service, 68

D

Delivery dates, 102
Description of the product, 33
Design documents
    Detailed/final design document, 70
    Initial design document, 69
    Product proposal, 69
    Technical design document, 71
Design flaws, 14
Design review, 170
Detailed control description, 43
Detailed design document, 70
Detailed editing, 212
Detailed menu description, 42
Detailed mode description, 42
Detailed toolbar description, 43
Detailed window and dialog description, 43
Development Team, 61
    Artists, 65
    Designer, 64
    Engineers, 65
    Producer, 61
    Product manager, 62
    Testers and QA, 66
    Writer, 67
DOS, 85
Duties, 26
Duty to customer, 26
Duty to employer, 26
Duty to product, 26
Duty to self, 26
Duty to team, 26

E

E-Help, 57
Electronic documentation, 54
Email, 80
Establish project goals, 101
Establish the reader, 104
Establish the system, 96
Exhibits, 249–258

F

Feature freeze, 30
Final design document, 70
Final draft, 176
Final edit, 229
Finished outline, 120
First draft, 128
Flowcharting programs, 80
Focus groups, 63
Foreword, 9
Format, 127
Foundation seekers, 29
FPO, 65, 85
Friend, 20
Front matter parts, 32
Functional overview, 42
Future of manuals, 89

G

Game designers, 64
Gantt chart, 103
General to specific, 44
Glossary, 46
Gold Master, 30
Grade level, 47
Grammar checker, 47, 78
Graphic artist, 226
Graphics programs, 80

H

Handy reference charts, 51
Happy writers, 83
Headings and subheadings, 24
Help file, 54
Help system creators/compilers, 80
Help systems, 55
Host, 20

How people read and use manuals, 28
HTML, 52, 56, 57
HTML Help, 56
Humor, 24

I

I18N, 87
Index, 46, 228
Initial design document, 69
Installation and startup directions, 34
Interface design, 31
Internationalization, 87
Intrepid explorer, 20
Introduction parts, 33
Introduction to reference, 42

K

Keeping the reader reading, 23
Keyboard commands and shortcuts, 43

L

Layout, 24
Lesson, 37
Lesson introduction, 37
Lesson summary, 38
Level of detail, 22
License page, 32
Line edit, 212
List of deliverables, 102
Lists, 23
Localization, 87
Lone wolves, 73
Long-term issue questions, 101
Look and feel, 22
Lunatic, 98

M

Mac OS Help, 57
Machine-specific file loading and saving, 51
Macintosh help systems, 56
Macros, 79
Manual grammar and style, 18
Manuals for hardware products, 15
Market-driven, 116
Marketing documents, 113

Mental models, 70
Middle ages of software, 72
Milestones, 102
Multimedia programs, 81
Multiple writers, 83
Multiple-platform products, 85

N

Names of things, 22
Neighborhood Nerd, 20
New Employee/Onsite Contractor Check-
   list, 250
Newfangled gadget, 48
Non-sexist language, 20
NotePad, 243
Numbering the graphics, 175

O

Online and onscreen help, 52, 53
Open-ended products, 16
Outlining mode, 79
Overall quality, 23

P

Page layout programs, 79
Parts of a manual, 31–58
   Additional information, 44
   Back matter, 47
   Front matter, 32
   Introduction, 33
   Parts of the Manual Checklists, 251
   Reference section, 42
   Tutorial, 36
Pencil and paper, 81
Personnel questions, 98
Poster, 51
Postmortem, 246
Power of the written word, 165
Pre-edit feedback, 119
Preparing a Draft for Layout Information
   Sheet, 255
Preparing for the line edit, 212
Preparing graphics, 221
Presentation, 127
Presentation of information, 22
Presentation software, 80
Process questions, 99
Product complexity, 15
Product design, 31

Product proposal, 69
Product-driven, 116
Program installation instructions, 50
Program starting instructions, 51
Project flowchart, 95
Project goals, 101
Project management software, 80
Project overview, 92–95
Proofreaders' marks, 254
Prototyping programs, 81

Q

Quick-Start guide, 50
Quick-Start Guide (or Addendum)
   Checklist, 253
QuickHelp, 57

R

Reader Profile Sheet, 105
Reader's advocate, 18
Readme file, 52
Recommended reading, 306
Reference books, 81
Reference parts, 42
Registration card, 35
Remedial Film School, 309
Research, 111
Retesting, 176
Revision tracking, 79
Rewriting, 175
Risk-reduction model, 75
Rock-band model, 72
Rule of threes, 23
Rush techniques, 84

S

Sample edits, 213
Sample Project, 91, 240–243
   Addendum, 234–235
   Content editing and testing, 166–172
   Final draft, 176
   Finished outline, 120
   First draft, 126–128, 128
   Layout and final edits, 226–230
   Learning the product, 111–117
   Learning the system, 96–110
   Line edit, 212–217
   List of deliverables, 102
   Marketing documents, 113

Numbering the graphics, 175
Onscreen help, 236–239
Organizing the information, 118–120
Outline and structural Edit, 119
Postmortem, 246–247
Preparing for the line edit, 212
Preparing graphics, 222
Preparing the draft for content editing, 166
Preparing the manual for layout, 218–225
Printing and final production, 231–233
Project backup, 244–245
Project flowchart, 95
Project goals, 101
Quick-Start guide, 234–235
Research, 115–117
Rewriting and retesting, 173–176
Sample project documentation, 256
Schedule, 102
Setup and planning, 96–110
Source documents, 113
Style sheet, 220
Testing the tutorial, 168
Validating the information, 166–172
Writing the manual, 126–128
Writing the outline, 119
Scanners, 29
Scheduling software, 80
Screenshots, 88
Self-starters, 29
Sentence and word length, 47
Short welcome, 50
SimpleText, 243
Software Development Lifecycles
Code and fix, 75
Design to schedule, 77
Evolutionary prototyping, 77
Spiral, 75
Staged delivery, 77
Waterfall, 76
Waterfall variations, 76
Waterfall with risk reduction, 77
Waterfall with subprojects, 76
Software development lifecycles, 71
Software manual dilemma, 30
Source documents, 113
Sources, 111
Special topics, 83–91
Spelling checkers, 78
Spreadsheets, 80
State of the manual, 27
Structural edit, 119

Style guide, 99
Style sheet, 220
System requirements, 50

T

Table of Contents, 32
Tables, 79
Tape recorder, 81
Teacher, 20
TeachText, 243
Tech writer, 19
Technical design document, 71
Technical Support, 68
Technical writing, 17
Technogeeks, 27
Templates, 79
Test plan, 66
Testing the tutorial, 168
The organization, 59
The outline and the structural edit, 118– 120
The Personal Newspaper, 13, 92
The sample project, 13
The software user manual, 11
Thinking, 118
Thorough dry-labbers, 29
Thorough readers, 28
Throwbacks, 73
Title page, 32
Tools, 78
Email, 80
Flowcharting programs, 80
Graphics programs, 80
Help system creators/compilers, 80
Page layout programs, 79
Pencil and paper, 81
Presentation software, 80
Project management software, 80
Prototyping and multimedia programs, 81
Reference books, 81
Scheduling software, 80
Spreadsheets, 80
Tape recorder, 81
The World Wide Web, 81
Wall calendars and whiteboards, 81
Web publishing programs, 81
Word processor, 78
Tooltips, 56
Tour guide, 20
Translator, 19, 88
Tutorial introduction, 36

Tutorial parts, 36
Tutorial rules of thumb, 38
Tutorial summary, 38
Tutorial to reference ratio, 47

U

UnTechnical Press, 2
   Books for Writers series, 2
   UnTechnical Writing, 2
UnTechnical Writing, 17
User, 15

W

Wall chart, 51
Web publishing programs, 81
Welcome, 33
What's This?, 56
Where to get help, 51
Windows Help, 52, 56
Word processor, 78
WordPad, 243
Work patterns, 44
Working conditions, 97
World Wide Web, 81
Writers' contributions to layout, 227
Writing, 17
Writing for the screen, 237
Writing front matter, 33
Writing the additional information, 45
Writing the back matter, 47
Writing the introduction, 35
Writing the outline, 119
Writing the reference section, 43
Writing tutorials, 39
www.untechnicalpress.com/downloads,
   14, 92, 94

Order Form and Order Information

Fax orders—925 825-4601

Telephone orders—Call toll free: 888 59 BOOKS (592-6657)
Have your VISA, MasterCard, or AMEX ready.

Online orders—www.untechnicalpress.com

Postal orders—
UnTechnical Press,
P.O. Box 272896,
Concord, CA 94527, USA
Telephone: 925 825-1655

Please send the following books. I know that I may return any books for a full refund.

See our complete line of books at www.untechnicalpress.com.

Quant.	Title	Unit Price	Total Price
	UnTechnical Writing—How to Write About Technical Subjects and Products So Anyone Can Understand	$14.95	$.
	The User Manual Manual—How to Research, Write, Test, Edit and Produce a Software Manual	$29.95	$.
			$.
			$.
			$.
	*Sales Tax: Add 8.25% sales tax for books shipped to California addresses.	Subtotal	$.
	**Shipping: For books shipped to locations inside the United States, please	*Sales Tax	$.
	include $4.00 for the first book and $2.00 for each additional book. Call for	**Shipping	$.
	shipping charges for locations outside the United States.	Total	$.

Payment:

❏   Check enclosed, payable to **UnTechnical Press** (Please write phone number and driver's license number on the check to avoid a shipping delay.)

❏   Credit Card: ❏ VISA   ❏ MasterCard   ❏ AMEX

Card number: _____

Name on card: _____ Exp. Date: _____ / _____

Cardholder's signature: _____

Ship to: Name: _____

Address: _____

_____

City: _____ State: _____ Zip: _____

Email: _____

Order Form and Order Information

Fax orders—925 825-4601

Online orders—
www.untechnicalpress.com

Telephone orders—Call toll free:
888 59 BOOKS (592-6657)
Have your VISA, MasterCard, or
AMEX ready.

Postal orders—
UnTechnical Press,
P.O. Box 272896,
Concord, CA 94527, USA
Telephone: 925 825-1655

Please send the following books. I know that I may return any books for a full refund.
See our complete line of books at www.untechnicalpress.com.

Quant.	Title	Unit Price	Total Price
	UnTechnical Writing—How to Write About Technical Subjects and Products So Anyone Can Understand	$14.95	$.
	The User Manual Manual—How to Research, Write, Test, Edit and Produce a Software Manual	$29.95	$.
			$.
			$.
			$.
		Subtotal	$.
		*Sales Tax	$.
		**Shipping	$.
		Total	$.

*Sales Tax: Add 8.25% sales tax for books shipped to California addresses.
**Shipping: For books shipped to locations inside the United States, please include $4.00 for the first book and $2.00 for each additional book. Call for shipping charges for locations outside the United States.

Payment:

❏ Check enclosed, payable to **UnTechnical Press** (Please write phone number and driver's license number on the check to avoid a shipping delay.)

❏ Credit Card: ❏ VISA ❏ MasterCard ❏ AMEX

Card number: _____

Name on card: _____ Exp. Date: _____ / _____

Cardholder's signature: _____

Ship to: Name: _____

Address: _____

_____

City: _____ State: _____ Zip: _____

Email: _____

Order Form and Order Information

Fax orders—925 825-4601

Telephone orders—Call toll free:
888 59 BOOKS (592-6657)
Have your VISA, MasterCard, or
AMEX ready.

Online orders—
www.untechnicalpress.com

Postal orders—
UnTechnical Press,
P.O. Box 272896,
Concord, CA 94527, USA
Telephone: 925 825-1655

Please send the following books. I know that I may return any books for a full refund.

See our complete line of books at www.untechnicalpress.com.

Quant.	Title	Unit Price	Total Price
	UnTechnical Writing—How to Write About Technical Subjects and Products So Anyone Can Understand	$14.95	$.
	The User Manual Manual—How to Research, Write, Test, Edit and Produce a Software Manual	$29.95	$.
			$.
			$.
			$.
		Subtotal	$.
		*Sales Tax	$.
		**Shipping	$.
		Total	$.

*Sales Tax: Add 8.25% sales tax for books shipped to California addresses.
**Shipping: For books shipped to locations inside the United States, please include $4.00 for the first book and $2.00 for each additional book. Call for shipping charges for locations outside the United States.

Payment:

❑ Check enclosed, payable to **UnTechnical Press** (Please write phone number and driver's license number on the check to avoid a shipping delay.)

❑ Credit Card: ❑ VISA ❑ MasterCard ❑ AMEX

Card number: _____

Name on card: _____ Exp. Date: _____ / _____

Cardholder's signature: _____

Ship to: Name: _____

Address: _____

_____

City: _____ State: _____ Zip: _____

Email: _____